THE LOST ONES

KATHLEEN O'SHEA

THE LOST ONES

A NOVEL

A family torn apart and mistreated in Catholic orphanages

HARPER element

This book is a work of non-fiction based on the author's experiences. In order to protect privacy, names, identifying characteristics, dialogue and certain details have been changed.

HarperElement
An imprint of HarperCollins*Publishers*
1 London Bridge Street
London SE1 9GF

www.harpercollins.co.uk

First published as *Little Drifters: Kathleen's Story* by HarperElement 2014.
This edition published 2019

1 3 5 7 9 10 8 6 4 2

A catalogue record of this book is available from the British Library

ISBN 978-0-00-834904-2

Printed and bound in Great Britain by
CPI Group (UK) Ltd, Croydon

The Lost Ones is dedicated to Grace, a very special person who was always there in my time of need. Rest in peace.

And to all the survivors in all the institutions and to all those who sadly did not make it. This is for you.

When we were young, wild and free
The happiest times for all to see
Had its moments of sorrow and pain
But I would live them all again
Brothers and sisters sticking together
Mother and father in all kinds of weather
Life can be cruel and often unkind
Now it's a memory engraved on my mind.

('Memories', Anon.)

Love and compassion are necessities, not luxuries.
Without them, humanity cannot survive.

(Dalai Lama XIV)

CONTENTS

PROLOGUE

I never had any intention of returning to St Beatrice's Orphanage. And yet here I was, standing in front of the house I had called home for five years. A home filled with misery, cruelty and abuse.

My eyes scanned the large black front door rising up from the path, the heavy wooden gates, the tree in the front garden, and I felt anger swell inside me. It was just a house. From the outside, you would never have guessed the secrets and sadness this place had hidden for so long. Now, nearly 20 years after my escape, it was no longer one of the houses run by the Sisters of Hope from St Beatrice's Convent. It was no longer Watersbridge, a home for children made wards of the state from myriad different personal tragedies. It was just an ordinary house. You might pass by this house and not look at it twice. It was just like all the others in the road – two storeys, small front garden, large Victorian windows, nothing special. And yet that's not what I saw.

I saw the children of my past in every part of the grounds, so real I felt I could reach out and touch them. So vivid, I could hear their voices. Here, on the roof, Jake squatted – keeping a watchful eye down the road for Sister Helen in case she came trundling down the road on her bicycle, ready to send up the signal to the rest of us that 'Scald Fingers' was returning. That's when we'd all scurry through the gate to the garden at the back. There, sitting on the wall, was 10-year-old Megan, her bare legs swinging and kicking against the red bricks. Jake's brother Miles clambered over the gate, one dangling leg testing the ground below before dropping into the front garden, where we loved to play, even though we weren't allowed. Six-year-old Anne, the little girl I adored, sat in the crook of the tree's branch, shouting and laughing at the children below, her pure white hair blowing around her pretty face like a halo. Shay, seven, rested on the ground, a look of fierce concentration on his face as his small, bony hands dug a hole in the earth with a twig. And scattered about, I saw others: James, Victoria, Jessica and Gina. I could picture every one of them – saw their fleeting smiles, their innocence, warmth and energy. Dead now. All of them dead.

'You all right, Mum?'

My daughter Maya interrupted my thoughts and the visions started to recede from my sight. The voices drifted away and, as they left, I felt a familiar ache inside. I hadn't spoken or moved in minutes. Maya stood at my side, concern in her voice and eyes.

'Yes. Yes, I'm fine,' I reassured her. I pulled my cardigan around me tighter, though it was a warm spring day.

'Do you want to go in?'

I glanced again at the ghosts from my past as they played, carefree and happy. So much to look forward to back then. Now their voices would always be silent.

'No.' I shook my head. 'I'd like to go now.'

I said goodbye to the children in the house and left them there – still playing, still blissfully unaware of their future. Too much pain, too much horror and torture went on in this house. I couldn't bear seeing any more of those lost children.

The fact was, I had never intended to return to Watersbridge. It was purely by chance that my daughter and I, on a trip to visit my father, had decided to pass through this town again. But as I turned away, I realised that coming back was important.

You see, I made it.

Out of so many children that passed through these doors, I was among the very few that came out alive and in sound mind. I saw myself as no more than fortunate in that regard. I have struggled myself for years to fight down the demons from my past. I was lucky to come through the other side – many others did not.

So the fact that I was here at all was a symbol of defiance against this heartless place that tried to break us, my brothers and sisters, and those we came to look upon as our family. The fact that I came back with my own family was a sign that ultimately love won this battle for our souls, for our very survival.

But for those whom we lost along the way, I tell this story now.

For *all* the children who suffered in Catholic convent orphanages all over Ireland – the ones who died, the ones who lost their minds, the ones who drown the memories every day in a bottle of whiskey, I tell this for you. Because in the end we are all brothers and sisters – and if we don't feel that, feel the bond of love between each other just as human beings, because we *are* human beings, then we are nothing. We are no better than the monsters who ran the orphanages.

PART I
BONDED

CHAPTER 1

THE COTTAGE

I loved to hear the story of how my parents met. Sometimes at night, when we were all gathered around the fire, Daddy would entertain us with his music and stories.

'Tell us about meeting Mammy!' we'd beg him.

Mammy, standing by the big sink in the kitchen, would tut and shake her head: 'Sure, you've heard it a thousand times already!'

But Daddy, now flushed with the drink, didn't need encouraging. He loved to tell us stories. He'd take a long swig of his Guinness, wipe the foam from his lips, then fix us all with a roguish grin.

'I had never set eyes on your mother before,' he'd start, and we'd all smile in anticipation. 'Not before this day. I was 23, getting on with my own life, engaged to be married to a local girl. And who should turn up in our town but your mother with her mammy and sisters.

'I was out riding my bike one day when I caught sight of her in the chip shop window. I stopped then and there, right outside the window, and looked in. Jesus, but she was the most beautiful woman I'd ever seen in my life! Long golden hair, sparkling blue eyes – all of 17, she was a picture. That night I went home and I told my sister: "Mark my words, I'll marry that girl!"

'So I called off the wedding and my parents went mental. But I didn't care. The next day I found out where your mother lived and I went to call on her. And I just came straight out with it and told her she was the most gorgeous thing I'd ever seen and she'd be mad not to go out with me. And naturally, she said "yes".'

'Because you're brazen as anything!' my mother interrupted him.

'And pure handsome of course!' he added, a twinkle in his eye. 'And that was that. My family went mad at me because your mother is from a travelling family and they didn't like that, which is nothing but prejudice, so we ran away together, your mother and I. The police came looking for us but there was nothing they could do. We were madly in love. I bought a ring a month later and we got married.

'And that's how all you's lot came about!' he'd finish off, laughing and poking at us all.

It was so romantic, so beautiful, we could all picture it – our father, the tall, dark-skinned, raven-haired man, and the young, slim blonde beauty. We never got tired of hearing that story.

Even as the years went by and the harsh realities of our lives took their toll, I kept that special story locked away in my heart. I held it there, like a secret, and told it to myself over and over again. When the darkness took over and the loneliness seemed to open up a cavernous hole within me, I'd reach for that story. And then I could hear my father's voice again, coming to me through the night, reaching out to comfort me, stroke my hair and hold me close.

That was the time we were all together, I'd hear him say. *That was where you came from, Kathleen. All you's lot! You were part of something very special.*

By the time I was born my parents had already been together a long while and we were a large family, getting larger every year. I was just three but I can still remember the cottage we lived in, the hills, the river nearby and all the lush green fields where beets, spuds and cabbages were harvested according to the seasons.

The cottage sat pretty on an isolated hilltop, surrounded by wide-open countryside with a beautiful river running past the foot of the hill. Our nearest neighbour was about two miles away, a farmer who owned most of the surrounding fields. You could see horses and cows grazing within stone walls that defined the field boundaries. These walls stretched for miles, gliding up and down the hill, following the contours of the land. Groups of trees dotted the landscape, and there was a stream and a woodland close by, adding charm and tranquillity to the place. It was such an idyllic setting and, for us, the younger children, it was an adventure playground.

The cottage itself was built from local stone and was a single storey with a slate roof. It wasn't big, especially for 10 of us, but we muddled along. There were three bedrooms. The older children – Claire, 14, Bridget, 13, Aidan, 12, and 11-year-old Liam – shared a room, and the younger ones – Brian, five, Tara, four, Kathleen (that's me), and our youngest brother Colin, two – occupied the other bedroom. Our parents were in the third bedroom. Later my sisters Libby and Lucy and brother Riley would come along, making 11 of us kids in total.

Each one of us was either dark like my father Donal, or blonde like my mother Marion – we looked like a salt and pepper family! Tara had long dark hair, I was fair, Colin was dark, Brian was blond, Bridget dark, Claire blonde and the older boys both dark like my father.

Our mother kept the cottage neat and tidy as best as she could. Most mornings she put out a plate of sliced soda bread and a pot of tea on the wooden table in the parlour, where we all helped ourselves when we got up. We had a small parlour with a log-burning stove. Pots and pans hung around the stove on big metal hooks attached to the walls. The wooden table was under the window and we'd sit, watching her washing away with the laundries, squeezing and flapping the sheets loose before hanging them on the rope that was tied to two nearby trees.

Of course we all tried to help as best we could. In a family so large, everyone has a job, no matter how small. Water needed to be carried in buckets from the nearby river. Mammy would bring us to the riverbank where she'd find a safe spot and show us what to do.

'Now mind where you put your feet down,' she'd warn. 'Be careful you don't fall in the water.'

She'd scoop up the water and lift the bucket, moving away from the river's edge.

'Don't dip the bucket too deep,' she'd instruct. 'There'll be too much water and it'll be too heavy for you lot to lift it up. Just put it half way in.'

She'd let us do it ourselves as it always required a handful of us to make a few trips to fill up the big barrel. Usually it fell to Brian, Tara and myself as the older ones were with my father, working on the farm. But as the buckets grew heavier with each trip we'd set to squabbling, and by the time we got to the barrel we'd usually have spilt half the water on the ground.

That wasn't our only job. We also had animals to tend to –

some horses, a goat and a few dogs. My mother had a way with the animals; she was ever so gentle with them. Ginny the goat was a kid when my mother got her. Now she was a milking goat with just one horn as the other was snapped off during a fight with one of the dogs.

When my mother needed milk, she'd just walk up to Ginny and say: 'Come on now, Gin Gin. Come to Mammy.' And Ginny would come straight to her.

'Stand nice and still now,' my mother spoke gently, and Ginny would obey.

Then my mother would sit herself down on a stool, plant a bucket under her and support one of Ginny's back legs.

She milked and talked at the same time, praising Ginny like mad: 'Thank you, Gin. That's a grand bucket of milk there!'

My two favourite horses was a piebald we called Polly, who pulled the cart, and a big mare we simply called Big Mare. They were very gentle creatures. We played under the horse's bellies and in between their legs and they never once hurt us. The greyhound and the Alsatian were used for breeding and their puppies sold off for the extra cash, but Floss, a black and white sheepdog, was my father's favourite and his constant companion. He went everywhere with Daddy.

As our mother was always busy, we were left to our own devices for the rest of the day. We kept ourselves occupied playing with the animals or on the grounds. My mother would call on us occasionally from inside the cottage, checking we hadn't strayed too far.

In the evenings us younger ones got to spend time with Claire and Bridget. They were so loving and motherly to us that Tara and me jealously fought for their attention, trying to outdo each other to be closest to them.

'Bridget, can I do your hair to see if there are any nits?' I'd ask.

Bridget would lie down and put her head on top of my lap.

I'd part her hair carefully with my fingers and move her head around and then exclaim: 'Bridget, don't move! I found a load of nits! Don't worry, I killed them all for you!'

Then I'd click my two thumbnails and push down on her head making a sound like I was squashing the nits.

'Did you hear that, Bridget?'

'Yes, baby, kill them all.'

I'd be at it for ages, all the while Bridget praising me like mad, knowing perfectly well that she didn't have any nits, and I got the attention that I wanted.

We had no electricity in the cottage so our only light was from candles and the open fire in the parlour, where we'd gather and sit out the evening listening to our father's stories or his playing on the harmonica or accordion. He could play any tune even though he never learned how to read music. He'd have us dancing and singing along with a medley of old Irish folk songs, his feet tapping the floor, always in tempo. And he'd tell great stories too – sending us into howling fits of laughter. But always, always my favourite was the story of how they met.

My father was a tall, strapping, handsome man with jet black hair, swept back on his head like a film star. He always looked smart, dressed in suits and shirts, working away from home a lot in different villages or towns. He was a jack of all trades, trying his hand at anything from building to roadwork, farming and breeding horses.

Before he lost touch with his family, my grandmother, Daddy's mammy, would come to see us and tell us stories about my father as a lad.

'He was the Madman of Borneo, your daddy,' she'd cackle. 'They called him that because he was wild as anything. A real live wire. He would often be heard coming into town, shouting his head off, standing up on the horse and cart with the reins in his hands, his shirt sleeves rolled up, galloping as hard as he could, grinning, laughing, pure brazen without a care in the world. Everyone had to jump out of his way or risk being flattened to the ground!'

At the weekends, my father took Bridget and Claire to the village pub where they were paid to perform as a trio. For my sisters, it was the highlight of their week and they'd dress themselves up to the nines, putting on make-up and doing their hair.

'We want to come! We want to come!' Tara and I would beg my father.

'No, babas, you're too young. I'll take you when you're a bit older,' he'd console us.

I was always so envious, watching my sisters dolling themselves up, getting ready for the night out. The two of them, so beautiful, always attracted the attention of the boys in the village, who bought them drinks all night long. My father loved it too, knocking back Guinness and whiskey and chatting away to all the locals. My mother waited up all night for him to come back and always used to tell us he could talk the ears off anyone.

Since our only means of transport was the horse and cart, if we wanted to get anywhere we'd have to walk. It was three miles along a narrow winding road to the village, which had a grocery shop, church, garage and three pubs.

If we had a bit of money the four of us – Brian, Tara, myself and Colin – would walk into the village to buy our favourite sweets: Bull's Eyes and Silvermints. We knew all the routes so we'd take shortcuts through the fields and woods, often straying to climb up a tree to get a better view of the birds or some nestling chicks. Then we'd head to the hay barn, which was along the way, and have a wonderful time climbing the stacks of hay, pushing and throwing each other off. We found it hilarious. We'd get winded and bruised sometimes but we'd get up and get on with it.

When we got tired of the hay barn, we'd walk on to the village, always keeping an eye on anything we could turn into play.

Having had our sweets, we'd pop in and out of the pubs. We loved chatting with the old folks and the locals, people we knew, the ones that called us 'Donal's kids'. They would often get us a packet of crisps or a bottle of lemonade. We made sure we headed home before it got too dark to see where we were going but more importantly we wanted to avoid 'the headless horseman by the big tree'. We'd been repeatedly warned of this ghost by the elders and weren't that keen to see it in the flesh!

My mother had just finished giving us a bath one day after we came home soaking and muddy from a downpour.

'Empty out the bath and stay out of my sight,' she commanded as she raced towards the kitchen to prepare the dinner.

We were draining the bath water when we saw the school bus pull up and stop at the end of the narrow road. I saw Aidan and Liam walking up the hill together and Claire and Bridget lagging behind. The boys greeted us with a tap on the head as they walked in the door but Bridget dragged in behind them, not looking at all happy.

Bridget had big green eyes and her hair flowed in big waves down her back. The sun highlighted the different shades of auburn that ran through her hair. My mother called her Sophia Loren because she had beautiful high cheek-bones. She was so gentle and kind we all adored her. Bridget scooped me in her arms and gave me a big hug. But as she put me down her eyes crinkled and she sighed.

'What's wrong, Bridget?' I asked, concerned.

'Nothing, baby, just got a bit of a sore head,' Bridget replied as her hands reached up to massage her temples. She didn't look at all well. 'I think I'm going go to bed and sleep it off and hope the headache will go away,' she added.

That night we all ate dinner together as usual, tea and bread with half a boiled egg each, except Bridget didn't join us because she was still asleep. We weren't long into the meal when we heard a loud bang from the bedroom. We all jumped, startled, and my father raced towards the loud noise, with a few of us tagging along out of curiosity. There was a terrible stench and we could see smoke seeping through from under the bedroom door. Daddy quickly opened the door and thick smoke bellowed out – the room was on fire!

'Get away! Get out of here! All of you – get out of the house!' my father shouted frantically as he rushed in, pulling Bridget out of the bedroom.

'Aidan, Liam – get the water and blankets!' he yelled again, panic now rising in his voice.

The rest of us gathered outside the cottage, sheer terror in everyone's faces, all our eyes transfixed on the door as we waited anxiously for our father, Aidan and Liam to come out.

It seemed like a lifetime when eventually they emerged from the house, blackened, dirtied and pure exhausted from their efforts tackling the fire. My father was still shaking. Somehow they had managed to keep the fire under control and confined to one bedroom.

We found out later Bridget had switched on the transistor radio before she went to bed and placed the candle on top of the radio. The candle had melted down into the radio and caused it to explode, starting a fire which quickly spread from the curtains to the clothing strewn all over the bedroom. The room was blackened by the smoke and it smelled so foul nobody could sleep there.

Now we were crammed into the two remaining rooms, and the scuffling between us kids was getting more frequent. My father could have easily fixed up the room as he was quite handy but he suffered with nerves and paranoia. To him, the fire was a bad omen.

So one morning, just as we were tucking into our breakfast, Daddy came striding in with a huge grin on his face.

'Hey, lads, you won't believe what I've got!' he announced. 'We'll all be moving soon. You lot gonna love this. I've found us a grand new home and if you'll quieten down I'll show it to you.'

We all looked at each other, puzzled.

'You better not be joking around now, Donal,' Mammy warned him.

He smiled and gave her a wink: 'How about we go outside and have a look then?'

'You can't leave a whole house outside!' Brian scoffed and we all fell about giggling. The thought was so hilarious. A new house! Outside?

Our father led the way out of the cottage and, to our amazement, parked outside the cottage were two brightly coloured wagons with two horses pulling on one wagon and Big Mare pulling the other one. They were shaped like barrels and had been hand-painted with all the colours of the rainbow. They looked so pretty.

'There'll be plenty of room – that thing is 13 foot long and there's two double bunk beds where we can all sleep,' Daddy said confidently as we all ran around, touching and exploring our new homes.

In each wagon there was a small wood-burning stove with a little chimney poking out the roof and a tiny cupboard to store pots and pans. Daddy lifted Brian onto one of the horses and he was so thrilled, he tried to buck and shove the horse to make it move.

Tara and me laughed and screamed as we chased each other in and out of the wagons.

'I'll have my family and my home with me when I go to work,' our father said proudly.

Only Claire seemed apprehensive.

'I don't want people to be calling us gypsies or tinkers. I'd be too embarrassed,' she objected. A teenager already, Claire had long blonde hair and was small and petite. She liked the nicer things in life and she cared what people thought of her.

'Ah, don't be worrying about that,' Daddy replied, putting a reassuring arm around her small shoulder. 'If anyone has anything to say, I'll kick the shite out of them!'

CHAPTER 2

LIFE ON THE ROAD

'Come on, children, let's get a move on,' my father yelled. 'We want to get there before it gets too late. On the wagon now!'

Finally, the day came for us to move out of the cottage and onto the open road. We packed and transferred all our belongings into the wagons, which didn't take long as we didn't have that much.

I took a long last look at the cottage – I was sad to leave it behind but at the same time I was stirred up by the excitement of our new life and all the adventures to come.

It was the start of our life on the road!

My father moved around the wagons and cart, checking that everything was in place, giving it a final inspection, tucking and pulling, making sure that the horses were safely strapped in before he was ready to hit the road.

He lifted Colin up into the wagon. Brian, Tara and myself climbed in, then he hauled himself up at the front, reaching for the reins. My mother was already there, and next to her was Floss, seated in prime position between my parents.

'Giddy up,' my father called and he tapped Big Mare's backside with a stick. Big Mare moved forward and we began our journey.

We made ourselves comfortable, trying hard to contain our giddy spirits while looking out of the small window behind the wagon at the sights that passed us by.

The day was already brightening up and I could feel the warmth of the sun on my face. It was a glorious, gorgeous August day – just the right time to set off on an adventure!

My father was at the helm of the first wagon with Ginny tied up behind us. Claire and Bridget were on board the second wagon with our brother Aidan taking the reins. Our brother Liam took charge of the cart with all the other horses tied to the back. We travelled slowly in a convoy along narrow winding back roads through the countryside and small villages. After a few hours, my father pulled into a lay-by where there was a water pump. He fed and watered the horses before starting a small campfire to boil the kettle for our tea while my mother made up some bread and jam.

Then we scrambled back to our places and started up again. But the hours now dragged by, and Brian, Tara and myself were all restless. We'd had enough of sitting down at the back of the wagon. So Brian poked his head up to talk to my father: 'Daddy, we want to stay out and walk. We're bored in here. There's nothing to do.'

Brian was always the bold one – he could get away with it because Daddy was very fond of him.

'Stay out then!' my father snapped back. 'I'm sick of the feckin' lot of you making a racket back there. You lot stay off the road and keep into the side of the ditches. You better keep up with the feckin' wagons, you pack of blaggards!'

So we jumped down and ran around behind the convoy, playing along, trying hard not to lag behind too far but at times we were so engrossed that Daddy had to stop for us to catch up.

'What did I tell you kids? I'll kick the shite out of you lot!' Daddy warned whenever we got close to the wagons.

When we were tired of playing, chasing and keeping up with the wagon, we ran up to my father's side so he could lean over to pull us up into the wagon one by one. My mother, sensing my father was losing his patience with us, put her finger on her lips: 'Shush! Quieten down now, children. Your father doesn't like all that racket going on. He'll get really mad. Go and lie down on the beds.'

We were so tired from all the running around that we didn't even argue. I lay down on the bottom bunk bed, listening to the sound of the horses' hooves clip-clopping as they hit the tarmac, echoing like a lullaby, and the swaying of the wagon was so soothing and serene that before long I fell asleep.

I woke to a different feeling. We had stopped and I stretched out my arms and legs before poking my head out the wagon. Daddy had pulled us off the road to a spot near the river with a bit of woodland for shelter and firewood. It was now late in the day and the warm orange glow of the dipping sun filtered through the branches in a patchwork of light. Daddy set the wagons close together and untied the horses from the shafts. Aidan and Liam helped take them to the river for a drink before letting them loose to graze in a nearby field. They tied a rope around the horses' back legs so that the horses wouldn't wander off too far for my father to get them when he needed to. Claire and Bridget came and helped us down from the wagon.

'Come, we'll go get the water and the wood so we can get the fire going and get some food into us,' said Claire as she handed me a pail.

We collected firewood, tied them into bundles then carried them on our backs to the campsite, which was near the farm where my father was due to be working the next day.

My father got the fire going while my mother prepared a vegetable stew. By tea-time it would be pitch black but for the glow from our campfire. I felt peaceful and safe in the woods with all my family by my side. But after filling my belly with warm, soupy vegetables I could barely keep my eyes open. Exhaustion soon got the better of us all and we clambered into the bunks for the night, all of us young ones curled up together on the one bed.

In the morning our mother shook us gently awake and I was filled with excitement once again at the thought of being in a new place, far away from the cottage. We each had a slice of bread and cup of tea before heading up to the beet field to join a group of other farm hands waiting for the farmer to arrive with the sack of tools so we could start work.

Brian, Tara, Colin and myself stayed at the fringes of the field as my parents and older brothers and sisters spread out to work in rows. We watched closely as my mother showed us how to thin the beet, trimming the excess leaves off the stalks from each plant. It didn't look difficult so we started helping out, just tearing the leaves off with our fingers. Of course it wasn't long before we got bored and started messing around so Daddy told us to go play somewhere else.

'Just don't be causing no trouble,' Mammy called after us as we cantered off towards the campsite.

'We won't,' we yelled back, keen to get as far away as possible.

Now, with our family in the field all day, we were free to do whatever took our fancy, and it was Ginny the goat who bore the brunt of our exploits at first. We tortured the life out of that poor creature. We'd get under her, pulling at her teats, squirting her milk into our mouths for a drink and then all over each other. Brian had this notion of riding on top of

Ginny like a horse. Brian got on her back, one hand grasping her beard and the other holding on to her horn. Alarmed, Ginny legged it, bucking as hard as she could as she felt his weight on her back while we ran behind, laughing our hearts out at the sight of Brian riding on top of the goat. He held on tight, trying to stay on for as long as he could.

'Go on there now, Gin! Go on!' Brian shouted. He was in fits of laughter as he rode Ginny, with a stick flailing in his hand, shoving and pushing Ginny to move faster and faster. But Ginny had other ideas. She headed straight for the ditch full of nettles and bucked him off, head first. The sight of Brian emerging, muddied, stung all over and with his blond head covered in twigs and leaves was the funniest thing we'd ever seen.

Now Ginny ran away from us whenever she saw us coming and it was getting more and more difficult to fetch her. But Brian refused to give up. One day he came up with this idea of putting on my mother's headscarf and coat.

He wrapped the colourful scarf round his head and the long brown coat hung off him as he called out in my mother's voice: 'Come on now, Gin Gin. Come now to Mammy!'

Brian looked so comical with the coat hanging off him and the silly headscarf, we never thought for a minute that Ginny would oblige, but she did! We were surprised but pure delighted as Brian had fooled her and we got to join in the fun. As soon as he managed to hold on to her horn, he was up riding off like a cowboy again. Off and away they went and the rest of us followed behind until Ginny bucked him off again to the same painful ending.

One day my mother came back from milking Ginny. She was rather disappointed at the amount that she'd got from our goat lately and asked if any of us had been at her. Innocently, we recounted how we'd been tugging at Ginny's teats for her milk and how Brian was riding on top of Ginny and all the chasing we'd done – the full scenario in fine detail. We thought she would find it as funny as we all had. But she was so horrified and appalled that she gave Brian a good hiding, telling him that he could have broken Ginny's back.

'Leave Ginny in peace!' she warned us. 'Stop tormenting the goat. How would you like it if someone was at you all the time?'

She was incensed at what we'd done.

It didn't matter. We started exploring further and further from the campsite, miles away, and we only came back when it was time for our dinner. The four of us would wander off into fields, rooting about the hedges, woodlands and everything else that we stumbled upon. When we came across an old ruin or barn, we'd spend hours playing in it. Occasionally, as we wandered across the fields, we'd catch a whiff of the awful stench from the feral goats as they came down from the mountain and we'd run away, screaming, laughing and holding our noses against the unbearable stink.

Sometimes, when we were by the river, we caught frogs and raced them. Our older brothers had shown us how to find hollow reeds to use as straws. We'd stick the straws into the frogs' behinds and blow into them until the frogs inflated, their fat bodies all puffed up as their little legs stuck out at the corners. Then we'd all get in a line and pull the straws out from the frogs' behinds at the same time and away they'd shoot, up into the air, as they deflated. The frog that flew the furthest won.

After each race we'd scramble about trying to retrieve our frogs, but as we went to pick them up again they'd often make a horrible squawking sound.

'Oh, don't touch that one!' Tara would warn. 'He's putting a curse on you.'

So I'd find myself another frog and we'd start the race again.

Aidan and Liam loved building rafts. And once built, they'd tie a rope to the raft while we little ones sat on it and we'd ride through some fast-flowing water while our older brothers ran alongside the bank, holding the other end of the rope. Our older brothers also used to bring us to the rock quarry where they tied us up with ropes and we scaled up and down the sides. The drop was tremendous. We'd have died if the rope snapped. Sometimes we'd play by the railway lines, throwing stones to try to break the white cups on the electricity wire as we walked the line. There were plenty of occasions when the Garda came to pick us up and bring us back to our parents.

My father would erupt at my mother: 'Look at the lot of your feckin' bastards. Always causing trouble!'

He promised the officers that he'd give us a good hiding but he never did. We played dangerously, fearlessly, never realising the harm we could come to. We were wild, free and happy. There were never any toys to occupy us, no kisses and cuddles at the end of the day, but it didn't matter. We were uncomplaining and self-assured – we'd been raised to look after ourselves and that's exactly what we did.

For the most part Brian was our leader. Since he was the eldest of our group we usually played the games he wanted and explored the places he found curious. And what Brian loved most was birds. He was wild about them and we were forever following him up trees, looking at the birds, their nests, the eggs when they hatched and all the little nestlings when they were born. We'd walk miles into the woodland looking for crows. Brian was always high up the trees checking out the crow's nests in the highest branches. He was determined to have his own bird so we'd try to catch water hens, but without success. They'd glide through the water so fast that they'd be on the other side of the bank before we could even get close. So Brian started making cardboard traps instead. He'd tie a string to the crow's feet when he caught one and let it fly off just as far as the string would let it go. The crow would flap vigorously mid-flight, but, unable to move forward, it would struggle before falling towards the ground.

Now my father knew of Brian's interest in birds and was concerned about him climbing trees all the time, fearing he might fall. So one day he came home with a turkey for Brian. Needless to say, Brian was overjoyed at having a pet, something that he could look after and care for. He guarded his turkey tirelessly, never leaving it out of his sight. We young ones weren't allowed to come close to the turkey, let alone play with it. Brian defended his turkey like it was his own child. Tara would dearly love to have played with the turkey but was too afraid of Brian. We were all afraid of Brian when he lost his temper. Brian could be very vicious when he was angry.

One day Brian went out with our father and Floss to catch rabbits, leaving me, Tara and Colin to amuse ourselves.

'Come on,' Tara urged. 'Let's get the turkey. They won't be back for ages.'

'Brian'll be mad if he finds out.' I was worried.

'He won't find out,' Tara insisted. 'He'll never know as long as we put it back when we're finished.'

So Tara picked up the turkey and headed towards the riverbank where there was open ground to play on, while Colin and myself followed close behind.

We were all thrilled to be playing with the turkey at last.

'I want to see it fly,' Tara shouted. She grabbed the turkey and tossed it into the air, running after it as the turkey flapped its wings but landed, running rather than flying. We all chased after it and grabbed the turkey again, then threw it up into the air once more and then again, and again.

'Why doesn't it fly? Why is the turkey doing that?' Tara panted, breathless from all the running and throwing. We couldn't understand why the turkey wouldn't fly. We kept tossing it in the air, repeatedly, and even tried doing it from raised ground. We kept at it for ages, trying to make it fly until suddenly the turkey dropped to the ground.

And stayed there.

'The turkey's dead. Oh my God, we killed the turkey! What are we going to do? Brian is gonna kill us when he finds out!'

Tara was a bundle of nerves. We all were – I trembled at the thought of Brian coming home to his dead turkey. We all stood staring down at the lifeless bird, too shocked to say anything.

Finally, Tara made a decision.

'We have to leave it here and pretend not to know anything about it,' she insisted. 'We *have* to or he'll kill us.'

We all agreed and returned to the wagons, leaving the turkey at the riverbank where it had dropped dead. We went about our business as normally as we could, though our hearts raced with anxiety.

Later that afternoon Brian returned and went straight to see his turkey. He looked everywhere around the campsite but he couldn't find it.

'Where's my turkey?' he asked all of us, including my mother. He was panicky and worried. We all shrugged, innocent.

'Come on,' he shouted. 'You've got to look for it.'

So we all pretended to be looking around until eventually my father and mother found it where we'd left it by the riverbank. Brian burst into tears, distraught.

'Never mind, I'll get you another one,' Daddy said, patting Brian's shoulder. We all felt terrible – we knew how much Brian loved his turkey.

'No! I don't want another one. It's not the same!' Brian screamed back.

'I know that Tara killed my turkey. She always wanted to get at it. I'll drown her in the river if I find out that she has done it,' Brian sobbed as he held the limp bird.

'Now, Brian. Tara didn't do it,' Daddy soothed. 'You can bring the nestlings back to the wagon and look after them.'

Later that night my father buried Brian's turkey – a sombre moment but also one filled with overwhelming relief that none of us got found out. We never did tell him the truth.

CHAPTER 3

HARSH REALITY

Looking back now, I realise those first summer months in the wagons were the best. We played and explored with abandon, never realising the hardships that would come with the change of seasons. But as every week passed and the summer turned to autumn, a crisp chill filled the air and the days grew shorter and harder. At first there was work to be done – my father, older brothers and sisters went back to the farms to harvest the crop. Crowning the beets, they called it. Claire and Bridget hated the work, complaining how cold it was in the early morning to pull the beets out of the hard frosty ground. Their knees were sore. Their backs ached from all the bending, up and down. The work was hard and the blistering wind chilled them to the bone.

Us young ones also had to work since we now had to make a lot more trips gathering wood to keep the fire going throughout the day and night for warmth. Mammy simply got on with her jobs, cooking on the stove instead of outdoors, to keep the wagon heated. Of an evening she'd make us all mashed potato followed by our favourite dessert called Goody, which was just milk, bread and sugar, but we all loved it. Occasionally we got a sausage or a side of bacon but mainly she saved the meat for Daddy, who got fed separate from us kids.

Once the beet had finished and the horse fairs were all done for the year, Daddy was at home a lot more, and, with the short days, we noticed that lately he was quick to anger. He couldn't bear to be around all us kids making a noise all the time, so often he'd throw us out of the wagon.

We'd stay at the other wagon while we listened to his raving and screaming at my mother. You couldn't help but listen. Sometimes we could hear my mother trying to calm him down, her soft voice almost drowned by his shouts. There were days she could soothe him, but other times she couldn't and he'd take the horse and cart to the village pub where he'd drink himself silly. But no matter how much he drank, Polly the piebald always managed to take my father back home. We'd see them coming down the road, Polly clip-clopping away, my father flat out on the cart, one leg dangling free, fast asleep, with the ever-faithful Floss still at his side.

We preferred it that way – I would rather have my father coming home asleep than when he was still awake drunk to his eyeballs. Then he terrified us so much that we all ran out of the wagon and hid in the ditches before he could make his way up.

We had seen him giving our older brothers a good hiding and we knew he could fire up a fearsome temper. Those times we'd crouch in the ditch, hearing my mother screaming and pleading for my father to stop until, eventually, everything went quiet and Mammy would give us the go-ahead to come back and we'd creep back to the wagon. He would be fast asleep by then. She, black and blue.

At first Daddy's temper came in short bursts, but as the long winter dragged on they became worse and worse.

'Are you trying to poison me, woman?' he growled at my mother one day, throwing a plate of bacon and mash out of the back of the wagon. Floss, who was never far from Daddy's side, eagerly set upon the discarded food as we all looked on longingly at the fast-disappearing meat.

'What on earth are you talking about?' Mammy replied calmly.

'There's poison in that food you're giving me, you wicked woman!' he railed, furious.

'Don't be so stupid!' Mammy shot back. 'You're pure paranoid!'

But Daddy was serious. Silence filled the air between them.

We knew there was only a few seconds before he'd be up on his feet and across at her like a Rottweiler. The tension was terrible.

So we all sprang up and scrambled to get out of the wagon before we had to see any more. We leapt into the ditch just as we heard the pans and plates go flying across the wagon, clanging and rattling around.

That night we slept out in the ditch with just a few blankets and a plastic covering to shelter us from the cold winter. We snuggled close to each other to keep warm, Aidan and Liam cuddling into Brian and Colin while Tara wrapped herself around Claire and I hugged Bridget tightly. Later, I felt my mother's protective arm extend over me as she lay down next to us. The next morning Mammy limped around the wagon, covered in bruises, black-eyed from Daddy's lashings. I knew something bad was going to happen. I could feel it.

A few days later, I happened to be up high on a tree branch close to the campsite while the others chatted around the campfire. I saw the occasional smiles and giggles as I looked down at my siblings. I let my eyes wander while I started to day-dream. Then, just as sudden, I snapped out of it when I heard my father's ranting. I was just about to come down to make a getaway when I saw my father swing his foot and catch my mother right in her stomach. I was so shocked that I lost my grip and fell awkwardly, leaving me winded and unable to move. I could only watch, helpless, as events unfolded. The awful screams that came from my mother were pure haunting as the foot made contact and her body crumpled in pain.

Claire and Bridget went running over to her, as she knelt on the ground now gripping her belly.

'She's bleeding!' Claire shouted to Daddy.

He stood there, dumb with shock, unable to comprehend what was going on.

'Can't you do something?' Claire pleaded. Then he turned away muttering to himself before calling out to Liam: 'Take the cart to the village. Get an ambulance.'

Meanwhile, my mother was doubled over in agony and Bridget held her shoulders as she screamed out over and over again. I crouched in a nearby bush, breathing hard and rubbing my knees where I'd fallen, too frightened to come out in the open. They stayed that way for what seemed like an age as Daddy paced the campsite, talking to himself, Floss flat out on the ground a few feet away, his ears and tail down. Daddy shouted out to my poor, stricken mother: 'Just hang in there! Liam's gone to get help. You just stay calm. I'm sorry. I'm so sorry.'

At last the ambulance came and took my mother away to the hospital – the two men helped her up and put her into the back of the vehicle. And as they eased her slowly away from where she'd fallen, she left a pool of blood on the ground.

It was the first time my mother had left us and we missed and pined for her to be back home. But we couldn't rely on

Daddy to keep things going – he was lost to us now, always drunk and roaming the place, shouting and talking to himself all the time. The Legion of Mary, a charity for helping out families like ours, came to visit one day and saw the state he was in.

'You'll have to come with us now,' they told my father, who looked like a broken man. I think he would have gone with anyone at that time.

'Where are they taking Daddy?' I asked Bridget as he folded himself into the back seat of their car.

'Daddy's not well,' Bridget said, a dark look on her face. 'He has to go to the mental hospital.'

I nodded, pretending I knew what she meant, but really I had no idea what a mental hospital was. Later Brian explained: 'It's a place to fix Daddy's head so he thinks better.'

We all agreed that this was a very good idea because Daddy wasn't thinking too well at the moment. The only problem was that, with both our parents gone, we were left to fend for ourselves. It was Claire and Bridget who took on the responsibility of caring for us children: dressing, feeding and washing us every day.

There were days we had so little to eat they'd put us all in the cart while we travelled from one farmer to the next to beg some food. Luckily, all the farmers were kind and they'd give us eggs, milk and vegetables so we managed to get by until Mammy returned a few weeks later. We were so happy to see her and suddenly felt a lot safer.

A week after that, Daddy came back too. He was more composed and calmer than before and he'd sworn off the drink, which we all thought was for the best.

'Daddy, what was the mental hospital like?' Brian asked that evening.

'Ah, it wasn't all that nice,' Daddy said, a little sadly, as he stroked Floss, who probably missed my father the most when he was gone. 'They give me the electric shocks to get my head straight again.'

'What's that, then? Electric shocks?' Brian was in a curious mood.

'It's like being struck by lightning,' Daddy explained. 'Like a big bolt of lightning in your head.'

We all gasped in horror – imagine being struck by lightning to make you better! It sounded horrifying. But at least we had our parents back again.

Weeks later my parents announced they had to go into town to get a bit of shopping and they'd be back later in the day. We were desperate to go with them, but no amount of begging and pleading from any of us would change their minds.

'We have something important to do. We won't be long,' my mother said as she pulled on her heavy winter coat and they both started walking down the road.

So we spent the day roaming the fields and climbing trees as usual. On our way home we spotted Mammy and Daddy walking back towards the wagon just ahead of us so we all ran and surrounded them, happy to see them back. My mother was carrying a bundle of blankets in her arms.

Brian asked my mother: 'What's that you're carrying in your arms? In that blanket?'

'Ah, I got a little sister for you lot. Her name is Libby,' my mother replied as she gently bent down to show off the baby.

'Wow, a baby! Where did you get the baby?' I asked excitedly. We loved babies and we all tried to clamber over my mother to catch a glimpse.

'Well, we were walking past this farmer's field and there were cabbages growing there. Mammy saw a leg sticking out and Mammy pulled out this little baby!' She laughed as she grabbed my hand. We all walked back together, our attention focused on the new addition to the family – a new sister, Libby!

Brian, Tara, Colin and I were out and about the next day with nothing particular planned when Brian had an idea.

'I want to get myself a baby like our mother did!' he said. 'Didn't she say she got it from under the cabbages? There must be a cabbage field somewhere and we'll get our own babies to look after. That's what we'll do. We could get a few babies each. Now what do you lot think about that? Ain't that a grand idea!'

Brian beamed. He was always so clever and smart, always the one thinking up the new schemes and games. And this one seemed like a really good idea, one of his best!

So we crossed the fields, skipping along, our strides quickening until we got to the farm. There we saw all the cabbages with the white heads peeking out of the soil.

There were rows and rows of cabbages, hundreds, thousands of them! Where to start? We were already bursting with excitement at the prospect of having all those babies.

Brian went first. He stepped up to the cabbage nearest to him while we stood watching, full of anticipation. He bent down to grab it and started pulling it out of the ground. It wasn't that easy. He yanked it, left and right, loosening up the soil before giving it one mighty heave and, with a sudden jerk, the cabbage came loose and he stumbled backwards. He threw it to the side then went to investigate the hole that it had left behind. We all peered in beside him, eager to see the baby – but there wasn't one! We were shocked.

'I don't understand.' Brian was baffled. 'Mammy said she'd found it under the cabbage.'

Tara chimed in: 'Maybe there ain't one under that one, but there could be one under this cabbage.' And she headed over to another cabbage to start work.

Then we all started pulling up the cabbages, all of us criss-crossing each other as we pulled out the vegetables, then cursing at our luck as we glared into empty holes. We pulled out one after another after another, but there were no babies. Not a single one.

We were all confused and bitterly disappointed.

'I can't find one, Brian,' I spoke out. 'Maybe there is no baby here or it might be somewhere else. Maybe you have to find a special one or a magic one.'

'Yes, Brian. I'm tired. Maybe we should go and do something else,' Tara added while Colin sat on the ground poking a stick into the mud, waiting on us to see what we'd do.

'No! There must be a baby! Mammy said so. Go and pull out a bit more,' Brian shouted back, angry and frustrated. By now we were all covered in mud – it was in our clothes, our faces and our hair – and so tired of digging that we gave up. The field was a mess with cabbages strewn everywhere and we walked back to the wagon dejected. We were so sure about the babies that our failure was hard to comprehend.

As we walked into the campsite Brian was still going on about finding babies: 'I'm going back there tomorrow. I'll find one.'

'Jesus Christ!' Suddenly we heard our sister Bridget's incredulous shout. 'Look at the lot of you! You're covered in mud!'

Claire seemed equally horrified as she caught sight of us: 'Lads, what have you lot been up to? Oh my God, look at how filthy you are! Mammy will go mad seeing you lot like that.'

They both shook their heads as they turned us about, examining us from head to toe. Mud clung to every part of us.

'Come, let's get down to the river to get all that filth off you before your parents see you,' she added.

Bridget grabbed a towel as she quickly ushered us towards the river.

As she was washing us down she asked: 'Anyway, how did you manage to get this filthy?'

'We were digging up cabbages in the farmer's field,' I answered.

'You what? You did what?' Bridget was stunned.

I thought that Bridget didn't hear me properly so I told her of our day on the field looking for babies as Brian, Tara and Colin nodded along. Claire and Bridget were completely gobsmacked and after I'd finished my story they just looked at each other before bursting out laughing. They were in stitches. They couldn't believe what we had done.

Finally, when they calmed down enough to talk, Bridget warned us not to go back to the field.

'The farmer will be going mad after you lot destroyed his crop. There is no baby under the cabbage and there never will be. The baby came out from Mammy. Your Mammy was only playing with you lot when she said about the cabbages.'

'But Bridget, she did say it,' I insisted, unconvinced.

'Look, you lot better not go round saying this but that day when your father kicked your mother he kicked the baby out of her. She was pregnant – us older ones knew but you lot didn't have a clue. All that blood on the ground, that was from the baby. And she was too early and little and that's why she had to stay in hospital all the time, to get stronger. Now stay away from the farmer and let that be it.'

We walked back to the wagon in silence. The river water was cold and I shivered as my mind returned to that frightening day that I saw my mother get hurt. I saw the blood stain on the ground. I recalled her haunting cries and the ambulance coming to take her away. I know now how our sister Libby came into this world. Libby was born prematurely, and by the time our parents brought her home she was already four months old.

With the new addition in the family, the wagon felt more cramped than ever. We were forever climbing over one another, and one day, when Tara and I were playing, Tara was clambering round the stove to get to me when, suddenly, she slipped. One second I saw her, and the next she was gone. She'd fallen straight into the middle of the stove's chimney stack. Her pitiful screams as her body touched the hot chimney were awful. Mammy bolted to grab Tara, who was now in hysterics, her small body scorched and singed from the fire.

I watched on, petrified, as Mammy ripped the smouldering clothes off my sister to reveal the red raw burns on her legs and body and her skin bubbling up into sacks of liquid. Mammy worked quickly, dousing Tara with pails of cold water while my father rushed to get the horse and cart. Everything was chaotic. I was glad to see the horse and cart galloping away with both our parents and Tara, who was still crying her eyes out over the pain. At least I knew she was going to get help but I missed Tara terribly. She was much more than my sister; she was my friend and companion. Of all my siblings, we were the closest, and every day without her felt like an age.

Tara was badly burned on the inside of her thighs and her stomach and she had some smaller burns on her hands. It was a pitiful sight when she finally returned from hospital, struggling to walk because of the pain. She was so miserable that she stayed in bed most of the time. I stayed with her to keep her company and cheer her up as much as I could. She had to go to the clinic a few times to get the bandages re-dressed and it was a week before the pain started to ease and she was able to smile again.

As if things weren't bad enough, even the weather conspired against us. It was early winter now and the sky looked constantly dirty and gloomy, never-ending clouds blocking out the sun. One day the wind was so strong and blustery we young ones found it hard to get about. Each time we tried to move from one place to another we were pushed off course by the powerful gusts. At first we laughed as it blew us off our feet but then the leaves and debris started to fly about and we got scared. Daddy was worried too and he called for everyone to come outside the wagons as he threw ropes over them to try and pin them down. But the winds were only getting stronger and the wagons started pitching and shaking from side to side.

Now the rain pelted down and every minute it seemed the storm was getting worse.

'We need to get to a sheltered area,' Daddy shouted over the deafening gales. 'These wagons could go over at this rate!'

Aidan and Liam nodded, working quickly to tie the horses up to the wagons to drive them down the roadside. There they waited for all of us to get on. We moved as quickly as we could, the air around us now stirred up and swirling with debris. Every second this storm seemed to be gathering momentum and power. The wind pushed at the trees' branches so they lashed at us like long arms. We were terrified, each of us jumping up into the wagons for safety. Once we were all aboard Daddy let out a massive 'Yarhh!', cracked the reins and galloped the horses hard. We rocked and bounced down the road. I could hear the wagon brushing against the trees as we all held tight, petrified for our lives. Daddy drove us as fast as he dared into the woodlands, hoping that the trees would provide us with a bit of shelter. As we came into the thickest part of the wood we all felt the wind lessen around us.

We stopped, listening, Daddy breathing hard, and just at that moment we heard a tremendous crack, followed by an ear-splitting crash.

The horses reared up, their ears pinned back in alarm, and we all scrambled out of our wagon to see what had happened. There we saw a tree lying right into the middle of the second wagon. We were stunned. I was so fearful that somebody must be hurt inside but then my brothers and sisters popped out of the wagon one by one, completely unharmed. That night we all slept in the one wagon in the middle of the woods while my father kept watch over us.

By morning the storm had moved on and we woke to see the second wagon buried under leaves and branches while the tree trunk rested slanted with its root jutting out at the other end. It had fallen right into the middle part of the wagon, leaving a gaping hole in the ceiling. Luckily, Daddy said it looked worse than it actually was and he quickly set about fixing it up with Aidan and Liam.

Secretly, Tara and I were disappointed. We'd had enough of the wagons now and we'd hoped the storm might signal an end to our hard life on the road. But Daddy wasn't giving up, even when the weather turned bitterly cold and snow started to come down in thick white clumps. That first winter was so cold that, even huddled together under a blanket, we shivered while we slept. Yes, life aboard the wagons was certainly harder than we'd imagined. I was quietly yearning to be back in a proper house. By summer we could play out and enjoy ourselves again, but as the second winter approached I felt a horrible dread rising up in me. Things were tough but I had no idea of the terrors another winter would bring.

CHAPTER 4

A BIRTH AND A DEATH

We knew the snow was coming long before it arrived. It was exceptionally cold that year. Daddy said it over and over. He could always tell what the weather was going to do and he'd been looking up in the sky for days now, tutting and shaking his head: 'There's snow coming. Big snow.'

Of course, all us kids were excited – we loved playing in the snow. But none of us could have imagined how hard and heavy it would come down that year. Once those large flakes started drifting to the ground, it didn't stop. For days it snowed and snowed until afterwards the fields, roads and everything else as far as your eyes could see was buried deep under a white carpet, truly transforming the landscape. It was just as well that we knew our surroundings like the backs of our hands or we could have got lost just by walking out of the campsite.

Now the deep snow made life a lot harder for us to move around, and our daily chores of fetching water and collecting wood became almost impossible.

Still, we always tried to have fun and often we'd start off on a chore before ending up in the middle of a snowball fight, ducking, diving and laughing as the snowballs found their marks. We built huge tunnels in the snow and massive snowballs which we'd push down the hills, watching in fascination as they grew bigger with every turn.

It was always great fun until our hands froze and then we'd have to go back inside the wagon, crying from the pain.

'Mammy, our hands hurt. It hurts, do something, Mammy!' Tara and I cried out as soon as we saw her.

'There, didn't I tell you lot not to overdo it playing in the snow,' Mammy chided, placing our hands in a basin of warm water and gently massaging them to relieve the pain and the numbness. Of course, it wasn't long before we'd get the feeling in our fingers back and we'd be at the snow again. There really wasn't much else to do as we were stranded about a mile from the village.

One night I woke up with the cold, despite the warm blanket and the body heat from Tara, who lay curled behind my back, her breathing deep and relaxed. My mother was asleep on the bunk below us with my brother Colin and Libby. I climbed carefully down the small ladder and reached for the box under the bunk, where my mother kept the socks. I could hear the wind howling outside and the wagon swayed when a gust of wind whistled past. It sounded so wild and scary that I hurried to pick up two pairs of my father's socks, rolling them as far up my legs as I could before creeping back up the ladder to my bunk and huddling up to Tara. I was slowly regaining a bit of warmth and was almost asleep when I heard my mother groaning beneath me.

Instinctively, I leaned my head over the bed to look down.

My mother was sitting up panting, gripping the pole of the bunk so tightly her knuckles were white while her other hand held her belly. Her face was misshapen as she grimaced, gritting her teeth with pain.

Sweat dripped from her brow and her eyes were shut tight in intense concentration.

'Mammy, you look sick,' I said as I came down the ladder, scared at what was happening to my mother.

'Go and get Claire and Bridget!' she spoke between rapid breaths.

I didn't need to be told twice. I threw on my coat and Wellingtons, jumped down off the wagon into fresh snow and ran across to the other wagon. Thick snowflakes rained down heavily, and the cross-wind was so cold and fierce that my cheeks were already stinging by the time I got to the door.

As soon as I opened it up, I shouted for Claire and Bridget. Groggily, Bridget sat up in the bed: 'Are you gone in the head, Kathleen?'

The breeze blew in behind me and the others sat up in their beds.

'You gobshite! Shut the feckin' door! It's freezing!' Liam shouted from the top bunk. Breathing heavily, I managed to tell them that Mammy was in pain and she needed them to come quickly.

The fear in my voice must have convinced them of the urgency for they all jumped out of their beds and grabbed their clothes in a flash. Bridget rushed to my mother while Claire took charge of the rest of us, ushering us into the second wagon. Aidan and Liam were instructed to go to the village to get our father from the pub and also a midwife as my mother was about to have a baby! My brothers had to trek a mile across deep, snowy fields in a blizzard to fetch help. Meanwhile, my mother's groaning turned to screams. We were all shaken by the terrifying sounds coming from the other wagon. Claire's face was almost frozen in fear.

'You lot stay in the wagon now,' she told us. 'I have to check on Mammy.'

She ran outside into the snowstorm as the screams came louder now – then suddenly the screaming stopped. We all waited anxiously, not knowing what was going on, holding each other for comfort and warmth. None of us spoke. Finally, we were relieved to hear the voices of our brothers and father accompanied by another voice which we reckoned must have been the midwife. Soon after, Claire clambered back in the wagon.

'Mammy is all right and she is being attended to by the midwife,' she said, smiling reassuringly.

'Bridget and our father are with her. She has given birth to a baby girl. We knew she was going to have another one but no one thought she would come so quick. She had her before the midwife even arrived. We had to wrap the poor little thing up in newspapers to keep her warm, but the baby's fine. There's nothing more to do but to wait till the ambulance gets here. Lie down and try to get some sleep.'

Claire spoke calmly, and as her words registered in my mind all the tension and stress of the past few hours left me. I had been so scared for my mother. Everyone sighed with relief that all was well.

In fact, it would take hours for the ambulance to arrive as the snowstorm had made our road impassable. A snow-plough was brought in first before the ambulance could come through and take my mother and the new baby to the hospital. And that is how our baby sister Lucy arrived in the world.

Mammy and the baby returned a few days later, along with the Legion of Mary workers who had now been alerted to our plight out in the middle of the fields, cut off from the village by the snow. They brought winter jackets, Wellington boots and blankets to fend off the worst of the cold and gave Mammy food vouchers to help feed all of us children. We were all grateful for the extra warmth and food. But in truth I never truly relaxed until I woke up one morning, well over a month after the drifts cut us off, to see the first thaw and the green and brown fields re-emerging from under their winter blankets.

'Have you seen Floss anywhere this morning?'

Daddy was up and about early that spring morning, tending to his horses as usual, bringing in the hay, grooming their coats and changing their shoes. But now he was searching the campsite, a concerned look on his face.

'It's probably nothing but it's a bit strange that he's not about,' he added, absent-mindedly. 'Have you seen him?'

I was not long woken up and still had a bleary head, full of sleep.

'No,' I replied. 'I've only just got out the wagon, Daddy.'

I was keen to help so I got Tara up and we set about looking for Daddy's favourite dog. We didn't have to walk far, just about 50 yards from the wagon, when we came across Floss lying under a tree.

Thinking he was asleep, I started calling out: 'Hey, Floss! Come here, boy.'

We waited a while but Floss didn't move a muscle.

'God! That Floss must be asleep,' I said to Tara and we crouched next to Floss as I said again: 'Come on, get up, you lazy dog!'

I went to give Floss a shove, but when I touched him his body was stiff. I tried to heave him to one side but Floss just flopped back, lifeless.

'Oh my God, Tara. Floss has died. He ain't moving.'

We both started to cry – Floss wasn't just like a dog, He was one of our family. We ran back screaming: 'Daddy! Daddy, we found Floss but he's dead. We found him under that tree over there.'

I pointed in the direction of the tree.

'You what …?' My father didn't get out two words before he ran to the tree and threw himself down on the ground where Floss lay.

I heard him shouting out: 'No. No. No!'

Tara and I followed behind and came upon my father, utterly distraught. Daddy was sobbing his heart out at the death of his friend and companion. I couldn't help but cry seeing my father in so much despair, and so did Tara. As my father's cries could be heard all round the campsite, gradually the others came to see and each of us shed tears at the loss of our dear Floss.

Daddy was inconsolable. He lay down next to Floss and stayed there, by his side, crying and talking to him. The day went on. We got ourselves some food but Daddy wouldn't move. As day shifted into night Tara and I came to sit with our father.

'See that dog Floss,' he said to us, now taking long swigs from a bottle of Guinness. 'We've been everywhere together. That's the smartest dog you'll ever find. You know, I sold that dog to a lot of the farmers and got quite a bit of money for him but the dog never stayed. He always found his way back home.'

Daddy laughed with the memory but then his sadness consumed him and he started crying again. Daddy didn't come in the wagon that night – no matter how much my mother coaxed him he refused to leave Floss's side. For three days Daddy slept outdoors next to his dog until eventually Mammy managed to persuade him to bury the remains, which were now beginning to decay and smell.

A little bit of Daddy died with Floss. You could see that his heartache weighed heavy on him for a long while. I hadn't seen him like this before, even after the time a man came to get Daddy to tell him his mammy was dying from TB. Daddy had gone back to his home town, and though he was still banned from his parents' home he saw my grandmother in hospital. He told us she had died in his arms and for a while he was sad and quiet. Daddy was always devoted to his mother and she adored him too. But when Floss died, Daddy was a wreck. Eventually he pulled himself together. The horse fair was coming up and he had to prepare all his horses, making sure they were in top nick. Eventually, Daddy left for the fair with Liam and Aidan. They returned two days later, pleased with their trades. They'd managed to sell off the horses and buy a good-looking chestnut mare.

She was lively and energetic, though she could be snappy and headstrong. My father seemed contented with the sale but he was still tortured over the loss of his dear Floss. Now he spent a lot of his time and money in the pub, drunk in the company of his friends. Mammy was left in charge of us all with no money and nothing to feed us, and this started a lot of arguments between them.

One night Mammy said she'd had enough and marched off towards the village to find Daddy and bring him home. We waited up, listening for the sound of my mother and father returning – it was late by the time we went to sleep and they still weren't back. The next morning they were both there and Mammy didn't say anything to us about what happened. Instead, she went out with my daddy the next night and they stayed out all night again. This happened night after night as Claire and Bridget were left, struggling to look after us, as well as the babies, Libby and Lucy.

'Mammy, why are you leaving the children with us so much?' Claire complained one night as Mammy put on her coat to accompany our father to the village again.

'It's not fair on us having to miss school to look after your babies. If this carries on, Mammy, I swear I'll leave! I am not going to be looking after your babies while you pop them out year after year. I want a better life than this. You don't even leave us with anything to eat. What kind of mother are you? Now you're both irresponsible parents – how is this going to make our lives better?'

Mammy didn't say much. She just went on with her work but we were all waiting for an answer.

We couldn't understand it – why did Mammy leave us? It was hard enough with Daddy out drunk every night.

Then one day, as my father was preparing himself to go to the farm, he shouted at Claire to put the reins on the new mare that he had bought at the last fair. Claire had done this many times and thought nothing of it but today the young mare was in a skittish temper.

As she tried to fit the reins over her head, the mare got snappy and bit Claire's face. Claire let out a sharp scream and pulled away, running back to my shocked father, crying in pain, both her palms covering her face. We could see blood streaming out the side of one hand. The next thing I knew, Daddy picked up a hammer and dashed across to the mare, bringing it down, smack, straight on top of her head. The horse came crashing down to the ground like a sack of potatoes. She was out stone cold. I was stunned at what my father had done. I thought he had killed the mare.

Meanwhile, Mammy started tending to Claire's wound. The horse had severed the right side of her nostril from her face. Blood dripped everywhere as Mammy helped her to get on the cart so they could take her to the hospital. A few minutes later I was relieved to see the mare stagger to her feet, a little groggy, but otherwise no worse for her bash about the head.

Later, Claire returned with stitches to her nose, covered with a patch. And Daddy was so stressed by the whole episode that he stayed the night at the pub. Claire, horrified at having her nose half bitten off, was in such shock and pain she vented angrily at my mother.

'I'm going to be left with a massive scar now. I hate this life. I'm not going to do this any more. I'm going off to get myself a job. I don't care. I can't watch any more what you and Daddy are doing to all of us.'

Mammy could say nothing to calm Claire down. And the more she tried, the more Claire ranted and screamed at her.

Bridget held Claire tight, trying hard to console her: 'Hush now, Claire. You're upset.'

'No, Bridget!' Claire wept. 'I'm going. I'm really going. I've had enough of this miserable life.'

'Now, now, Claire. Mammy needs you. You just can't get up and go. Daddy won't allow it. Besides, you'll be better soon and it'll all be forgotten.'

'Forgotten? How can I forget all that's happened to us? They don't care. Why should they care if I leave? The only thing that's stopping me is the children.'

They hugged each other now and all us young ones rushed to offer our comfort, burying ourselves in our elder sisters' embrace.

Later, when Claire had calmed down we all decided to take a walk. My mother, Claire, Bridget, Tara and myself talked and joked about, and we teased each other as we walked. We were not far from the river when we saw our father about to cross the bridge from the other side. The bridge itself was only wide enough to allow a cart to pass through, and on either side, about a foot thick, there stood a three-foot-tall stone wall. We saw Daddy staggering towards us, so drunk he could hardly keep himself upright.

'Look at that old fool!' Mammy scoffed. 'Your father's as drunk as a skunk! He can't even keep himself up. Mind, he'll fall over the bridge if he's not careful.'

I worried in that moment that my mother was right. He was veering uncontrollably from one side to the other.

'Daddy! Daddy!' I called out.

Daddy saw us, stopped walking and smiled wonkily. He looked like he was just going to sit down for a quick rest, backing himself into the wall on the bridge. But he went too far and toppled over backwards into the river. We heard a loud splash as my father hit the water.

'Oh my lord!' Mammy shouted. 'What did I tell you? That flipping eejit just fell over the bridge!'

We all ran down the bank of the river to see what had happened to our father. Though the river was only about waist height Daddy was struggling to get his head out of the water, and every time he got up he fell down again as the river swept him off his feet. I watched anxiously as Mammy, Claire and Bridget waded into the river to rescue him. Mammy managed to catch hold of him and we all helped drag him to the bank. Claire took hold of one side of our drenched father and Bridget the other as they helped him home, all the while my father rambling on and on about the mare, not even realising he'd nearly drowned. We laughed about it the next day but Claire was quiet. The horse bite had been the final straw for her.

Now a change was coming – the family I'd known and loved all my life was about to break apart.

CHAPTER 5

NEEDLES AND HAYSTACKS

Claire had had enough of our hard life, and though just 15 and 16, she and Bridget decided to strike out on their own. The Legion of Mary charity helped them get nursing apprenticeships in Dublin, and just a few weeks after the horse's bite they both left. Daddy couldn't believe it – he was terribly fond of them both, but especially Claire. We all cried when they had to go – we loved our older sisters so much, they had brought us up and cared for us for so long. I didn't know it then but I wasn't to see Claire again for another ten years. Now we were left alone and, when Mammy was gone, it fell to me and Tara to look after the little babies. We did our best but it wasn't easy – we were just five and six ourselves. One time Lucy found a bottle of medicine and drank it all. She was limp and floppy by the time Mammy got back and rushed her to hospital but luckily she survived.

One day, not long after Bridget and Claire left, a car pulled up by the wagons. Four people got out – a worker from the Legion of Mary whom we knew, a man that looked like a doctor and two others.

From what we could make out, they were chatting to my mother about the 'im-you-nice-ay-shun' of the children.

'We've been looking to do it for a long while now,' they were telling Mammy. 'But we kept missing you. Every time we came to find you you'd moved on.'

We all listened curiously, not having a clue what they were going on about. Mammy went into the wagon and brought out Lucy. We saw the doctor open a large black case then a pull out a giant needle.

He attached a little vial of liquid to the top, tapped the needle then sunk the whole thing into Lucy's chubby little leg. Poor Lucy screamed her little heart out but the doctor just went on with his work, pulling out another vial now and asking Mammy to bring Libby.

Just then the penny dropped and Brian, Tara, Colin and myself realised that we were next! Brian was out of the back window of the wagon like a shot of lightning and Tara, Colin and myself scrambled out quickly behind. We knew we had to get as far away as possible from that gigantic needle so we scattered all about the place. The folks from the Legion of Mary saw what we were doing then and shouted at my brothers: 'Quick! Catch them!'

Aidan and Liam set off in pursuit but, try as they might, they couldn't catch us because they were laughing so much. We darted in and out of the campsite, Mammy shouting at us to come back, Liam and Aidan dodging and weaving about, trying to pin us down. Eventually I felt Aidan's firm grip on my leg and I fell face down into the dirt.

'No, Aidan! Don't let them do that to me!' I begged, bucking and kicking at my brother.

I could hear Brian a way off, shouting and swearing his head off: 'Let go of me, you feckin' bastard!'

Someone else had hold of Tara.

'Mammy!' she screeched, petrified. 'Save us, Mammy!'

But Mammy just looked on, unconcerned, now holding two bawling infants. Our brothers dragged us back to the doctor and I was trembling with terror as I saw the needle and felt it prick my leg. The pain seared up the side of my thigh and I cried out, terrified, until I felt my brother's grip loosen and the doctor, having completed his task, moved on to the next one.

The next day Tara, Colin, Brian and myself resolved to get as far away from camp as possible. We didn't want any more nasty surprises.

'Come on!' Brian yelled when he spotted the hay barn we loved to play in. It was one of our favourite games – we liked to pile bales of hay one on top of the other so that eventually we had a hay tower all the way to the top of the barn. That day we'd just built our tower to the top and we were climbing down again – I was in front with Tara and Colin behind me. There was just a little ledge at each level so you had to go down carefully from one level to the next. But Colin was impatient and pushed me from behind before I could get down. I missed my footing and fell all the way from the top of the tower to the very bottom. On the way, my leg got caught between two bales and my body twisted round. I felt something snap then and a stinging sensation in my leg as I came to a stop at the bottom. The others followed quickly behind and jumped down to the ground before running out of the barn, hardly paying me any mind. I wanted to run after them but I was dazed from the fall and my leg was still stinging. I tried to ease myself off the ground but my leg refused to move. So instead I crawled out of the hay barn with my arms.

I'd just got myself out into the yard of the farm when Tara came running back.

'Come on, come on, Kathleen,' she urged. 'What's wrong with you? Get up and walk.'

'Tara, I can't feel my leg,' I told her. 'I can't even move it.'

All I could feel was this dreadful stinging.

Then she looked down and let out an awful scream. I followed the path of her gaze down my leg and got the fright of my life. All along my ankle I could see my white bones sticking out.

'Oh my God!' I screamed. 'I'm dying! I'm dying!'

Before that moment I had no idea I was seriously hurt, but now I went into shock. Tara did what she could – dragging me through the yard, out the gates and putting me onto the side of the road.

Then she went and got my mother. Mammy came and she started screaming too and that alerted the farmer. Just then Daddy pulled up in a van with two other people I'd not seen before.

'Look at the child's leg!' she shrieked at him. 'Look at it! It's destroyed. Look at them bones sticking out. Get out of the van and pick her up!' Mammy's screams were more terrifying than anything else – I couldn't even cry because she was going so mad. But Daddy didn't say a word. There she was, ripping her hair out, and he just drove off. So the famer put me in his car and drove me to the hospital, Mammy still ranting and raving.

Everything seemed to happen in a blur. We got to the hospital but they told us they couldn't fix up my leg because they didn't deal with broken bones. Instead, they put Mammy and me in an ambulance and drove us to another hospital. Here, they cut off my sock and shoe and said to Mammy that they were sorry but they would have to amputate my leg because I'd been too long without blood circulating.

Mammy turned on them fiercely: 'There's no way you're taking that child's leg! No way!'

So the doctors went away and when they came back they told us we were very lucky because it just so happened that a surgeon from America was visiting and he was a bone specialist. And he was going to try and save my leg.

'Mammy, am I going to die?' I asked her as they prepared me for surgery. I really didn't know what was happening but judging by my mother's hysterical reactions I reckoned it must be pretty terrible.

'No, baby,' she said, though her eyes didn't look so sure. 'They just have to put you to sleep for a bit so they can fix your leg back on again.'

'You will stay, Mammy?' I begged her. 'You will stay until I wake up?'

'Of course, baby. I'll stay with you.'

I felt reassured at least that Mammy would be there when I woke up and she held my hands as they led me on a trolley into the theatre.

The last thing I saw were the bright fluorescent lights overhead, racing past. Mammy's worried eyes. And then I was gone.

I came round in a dark ward, lit only by a few dim bedside lights. There were other beds all around me but everyone seemed asleep, except a couple of nurses going about their business in hushed tones.

I looked down to see my whole leg was encased in a hard white material, all the way from my toes to my hip. And Mammy was nowhere to be seen.

I had to stay in hospital for two whole months and I cried the whole time I was there, thinking nobody was ever going to come back and get me. There were other children in the ward too but they all had visitors – nobody ever came to visit me. For the first few weeks I was confined to bed, unable to walk, but as my leg healed I was given crutches to get me back on my feet. I couldn't use them so I ended up sliding across the floor on my bottom to get around. I knew that if nobody was coming for me I'd have to make my own way home, so once I was out of bed I tried everything I could to escape. Each time the nurses' backs were turned I was down on the floor and out the door. It drove them mental. Eventually they put me in a room on my own, and tied my hands and legs down to stop me escaping. I cried my heart out then.

Though, really, I didn't have any reason to complain. In fact it was quite nice in the hospital. We had regular meals, new clothes and the doctor who fixed my leg even bought me a doll, a bribe to try and stop me escaping. I enjoyed playing with the other children on the wards. We'd all be putting bandages on ourselves and each other and there was even a school where we did lessons. They tried to teach me things but I couldn't learn. I'd never been to school or been made to sit and listen to anything before in my life. I didn't have the patience for it. All I wanted was to go home. I was missing everyone so much.

Every day I asked the ward nurses: 'Are they going to come back and get me today? When is my Mammy and Daddy coming for me?'

But no one could answer my questions. I really thought they were never coming back.

One of the nurses had the idea of letting me sit and chat to the older folk in the next ward and that seemed to calm me down. So every day they sent me to the old people where I'd pass a pleasant couple of hours telling them all about Tara, Colin and Brian and all the things we liked to do. Eventually, one day the nice doctor who had fixed my leg came to me and said: 'You're going home today, Kathleen.'

I was so excited! My leg was still in plaster but now I'd learned how to use the crutches and I could get about quite well. I said goodbye to all the friends I'd made in my ward and also the old people's ward, who seemed a little sad I was leaving, but happy for me when I told them over and over: 'I'm going home. I'm going home!'

The hospital took me back in an ambulance and I asked the nurse in the front to let me know when she spotted our wagons.

Suddenly, she announced: 'I can't see any wagons, Kathleen, but I do see a pretty cottage.'

I was confused. We came to a halt and the nurse opened the back door of the ambulance in front of a long drive leading up to a large house in the middle of a skinny lane. The nurse helped me out the back and that's when I saw my Mammy, Daddy and all my siblings emerging from the front door. A house! We had a new house!

Tara ran the quickest and she was upon me in a flash, cuddling me and kissing me all over.

'Oh, Kathleen! We thought you were dead! We kept asking Mammy when you were coming home and she always said "soon" but then you never came so we honestly thought you were dead!'

'I missed you!' I said. 'I missed all of you's!'

Tara seemed fascinated with my leg, now encased in plaster, and she watched, intrigued, as I used the crutches to help me hobble up the drive.

'We've got a house!' she said proudly. 'Look, a proper house! Come inside, I want to show you around!'

As I came to the doorway, Daddy knelt down to wrap me in a loving embrace, tears welling up from the sight of me. The others cuddled me too. Mammy was now holding a new little baby who screamed away in her arms.

'Now just you be careful with that thing,' she called, pointing to my plaster cast, as Tara led me inside the new house. 'You mind them stairs!'

There were no hugs or kisses from her. Nothing. I didn't even stop to ask why nobody had come to visit me in the hospital.

I was just happy and grateful to be reunited with my family. And in a house again. That was just grand!

CHAPTER 6

A NEW HOME

'Come on! Come on!' Tara was breathless with excitement. She couldn't wait to show me around our new home. I shuffled in through the big old-fashioned door with the latch and immediately I could see we had a large open parlour with a fire in the middle.

'This here is our room,' Tara beamed proudly, swinging open the door of a room on the ground floor to reveal two beds and a pile of clothes on the floor. I was pleased to see my dresses among them.

'Let's go upstairs!' she shouted. But I was still on crutches and I looked at the steep stairs up to the second floor.

'I can't climb that,' I told her, nodding towards my leg, still in plaster from my hip to my toes.

'That's okay – Aidan and Liam will carry you,' she said, undeterred, yelling for the older brothers to pick me up so I could see upstairs. There was a second room for Mammy and Daddy and the little ones. And next to the bed I saw a brand new cot in the corner.

'That's for the new baby,' Tara said authoritatively. 'He's called Riley. Oh, Kathleen, you're going to love him! He's just the most beautiful thing in the world!'

Afterwards, Tara showed me the outdoors – we had two acres to the front of the house with sheds all around the walls.

'That's for the dogs,' explained Tara. Now Daddy had been busy while I was away, breeding pups, and the sheds were full of yapping dogs as well as Nellie our greyhound, an Alsatian and a little white terrier.

It didn't take long for me to settle into our new life and I was so pleased we were back in a house. Of a night me and Brian, Tara and Colin would all curl up together on one bed, as we were all used to doing, even though there were two beds in our room. And during the day we'd go out exploring the fields and woodlands, though at first I couldn't go very far because of my plaster cast. I was bursting to get it off so I could climb trees again with the rest of them.

It should have been a wonderful new start for us but Daddy was still troubled. And still drinking. One day the Legion of Mary came round with a present – a brand new television set.

'Ohh!' we gasped in wonder as we ran our hands over the smooth wooden box.

I'd seen a television before in the hospital but I never imagined we could have one ourselves at home so it was a real surprise.

'Let's get this thing working now,' said Liam, and he set to fiddling about with all the wires at the back. Tara and I jumped around him excitedly while he shooed us away.

'Get back.' He swatted at us good-naturedly. 'Can't you let a man get on with his work?'

He was still only 15 himself but in our eyes Liam was already fully grown, tall and strong, just like our Daddy.

Finally, he looked up at us, satisfied: 'Okay now. I think we're ready. Tara, press that large button at the bottom, will ya?'

Tara did as she was told and at that moment the screen flickered into life and we found ourselves staring at a row of black and white lines.

'Okay, give me a minute,' said Liam. 'I'll just have to tune it up.'

Between the blasts of white noise we could just about make out the sound of two men talking. Liam twiddled a dial just above the 'On' button and eventually an image flickered, disappeared then reappeared and stayed steady – we could see two people sat across from each other on chairs, talking. We all cheered loudly at his success.

'What's that feckin' racket?' Suddenly we heard Daddy's angry shouts as he strode in the front door.

'Daddy! Daddy!' we all clamoured. 'Look! We got a television!'

'No we bloody don't,' he growled. 'Not with that racket.'

And he crossed in front of us, ripped the television free from its wires and flung it straight through the window.

It came down in the garden with a loud crash. We jumped up to look out at the television set, all broken up and smashed on our garden.

That was it. We'd had a television for about two hours. Then it was gone. We hadn't even managed to watch anything on it.

Daddy's tempers seemed to be worse than ever in the new house and poor Mammy bore the brunt. There were times he got so mad with her he'd fight her like he would a man, slapping, hitting and throwing her about all over the place. For us it was frightening and we all tried to run out the house whenever we felt the threat of a violent outburst. Now Daddy had a new grievance – the baby.

'That feckin' child ain't mine!' he'd tell her whenever he heard Riley screaming out from his cot upstairs.

Mammy would sigh, pure exhausted with the constant fighting.

'Of course he's yours, Donal,' she'd reply, just like she'd said a million times before this.

'No, he's not. That child ain't mine. I know he's not mine.'

During these moments we'd dodge and weave through their legs, hoping to reach the front door to escape out of the house before things could get any worse. If they were fighting near the front door we had no choice but to run upstairs and hide in their room instead, hoping Daddy wouldn't come up while he was still mad. None of us really thought too hard about what Daddy was saying – we all knew the baby was his too. It was beyond our comprehension to imagine anything else. Daddy was sick, that was the trouble, and his paranoia told him all sorts of things that just weren't true.

One day Daddy's rage started early and went on all day long, gaining power and momentum every time he came in the house. There was nothing Mammy could say to calm him down, and by evening he'd already drunk himself into a storm of fury.

'Why don't you just admit it, woman?' he bawled at her, sending plates and cups flying as he swept a heavy arm across the kitchen table.

'Admit what?' she yelled back, darting behind the table to get away from him. 'I ain't done nothing, Donal. It's all in your bloody head. You're just so ...'

But she never got to finish her sentence. Daddy flew across the room and jumped on top of her, pushing her back onto the ground. He had his large hands around her neck now and his eyes were like a man possessed – frenzied and demonic. He was pushing hard onto her throat, putting all his weight onto his taut arms, and she was choking, gasping for breath while her eyes bulged with terror. We had been playing by the fire but when we saw them like that we all ran out the house, terrified.

'He's going to kill Mammy!' I whimpered, as Tara and I clung tight to each other in one of the dog sheds in the garden, a place where we liked to hide to get away from their fights.

'For sure, he's going to kill her this time!' Tara agreed. Colin was sat in a corner, making marks in the dirt while Brian kept watch at the opening.

'We can't go back,' Brian declared. 'We don't want to see poor Mammy dead in the kitchen.'

Brian was always the grown-up one of us – making the decisions that were best for us all. He was right. We'd seen it for ourselves – Daddy had lost control completely this time and there was no way Mammy could survive this attack. We let the hours pass by and must have dropped off for a while because the next thing we heard was my Mammy's voice calling all our names.

'Brian! Tara! Kathleen! Colin! Come on, you lot. Come inside now.'

We all looked at each other in surprise – she was alive!

We scrambled to our feet, shivering from being outside so long and having had nothing to eat for our tea. I was so happy to see my Mammy was alive I ran straight into the kitchen to see her, but when I caught sight of her face I almost recoiled in horror. She had the most terrible red eyes you've ever seen in your life – like the devil.

I must have looked pretty upset because Mammy said: 'Now, don't be making a fuss there, Kathleen. Have your tea now.'

We sat at the table, eating our bread and drinking tea in silence.

Finally Brian asked: 'Where's my father, Mammy?'

'Your father's down at the pub,' she replied, busying herself with the cleaning and washing up.

Some time later, when we were all finished and warming up by the fire, Aidan and Liam came back from working in the fields.

They were talking loudly and being boisterous between them until they caught sight of Mammy.

'Jesus! Mammy! What did he do to you?' Liam exclaimed loudly.

'What did he do to me?' Mammy spat bitterly. 'What does it look like he did?'

'That's it, Mammy!' he said. 'That's the final straw there. I'm going to kill my Daddy for what he's done.'

Liam was boiling with rage. He couldn't bear to see what my father had done – none of us could. We couldn't look Mammy in the face. It was horrible to see those red swollen eyes.

'Don't be saying that now, Liam.' Mammy shook her head.

'No, really! I'm going to kill him!'

'You can't kill your father,' she repeated. Now she was stood against the wall as Liam paced back and forth in the room. 'You better not be touching your father,' she warned him again. Aidan meanwhile was sat silent next to us, staring into the fire, a look of utter despair on his face. He caught Liam's eyes – I could tell what he was thinking right there. We all could. He wanted Daddy dead too.

Nothing more was said but Mammy set about getting the older boys their tea. None of us wanted to go to bed that night.

We were all too shaken up by what had happened and we needed the comfort of the fire and each other. Liam went upstairs. He seemed in a strange mood but we tried not to pay it any mind. Liam was always trying to protect our Mammy but it often left him battered himself from Daddy's violent outbursts.

It was late when my father finally staggered in, up to the eyeballs with the drink. He didn't look at my Mammy. Nobody said a word. He just plonked himself on a stool by the range and sat there, warming his hands and feet at the fire. He couldn't have been there more than a few minutes before we heard the clump-clump of Liam's feet overhead. Then he flew down the stairs in a second and before we knew what was happening he came up behind my father and whacked him over the head with a large ashtray.

In a stomach-churning whump we heard the ashtray make contact with Daddy's skull and then his head split open and blood started pouring out.

'Liam! No!' Mammy screamed.

But it was too late – Daddy's head was oozing thick dark blood. He hadn't even fallen off his stool – he just rocked back and forth slightly, not saying a word. Then he staggered to his feet as Liam stood back, breathing hard, a look of pure hate on his face.

We could all see he was drawing his arm back to go at Daddy again.

'Stop, Liam! Don't!' Mammy screeched, racing over to Liam and grabbing hold of his arm, pinning it back at his side. They struggled like that for a bit as Daddy swayed from side to side before stumbling out the front door.

'Let me go, Mammy!' Liam was shouting. 'I'm gonna kill him!'

Mammy ran to the door and shut it against my father, then leaned back on it to stop Liam from following Daddy outside.

'Please, Liam, don't do this!' she was crying, pleading with him now. 'Think of the little ones!'

'I am!' Liam roared. 'I AM thinking of the little ones. He's killing us all!'

'No, no, no,' Mammy sobbed. 'You can't do this. You can't kill that man.'

We were all too shocked to move or do anything for a while as the two of them stood there at the door, my Mammy distraught but determined not to let my brother out, Liam, shaking and hollering.

Finally, Tara and me got up and went to stand with Mammy, by her side. We couldn't let Liam kill our daddy. For all the wrong that he'd done, we all still loved him. Tears now were pouring down my cheeks as I shouted at my brother: 'Leave him alone, Liam! You've can't kill our daddy. You leave him be!'

He looked down at us then and his eyes filled with tears. Just then all the fight seemed to go out of him, his body slumped forward, he dropped the ashtray and he turned and walked back to the fire. I buried my head in Mammy's skirts then and she held onto the back of my head and we stood there like that, all crying and heaving with the terror of it all.

Now it was Daddy we thought was dead. There was no doubt about it, Liam had given him a fearful crack on the skull. How could a man survive a thing like that? After a while, Mammy wiped her arm across her face and we all went back to the range. Once she was convinced Liam had finally calmed down she said to us: 'Come on. Let's see if we can find your father.'

So we carefully opened up the front door, half expecting to see him laying down dead on the path. But there was nothing, just a few spots of blood on the path leading out the front gate to the lane.

'Where is he, Mammy?' Tara asked.

'I don't know, baby,' she replied, herself looking confused and worried. We searched all over the place that night but there was no sign of Daddy at all. We crawled into bed later, the four of us, and Brian said he thought maybe Daddy had gone to the woods to die.

Tara and I cried quietly into each other's shoulders then, sorry for Liam killing our daddy.

It was a pure miracle Daddy survived that night. A farmer found him unconscious on the road and picked him up and took him to the hospital. The next day, as we were having our breakfast, the Garda came knocking at the door. They told my mother Daddy was being looked after in the hospital and he should be back in a few days.

We all held our breath, half expecting them to take Liam off to jail, but they didn't say anything else. Mammy nodded and thanked them. They couldn't have helped seeing her eyes, all still red and bloodshot from where Daddy nearly strangled her to death. A few days later Daddy was back and nobody said anything about what had happened. We thought it would all blow over, just like all them other fights they'd had before. But, though we didn't know it then, Mammy had made a decision that night, a decision that would change all our lives for ever.

PART II
BROKEN

CHAPTER 7
GLOUCESTER

It was a few weeks later that Bridget came back. We were so thrilled to see her, we jumped all over her, kissing her like mad and hanging round her neck.

'We missed you!' we told her over and over again. We thought she was coming back for good – we were so excited, we hardly even noticed the strange look that passed between her and my mother as she set her case down on the floor. We all went to sleep that night, happy that our older sister had returned.

But the next morning she shook us awake and whispered: 'Come on now, lads. Wake up and get ready. We've got to go.'

We all pulled on our clothes, unquestioning, not having a clue what was going on. When we came into the parlour Mammy had the babies all dressed and Bridget was standing next to three cases. Aidan and Liam were there too, looking grim-faced. Next to them was a man we didn't recognise.

'This here is Fergal,' said Bridget. 'He's my fella and he's gonna be helping us.'

Mammy was bustling about, getting all our sandals out and ordering us to put on our coats. She seemed tense, nervous.

Once they'd ushered us all outside I asked: 'Where are we going?'

It was Bridget who replied: 'We're going to England.'

England? I didn't know where England was. I'd never heard of the place – but in that instant I knew one thing. We were all leaving without Daddy! I started to sob. My heart ached. We couldn't leave Daddy. Despite everything, I worshipped my daddy and I knew he loved us all to death.

'But Mammy,' I tugged at her skirt. 'We can't leave Daddy behind. Why isn't Daddy coming with us?'

'Hush now,' she said. 'Stop your crying.'

I didn't really have to ask – I knew why we were leaving but I couldn't bear the thought of Daddy coming home to find all of us gone. But there was nothing I could do. We set off then across the fields to get to the village, not daring to walk along the road. Fergal and Bridget took the cases while Mammy, Liam and Aidan carried the little ones. It was three miles to get to the village but for us this wasn't a long walk. We tramped along in silence, and once we arrived we sat at the roadside until the bus came along to take us to the main town.

I was too sad and preoccupied to talk. I didn't know where England was but it sounded a long way away. How would Daddy feel finding an empty house? It was horrible to think how lonely he would be without us all. We all got on board the bus and Mammy ordered us to sit down and quieten while she settled the little ones. The bus started up but since we were going along small, winding country roads, it couldn't go too fast. Just then, up ahead, I spotted Daddy, strolling down the road in his white shirt with his sleeves rolled up, his hands in his pockets, his lips pursed to whistle. He was on his way home and looked so happy, not a care in the world.

My heart soared to see him and I called out: 'Look! There's Daddy!' and started banging on the window.

But Mammy must have caught sight of him at the very same moment because she screamed at us all: 'Get down!'

She grabbed my arm and pulled me to the floor of the bus. All the others hid down behind the seats as we passed by my father, clueless that we were all in the bus, escaping from him. Then the bus was past and he was gone. Mammy, who had been laying half on top of me on the floor, pulled herself up and dusted herself down. I was devastated. I sat silently for the rest of the journey, watching all the green fields pass by, imagining Daddy, all alone and sad in our house.

To us country children, arriving in a large town was something incredible. We'd never seen so many people before and the buildings seemed to tower over us, giant structures that rose majestically into the sky. All the crying stopped then as Mammy led us from the bus station to the train station. We all gaped in open-mouth wonder as we caught sight of the huge engines on the tracks. We'd never even seen a train up close before, let alone been on one. All thoughts of Daddy flew out of my head as I admired the enormous, steaming machines in front of us. Mammy found our train and she hustled us all aboard. This was surely the most thrilling thing in the world and now there was no controlling any of us as we ran up and down the carriage, exploring our surroundings.

The train set off and we were still flying around, jumping on the seats and hanging round the door to look out of the window.

'Would you leave that bloody window alone, Brian!' Mammy shouted from the table where she and the older ones sat as Brian pulled the window down for the hundredth time. If they had let us we would have run through the whole train, going from one compartment to the next. As it was we contented ourselves with just playing havoc in one carriage. We were almost sad when the journey came to an end, but then the older ones led us towards the port where we had to get on a big boat.

'A boat?' Brian kept on at my mother. 'Are we really going on a boat?'

'Yes, Brian,' Mammy replied, sighing. 'We really are.'

'I can't believe it!' he said to her. Then to us: 'I can't believe it. Can you believe it, Kathleen? We're going on a boat!'

Once on board we went completely berserk. We were everywhere, up on deck, down below, all around the whole place. We ran through the corridors, in and out of the toilets, slamming the doors behind us, and even climbed onto the railings to look down at the sea below. But that scared us because it was so high up that we didn't do it a second time. Mammy didn't pay us much mind – she just got on looking after the babies. She never did seem to mind what we were doing – we must have been in danger most of the time but Mammy reckoned we must all learn to look after ourselves so we were left free to make our own entertainment.

About half an hour into the crossing, we were stood on deck, spitting into the sea below to see whose spit could go the furthest while the wind whipped our hair and skirts about us. Just then Brian let out a terrible scream.

'It's a monster!' he jabbered. We all turned to look where he was pointing and we saw, coming towards us on the deck, a man who was as black as the night. Brian was right – the man was so black we thought he must be a monster too and we all started screaming.

Now Brian was shaking like a leaf and the monster was coming towards us, a confused smile on his face.

'Is there a problem?' he asked us politely.

But none of us could speak, we were all scared witless by the monster. And just then Brian took off. We all followed swiftly behind him but the monster came right after us!

We dived below deck, searching out Mammy and our older siblings.

Brian was the first to speak: 'Mammy! Mammy! Mammy! There's a monster on the boat! And he's chasing us!'

Indeed, just behind us, now panting and looking pure distressed, was the black monster.

'They just started screaming when they saw me!' he explained apologetically, clearly rattled by our hysterics. 'I didn't do anything to them but they seem very upset.'

He was right – we were all crying by now, clawing at my mother for protection, begging her to save us. But Liam and Aidan just started to laugh.

'I'm sorry,' Mammy said to the man. 'They were brought up in the countryside and they've never seen people of different colours before. It's all new to them.'

The man nodded, looking a little relieved, then he left us.

'That's not a monster,' Aidan laughed at us. 'He's just a black man.'

Now Brian was confused: 'But *why* is the man so black? I don't understand it.'

Mammy explained: 'There are people of all different colours in this world. Some are black, others are yellow or orange. You're going to be seeing a lot of different coloured peoples once we get to England. Now just you all calm down. Look at the poor man! You scared the living daylights out of him!'

Later, as Mammy handed out egg sandwiches that she'd bought at the ship's canteen, Tara whispered to me: 'Kathleen, can you imagine a yellow person?'

'Or an orange person!'

'Wouldn't that be strange! Do you think they have purple or blue people in England?'

I started giggling: 'I'd like to see a blue person, Tara!'

It was night-time when we arrived in England. We hadn't slept at all on the long, five-hour crossing, and by now we were all groggy with tiredness. The older ones gently herded us all onto another train and there we laid our heads down on the seats and let the gentle swaying of the carriage rock us all to sleep. We were so tired and sleepy when we got off the train that we walked hand in hand up and down the dark streets, hardly able to stand up, let alone take in our new environment. We were led past row after row of grand, old-looking houses, turning into one street and then the next. God, it felt like it would go on for a lifetime, until eventually we came to a large, three-storey house where Mammy climbed up the three stone steps to the entrance and knocked. A man we'd never seen before opened it. But he must have known Mammy because he started chattering away. The man led us all into a spacious living room on the ground floor where he'd put out a load of blankets and we all just lay down and cuddled up to sleep the rest of the night.

By the time we woke up the next morning Mammy was already in the kitchen, making a mouth-watering breakfast of sausage and eggs. It was the first thing we'd eaten since the sandwiches on the boat and we set about devouring our food, ravenous.

'You can all go now,' she said when we finished. 'But just mind you don't be playing in the rooms at the top. That's not for us.'

We were all looking forward to exploring the house, which seemed enormous to us. In the hallway there was a large staircase with a wooden banister and all the way up the stairs were tons of different rooms, some with beds, but mostly empty. We climbed all over the banisters, hanging off them and sliding down. Later we went outdoors to find a big garden with a shed in it and, behind the garden, a river. Then we went out into the street. The house was on a road with shops at one end and rows of houses down our end.

'What is this place, Mammy?' Brian asked as we passed her in the kitchen.

'It's a squat,' she told him. 'In Gloucester. Now just you kids mind to stay out of trouble.'

We later learned that there was a mother with three little girls living in the squat with us and when they returned they opened up the shed to let us play on their bikes with them. It was exciting being in a big new house but we couldn't help thinking of Daddy and how lonely he'd be back in our home, all by himself.

At first we just spent our time playing in the street. We were desperate to see the different coloured people Mammy had talked about so we wandered up and down, looking for the yellow and orange people. When we didn't see any we just amused ourselves on the bikes and by the river behind our house. Aidan got himself a job working in a hospital at the end of the street, Liam was out mostly and Bridget stayed with us, looking after the little ones. At nights we had two rooms to sleep in – the older boys in one and the rest of us in another.

We didn't see much of the man who had first opened the door to us – from what we could gather from overhearing when the older ones spoke, it sounded like he was married to one of our aunts, but none of us knew which one. There was a pub across the road from us, and from the moment we arrived in Gloucester Mammy spent most of her days and nights in there. From the very beginning she warned us against ever coming into the pub.

'That's not a place to play!' she snapped at us. 'You're not even to cross to that side of the road. You understand? Don't even look at it!'

Mammy didn't seem the same to us. It was strange. She was never home and she didn't seem to have time for any of us. There were even some nights she wouldn't come back to the house – we'd wake up in the morning, just us kids and Bridget watching over us. But after a few days we cottoned on to what was keeping her away so much – there was a man she was with and they were talking and laughing. One time Brian said: 'I'm going to get a closer look at him!'

But when he went up to the front, Mammy spotted his little blond head peeking through the glass window of the door and she came belting out, giving him an earful!

It was late one night, about two weeks after we first got to Gloucester, that she brought the fella back to the house. Tara and I were playing in the hall, climbing up the walls, seeing if we could get about the whole house without touching the floor. We heard my mother's tinkly laughter as she pushed open the front door and he followed in behind her. He just seemed a very normal-looking fella, not greatly tall, with dark, curly hair. She barely looked up at us as we stopped messing about to see this man up close. Mammy carried on walking right through to the kitchen but the man stopped there in the hallway.

'Hello,' he said to us.

'Hello,' we chorused back, curious.

'I'm Frank. I'm your mother's friend.'

'This here is Kathleen and I'm Tara,' my sister said, bold as anything.

'Why don't you come over and give us a kiss hello?' he said.

We didn't think anything of it – we both went over and gave him a peck on the cheek.

Then: 'Do you want some money?'

We both nodded eagerly – of course we did!

'Right, well, I'll give you some money if you give me another kiss.'

That seemed like a good deal to us so we each stretched up on tiptoe to give him another kiss on the cheek and afterwards he held out a ten pence piece for each of us. We ran away laughing. We had no idea why the stupid man wanted to give us money for kisses but we weren't going to argue!

Frank stayed with my mother in another room that night, and the next day we didn't even wait around to see anyone. We went straight out to spend our money on toffees in the shop up the road. Two days later Frank was back in the house and asking us for kisses again.

This time, instead of kissing him on the cheek, he wanted to kiss us both on the mouth. Again, we didn't think about it and just went right ahead to get our money. But by the third occasion I realised something wasn't quite right. This time he wanted to keep his lips on mine for longer and he held my shoulders tight and squeezed, not letting me go. Eventually I managed to squirm away from him because I'd had enough. Then it was Tara's turn.

She stood on the staircase so he didn't have to bend down to kiss her and he did the same again, holding her little shoulders so she couldn't get away. He was at it a long time, so long in fact that Mammy came out of the kitchen at that very moment and caught them kissing!

'Tara!' Mammy erupted in a fit of pure fury. Frank dropped my sister and Tara quickly jumped down from the stairs and ran away, through the rooms of the house.

'What were you doing, you dirty little girl!' Mammy shouted, going after her. By now Frank had walked silently into the kitchen.

Tara's terrified shrieks could be heard all around the house as Mammy chased her and finally caught up with her. I came upon them in time to hear my mother demanding: 'What were you doing?'

She was holding Tara roughly by the back of her dress.

'I wasn't doing anything, Mammy,' she pleaded. 'He kissed me. He give me money for it.'

She held out her trembling hand and uncurled her fingers to reveal the ten pence piece she'd just earned.

'He give me the money too, Mammy!' I said and I showed her my coin.

Mammy was still angry but now a wave of uncertainty passed over her face. She blinked twice.

'Well, that's enough!' she admonished. 'You better not be taking any more money off him. Leave the poor man alone.'

We scurried away to our room then, confused and upset. We didn't know what was happening at all. It wasn't our fault he wanted to give us money for kisses. We'd never come across anything like it before in our lives.

One morning a week later Mammy's sister arrived at the house – we'd never even met her before but Mammy said it was her sister, our Aunt Elizabeth, and we should get dressed because we were going home to see our father. We were so excited we all got dressed in a hurry – this was brilliant news! Mammy made us all some bread and tea and as we were eating Brian asked her when Aidan and Liam would be here.

'Oh, it's not all of us,' she said casually. 'It's just the four of you.'

My hand froze in mid-air and I looked straight at Tara. In that split second we both understood – we were being sent back to Daddy for good. We were being punished for the kisses and now we were going to be separated from our siblings and our mammy.

I bolted from the table and ran upstairs where I hid under the bed, hoping nobody would find me there. But I heard Mammy's heavy footfall as she climbed up the stairs slowly and walked into the room. I lay under the bed, breathing hard, looking at her stockinged feet and the buckles on her worn brown shoes.

'Come out from under the bed!' her voice boomed from somewhere over my head. I didn't respond.

'I said COME OUT!' she shouted now. 'I swear, if you miss your train I'll kill you!'

But still I refused to budge. Then I saw her legs bend and her bottom lower to the floor. At the same time her arm shot out, making a grab for me. She yanked me out from under the bed, even though I tried clinging onto the leg, and I cried out: 'I don't want to go, Mammy! Don't send us away!'

'Don't be stupid, Kathleen!' she chided, roughing me all the way down the stairs again. 'It's only a little holiday. You'll all be coming back again.'

But I knew it wasn't a holiday – we all did. Mammy just wanted us gone. We could see that. Now Brian was crying but she wasn't putting up with any of it. We'd never seen Mammy like this before. She was impatient, aggressive, like she couldn't wait to get shot of us.

Mammy dragged us outside and Brian kept crying and kicking at her. It was awful.

'Please, Mammy!' he begged. 'I won't be naughty any more. Just let me stay. Please!'

She marched us down the road towards the train station and after a while we stopped crying and fighting with her. It wasn't making any difference. We hadn't even had a chance to say goodbye to Bridget, Aidan, Liam or the little ones. Once on the train, Mammy didn't even kiss us goodbye. She just looked at us all sternly and ordered: 'Now you all be good for your aunt. She doesn't need you causing trouble for her.'

We got on board and Aunt Elizabeth followed on behind us – we had no bags at all, just the clothes we stood up in. Now it was sinking in what was really happening Tara started to sob. I put my arm around her and tried my best to console her: 'Don't be sad, Tara. Just think how happy Daddy will be when he sees us.'

But she couldn't be comforted.

Eventually Aunt Elizabeth snapped at her: 'Stop your bawling, Tara! I don't need to be listening to you lot crying all the way back to Ireland.'

It was a sad journey home. None of us jumped about or ran around the train; we hardly even went on deck during the boat crossing and all the way back we were teary, silent and miserable. But we didn't go straight back to Daddy's. Aunt Elizabeth took us first to her home. Though Mammy's family had been travellers when they were all growing up, most of them had now settled into houses. When we got there it was late at night and there was an old man with a wiry brown beard standing in the kitchen. He must have been our uncle, but he didn't greet us. He didn't even look at us. He just pointed his finger towards the staircase and said: 'Straight upstairs.'

And that's where she took us – to a room upstairs, where we stayed for the next two weeks.

CHAPTER 8
DADDY

Locked away in that one small room upstairs, the four of us lost heart. For two weeks we did nothing at all, just lay down on the mattresses Aunt Elizabeth had brought into the room and talked about where Mammy and Daddy would be at that moment. There was no TV, and we weren't even allowed to look out of the window at the children playing below on the streets. At mealtimes Aunt Elizabeth brought us a tray of tea, bread and jam and we were allowed to relieve ourselves in the toilet across the hall. Time seemed to go on for ever. It felt these long days and nights would never end until suddenly, one day, Aunt Elizabeth came in and announced: 'You're going to see your father now.'

We couldn't believe it – we were so happy. Just to be allowed down the stairs and out the front door into the world outside felt like freedom. Now we were walking along the street and our high spirits brimmed over as we laughed and skipped, holding each other's hands. But we didn't see Daddy straight away – our aunt took us first to our grandmother, her and my mother's mother. She had been a traveller all her life but she now lived in a house. We'd never even met her before and our first impression was one of a fierce, angry-looking lady. She shooed us into the house before giving out to Aunt Elizabeth, there on the doorstep.

'You and your sister should be ashamed of yourselves,' she shouted. 'You're a disgrace, what you're doing to these children!'

Aunt Elizabeth didn't say anything, she just turned around and walked away, not even a word of goodbye. At first we were all cowed and nervous around our grandmother – but once she was inside she talked sweetly to us, giving us all bread and bacon and letting us play in her garden.

'Your father will be here tomorrow,' she said. 'So just settle down here for one night and then you'll see your daddy again.'

Tara, Colin and I were just relieved to be out of Aunt Elizabeth's house, but Brian was curious. He started asking our grandmother all about her life. She told him that even though they didn't live in caravans any more they were still travellers at heart. They loved the outdoors and being close to nature, just like Brian. They seemed to get on really well.

'I think she's grand,' Brian declared later that night while we were all in bed. 'She treats us nice, anyways.'

But it was my father I was pure happy to see. When he got to the house he knelt down to give us all a massive hug.

'Oh children! Children!' he cried out, tears welling in his eyes. He picked up Colin and swung him about the room. Then he tousled my hair and held Tara's hand. We were so delighted to be together again. When it came time to leave, Brian shocked us all.

'I want to stay here with Grandma,' he said. 'She said it was all right if it's all right with you, Daddy?'

We were all surprised but Daddy looked a little sad too.

'Why do you want to stay?' Tara asked him.

'I like it here. Grandma says she can get me a job working on the farm and that's what I'd like to do.'

Just then Daddy broke into a smile.

'Ha! A working man, just like your daddy, eh?' he said, clearly proud of his son. He gave Brian a manly pat on the shoulder. 'Well now, Brian, if you want to earn your keep here and learn the working life, I don't see why's not. Just you make sure you work hard and don't make any trouble for your granny now.'

'No, Daddy, I won't,' said Brian earnestly. He was only eight, just two years older than me, but it was normal for us kids to work. We'd done it all our lives and we could see that Brian and my grandmother already shared a special bond.

We all hugged them both goodbye – we couldn't wait to set off across the fields back home with Daddy. It was a long walk back to our cottage some miles away but we didn't care – we were free again.

On the way back, Daddy put Colin on his shoulders and held mine and Tara's hands. He was silent a while; you could see he was preoccupied. Then he asked us straight out: 'What's your mother doing in England?'

'She's got a house there, Daddy,' Tara replied. We told him about the big house in Gloucester with the long banister and all the rooms. We told him about the family with three little girls with the bikes and how Aidan was working in a hospital. We didn't tell him about the man Frank – we didn't see any reason to upset him further.

It was strange walking back into our cottage again after six weeks – everything was exactly as we'd left it, clothes lying about everywhere, baby prams and cots. It was like we'd just stepped out for the day and Daddy expected us back any moment. We soon settled back into our usual routine – Daddy went out to work every day while the rest of us just took care of ourselves, wandering the fields, climbing trees, catching birds and playing with the dogs. It was the way we'd always known things so it seemed natural, but we couldn't help but think about our mother and our siblings back in England. We were grieving for Mammy, grieving for the woman who had looked after us all our lives. And we weren't the only ones.

At night Daddy would hit the drink hard, sitting and pouring it down his throat until he was so drunk he would start to cry. Then he'd go round the house, picking up the baby clothes and holding them to his face, all the time weeping: 'My babas! Why did she take my babas?'

Now Daddy had abandoned the room he used to sleep in with Mammy he slept downstairs with us children. Sometimes Daddy would be at the pub all night, and when he came back he brought the drink with him. He was still making us tea of an evening but there were times he got so drunk he forgot.

Now he stopped going to work in the day and just sat about the house instead, drinking and getting himself into a state. Sometimes he would erupt in a blaze of fury, punching the wall with his bare fists till they bled.

'I can't believe what your mother's gone and done!' he'd rage. 'Just left her children like this!'

Then he'd crumple up in despair and grab Colin, cuddling him and crying into his neck: 'Oh you poor babas! I know you miss your mammy.'

And it was true – we were all sad. We couldn't think of our mammy without a great empty hole opening up inside us, but we tried to hide our feelings from Daddy because if he caught us crying he would start crying too.

Now we'd pick our way through the empty bottles of whiskey and Guinness scattered about on the floor every morning as Daddy slept, helping ourselves to whatever we could find in the kitchen. Usually it was just a slice or two of bread. We were hungry a lot of the time but we didn't say it to our father. The place was a state – Daddy left all the cleaning and housework, and our clothes were constantly dirty and ripped. Daddy had given up. One night we found him just sitting in front of the fire, not talking or drinking or doing anything. He just sat there, staring at us.

The next day he started breaking up the house.

'I'm not living here no more,' he muttered to himself. He began smashing up chairs and tables and he dug a large pit in the back of the garden, next to the wall.

'Daddy, what's the hole for?' I asked him.

'It's for the dogs,' he said, distractedly. 'We're not doing this any more. We're getting the hell out of here.'

He went to see the farmer and when they came back together the farmer had his shotgun with him.

'Get inside the house!' Daddy ordered us all. We were terrified.

'What are you doing, Daddy?' we yelled.

'Just get inside NOW! And stay away from the windows,' he shouted. So we all scampered inside and sat on the bed.

We heard one shot accompanied by a strange, strangled yelp.

Then another, and another and another.

Eventually, after ten rounds, Daddy called for us to come out again.

All the sheds in the garden were open and empty. Daddy was busy covering over the pit at the back of the garden with fresh soil.

'Daddy, what did you do to the dogs?' I was shocked.

'Look what she made me do!' Daddy was weeping now as he worked at the ground. 'Look what your mother's made me do.'

Later that day two more farmers came and Daddy sold them the rest of our horses, all except Pieball and Big Mare.

That night he sat staring at the fire, drinking bottle after bottle of Guinness. We crouched next to him, fearful for both him and us.

The next day he told us all to get dressed because we were leaving.

He didn't say where we were going. We just pulled on our clothes, walked out the cottage and slammed the door behind us. Then we started out over the fields. We walked in silence, a sense of horrible dread between us all. Tara and I dared not speak but I knew we were thinking the same thing – Daddy had truly lost his mind this time and we didn't know what was going to happen next. He took us to the harbour in the town and we sat on the quayside, skimming stones as Daddy looked out over towards all the boats, coming and going.

'If she's going to be anywhere, she'll be here,' he said quietly to himself. Did he really think Mammy was going to just sail into the harbour that day and come home to him? Daddy went to get himself a pint from the pub and we children just played along the quay and shore while Daddy sat and drank. And drank and drank and drank.

We were there all day long, my father just staring out towards the ocean as the sun made a dramatic red setting against the harbour and the cold night fell around us. It was late now – the pub was shutting and still we hadn't eaten anything all day. It didn't matter – we were used to hunger.

'Come on,' Daddy said at last, slurring and staggering about. 'Let's get you to your granddad's.'

Out of nowhere it seemed a van turned up with a man whom we didn't recognise behind the wheel. We drove for a while before the van dropped us off in a town I'd never been in before. But Daddy seemed to know where he was going, even though he had obviously had quite a bit to drink by now, and he weaved his way through the streets, the three of us running along beside him, until we reached a house. When Daddy knocked an old man answered – he looked like our father but much shorter with wispy white hair.

'Just a minute, you lot,' Daddy said to us, while his father beckoned us inside. We went through to his living room and our grandfather stepped outside to talk to my father, shutting the door behind him so we couldn't hear them speaking.

After a few minutes the door opened and Daddy came into the hallway – he wouldn't come any further.

'Kids, this is your grandfather and you're going to stay here with him while Daddy goes off and gets better.'

We all nodded, then he bent down to give us all a kiss and cuddle goodbye. And that was that – he turned around and left us, left us with another stranger in another strange home. We were so sad to see him go – we'd only been with him a few weeks before everything had fallen apart. It seemed we couldn't stay anywhere long enough to get settled. Our grandfather didn't say much at first – he bustled about in the kitchen, making us each a fried egg before putting us to bed that night.

'Do you think Daddy'll be all right?' Tara asked me as we climbed into bed.

I shrugged. 'He can't get much worse. Maybe he'll go back to the mental hospital for some more lightning. I think his brain has stopped working again.'

Colin came and curled up in my embrace. I looked down at his peaceful little face, eyes shut to welcome sleep.

'We'll be all right, Colin,' I told him, stroking his cheeks. 'We'll be fine. We still got each other.'

It turned out that Grandpa was the best one of the lot! We'd been shoved around so much the past few months we were all wary of being moved on again, but it seemed our grandfather had a lot of time for us. He waited about a week and when it seemed Daddy wasn't coming back to get us he told us: 'Now you're living with me and you don't have to worry. You'll be fed and clothed and there'll be plenty of nice things to do.'

Then he went out and bought us all new clothes and skipping ropes. Grandfather still had two of my daddy's sisters living with him and Tara and I slept in their room while Colin slept in Grandpa's room. He had a nice bungalow with a large garden at the back.

And from the very start Grandfather looked after us all beautifully, doing all the cooking for us himself, cleaning and washing our clothes. He took us hunting up in the mountains for rabbits and he kept racing pigeons, which he let us touch and hold. He told us all about his pigeons and, when he wasn't taking care of us, he let us play out in his garden.

It was a relief to be looked after properly by an adult again. For a little while we could just be children, not worry about our father or our mother, how we were going to eat or what would happen the next day. The weeks turned into months, and as September approached with no sign of Daddy, Grandpa told us he thought we should all go to school.

'It looks like I'll be keeping you, at least for a while,' he said, smiling. 'So let's get you all some school uniforms.'

How exciting! None of us had ever gone to school before and we were thrilled at the idea of meeting loads of new children.

But we never got to wear our new uniforms because Daddy came back a week later. He turned up drunk in the middle of the night and we could hear him outside as my grandfather tried to reason with him.

'Donal, leave them children!' Grandad pleaded. 'You're not able to look after them. Leave them and I'll raise them for you.'

We could hear our daddy's voice then, loud and angry: 'You ain't having my kids. You hear that, old man? They're mine – they're the only things I have left in this world!'

'Donal, be reasonable. It ain't fair on …'

'Don't you be telling me what's fair. Their mother left us – now is that fair? Just get them or I'll come in and take them myself!'

'Donal, I swear on my life, if you take these kids tonight I will disown them for the rest of my life. You won't be able to bring them back again.'

'Just get them!' Daddy growled, a simmering violence in his voice.

Then, silence.

Grandpa opened the door and told us all to get ready because we were going home with our father.

I looked sadly at the crisp white shirt and brown skirt laid out on the trunk at the foot of my bed, all ready for school.

'Do I need these, Grandpa?' I asked.

'No, my love,' he replied. 'You don't. Just leave them there.'

Truth was, we didn't want to go with Daddy again. He wasn't better – we could see that – but it's not like we had any choice.

Daddy took us on a bus that night and then we walked across the fields back to the cottage, Daddy carrying Colin all the way. This time when we got back to the cottage it was worse than I'd even remembered. The place was a state, with barely a stick of furniture standing and clothes, bottles and rubbish strewn around every room. Daddy went about, trying to tidy up a little, mumbling: 'There now, this'll all be grand in the morning.'

But none of us believed him.

We'd had enough. We'd been shoved from pillar to post for so long now, it felt like no one truly cared.

'I just wish Mammy would come back and get us!' Tara wailed that night. I felt the same. Meanwhile, little Colin slept soundly next to me. Poor Colin was such a sweet thing, he never complained or cried. He just went along with us, holding our hands when we asked him, trusting us completely. But the next few weeks were to be the worst we'd ever experienced.

Daddy was all right for about two days, but then he went downhill fast and now he seemed to have little patience with us. If we made a noise at all he would kick us out of the house. Though he never lifted a finger to any of us, it was scary enough to hear the anger in his voice. We'd run out of the cottage and flee to the fields, where we'd pick berries and crab apples. Daddy had all but given up feeding us so we took to foraging food from the countryside and occasionally stealing spring onions from the farmer's fields, eating them raw.

The farmer's wife lived a couple of miles away and sometimes when we were desperate we'd go to see her.

'We're hungry. Can we have something to eat?' Tara would ask for all of us. The old lady knew us, and she knew our mammy was gone, so she took pity on us and gave us bread and jam. When we went home of an evening there was never anything there so we really didn't have a choice. It was either beg, forage, steal or starve.

Daddy had lost his mind and now we were lost too. We lived in squalor, out in the middle of the countryside, miles from the nearest village, not seeing a single soul from one day to the next. Unkempt, unwashed and starving, we drifted about, wretched and ragged. If we hadn't had each other, we might not have made it. But every night without fail, at whatever time we happened to fall into bed, we curled up next to each other and hugged each other tight, hoping and praying that tomorrow would be different, that something would change. Looking at my brother and sister's hollow cheeks and their stick-thin legs, I knew we couldn't go on like this much longer.

CHAPTER 9

NORTH SET

It was a relief when the police finally arrived, though to this day I have no idea who called them. Two Garda cars just pulled up at the house one afternoon without any warning. We were all playing outside the cottage and the policemen went inside to talk to Daddy. We could hear them, being sweet as anything with him, obviously sorry for him because he was such a wreck by now.

'Come on, Donal,' they urged, each taking an elbow. 'We'll take the children, we'll look after them and you go to hospital and then you can get your children back and we can tidy up the house.'

'I don't want you to take the feckin' children.' Daddy was swearing and cursing like anything but he had no fight left in him. He shuffled towards the car, his shirt hanging off him, his face unshaven.

We saw him start to cry helplessly as he stared forlornly out the window at us all, then the police car drove off and took our daddy away.

We were put in the back of the other car and once we were on our way we asked them where we were going.

'We're going to a place called a convent,' said the policeman. 'It's a nice place run by kind ladies called nuns. You'll get new clothes, lots of good food and meet other children.'

I'd never heard of a convent before – I'd never even seen a nun – but it sounded good. In truth, anything would be better than living with Daddy. Half an hour into our journey Tara shouted out: 'We have another brother!'

The policeman stopped the car and turned around to face us.

'What do you mean you've got another brother?'

'Brian – he lives with our grandmother. We should go and collect him.'

The policeman sighed – he obviously didn't want any extra work but he couldn't ignore this new information. We turned off towards the town where our grandmother lived and we stopped to pick him up.

Brian seemed unsure when he came to the door.

'But I like it here,' he protested when the policeman asked if he wanted to come to the convent with us.

'Please, Brian! Please come!' we urged. 'We don't want to go on our own and it's going to be brilliant with us all there!'

But Brian wavered. If only Tara hadn't remembered, if only we'd known what was in store for him, we'd never have asked him to come too. But how were we to know? In the end, Brian came with us, and it turned out to be the worst decision of his life.

Two hours later we pulled into a town and there we came to a large imposing red-brick building with massive gates leading up to a long drive. A tall nun in a long black dress I was later told was a habit glided out to greet us. The policeman introduced her to us as the Reverend Mother. We'd never known any other mother apart from Mammy so we took this as a good sign.

'And what are your names?' she asked, smiling down at us. We told her and then she asked our ages. We all looked blank – we'd lost track. None of us could say.

'Well, when are your birthdays?' she asked.

Again, silence. Looking back, I must have been around seven but I really had no idea at the time – none of us had ever known or celebrated a birthday.

'We don't know,' Brian spoke for us all.

The Reverend Mother just smiled and brought us into a big room to wait while she spoke to the police. Her habit was so long and she moved so smoothly she really seemed to float from one place to the next.

When she came back she told us: 'First, I'm going to take Brian because he needs to go to the big boys' house.'

This was disappointing – we'd assumed we would all be kept together but we thought maybe we would all be back together once we'd settled in. When she returned, the Reverend Mother led the three of us down a long corridor that seemed to go on for ever. We trotted along, trying to keep up with the Reverend Mother as she glided swiftly through the corridor that seemed to link one building after another after another. Eventually we came to a place she called the nursery.

Two more nuns were there to meet us and they were introduced as Sister Sarah and Sister Beatrice, then the Reverend Mother left us.

'Bath first!' Sister Sarah announced primly.

We were taken into a white room with two big baths – we covered ourselves at first, not wanting to undress in front of these strangers, but they didn't listen to our protests. They stripped us all and put us in the large baths, scrubbing us with flannels and washing our hair.

Then they gave me and Tara an orange nightie each to wear and put Colin in a pair of pyjamas. They led us through to a large room divided up into smaller cubicles and there, at a little table, they fed us bread and cheese, then led us to a small room at the back where they'd set up three white metal beds, all ready for us. The nun walked over to the large windows at the end of the room and turned the shutters down. There was a light in the middle of the room that Sister Sarah switched off.

'Now get to bed and go to sleep,' she instructed.

Then she closed the door behind her and we heard the key turning in the lock. Until this moment we'd been calm and obedient – it was all fascinating to us. But at hearing that click as the door locked, we panicked.

'Oh for feck's sake!' exclaimed Tara loudly. 'They're locking us in!'

Alarmed, we rushed over to the door and started banging away.

'Open up!' we yelled. 'Let us out! We don't want to be locked up!'

Sister Sarah, who had a small cubicle of her own in the nursery, came to the door and turned the key. As soon as we saw it open a little way, we tried grabbing the edge and yanking it hard so we could shove it wide open and run out. But she was strong, this nun, and she inched her body into the room, closing the door briskly behind her.

'Now what did I tell you?' she said firmly.

'We don't want to be locked up here!' I shouted.

'Now don't you be answering back, Kathleen,' said Sister Sarah sternly. 'We're locking the door for your own good. Just get back into your beds and settle down. And switch that light off! I won't tell you again.'

But we couldn't settle – for ages we were shouting and banging around, jumping all over the room, trying to get the nun to come back. After a while we took turns kicking the door, making as much noise as possible. We heard the nun's footsteps as she came towards us and we stood back, ready to jump as soon as the door was open.

But she was too big for us and she pushed us all back again.

This time she was mad. She took us each by one arm and slapped the back of our legs till they stung.

'That's enough!' she shrieked. 'Get into your beds! I don't want to hear another word out of you.'

By now we were all cursing the sister to hell but she didn't pay us any mind. She slammed the door on her way out and the key turned once more. Eventually we all crawled into one bed together, holding each other, terrified.

'Why are we being locked up, Tara?' Colin whispered. 'Did we do something wrong?'

'We didn't do anything wrong!' I fumed in frustration.

'And where's Brian?' The poor boy seemed so confused. 'Where did they take him?'

The next morning we were woken by Sister Sarah tutting and muttering above us: 'Oh, for Pete's sake!' She was standing over us all, hands on hips, disgruntled and complaining: 'What are you all doing in the one bed like this? You each have your own beds. You're not to sleep together.'

'Why not?' Tara asked.

'Don't be giving me any cheek, madam,' Sister Sarah berated her.

'Well, I don't understand why we can't sleep together,' Tara protested. 'What difference does it make to you? We always sleep in the same bed.'

'Well, not any more,' said Sister Sarah. 'And until you learn to behave and do as you're told, you'll stay in this room.'

'You can't be telling us what to do,' Tara shot back angrily. 'You're not my mother. Just let us out of here. I want to go home.'

'Yeah, let us out, you pig!' I shouted at her. 'We're not staying here and you're *not* going to lock us up and we're *not* going to do what you tell us!'

'Fine,' she replied. 'You keep giving the cheek and you'll just stay in this room until you learn how to behave.'

And she meant it too. For the next week we were locked in that little room day and night, only allowed out into the nursery area for our meals. Then it was back in the room again. At first we fought Sister Sarah on everything, swearing and cursing her out like crazy. But as the time dragged by we realised we weren't getting anywhere so we did as we were told, though it took weeks for us to learn to sleep in our own beds. Finally Sister Sarah said we were good enough to be allowed into the nursery area to play with the toys. But none of us were interested in those; we just wanted to get outside and find our brother. Another two days passed and we were let out into the playground.

'The more you behave, the better time you'll have,' the nun explained. 'And then you can meet the other children.'

One day, when we were in the nursery we heard our brother Brian shouting from the playground below: 'Where are you? Lads, are you here? It's me! It's Brian!'

'Brian!' we all shouted at once and ran to the large windows, but Sister Sarah was soon on our tail and she led us back to our room.

'You'll see him in good time,' she said. 'Just calm yourselves and keep behaving nicely and there will be plenty of time for seeing your brother.'

So we behaved and after a few days Sister Sarah said we were going to join the other children now in North Set and she took us back down the long corridors until we came to a house. There we were met by a man called Teddy and a lady called Mona, who weren't nuns but members of the convent staff.

'You be good children now for Teddy and Mona,' said Sister Sarah. 'I'll be back to check on you shortly.'

We weren't sad to see her go.

Teddy smiled at us warmly and said: 'Welcome to North Set. We hope you'll be at home here.'

Then he showed us around – there were children everywhere and, one by one, Teddy introduced us to them all. It was exciting to see so many other kids. Upstairs there was a large dormitory and on one side were a load of cubicles with a bed, a locker and a little sink in each. There must have been around 10 girls in our dormitory, and across the hall there was a larger dormitory for the 20 or so boys. The children seemed really nice and many, like us, were brothers and sisters.

That first night we each settled into our own cubicles but it wasn't long before Tara popped her head over the top of mine.

'Come on!' I urged and she nipped round to come and sit on my bed while we chatted. We both agreed that Teddy and Mona seemed a lot nicer than Sister Sarah from the nursery but we couldn't help missing everyone. Everything in our lives had changed in the space of a year and it seemed there was nobody we could rely on except each other.

'I just hope Daddy gets better soon,' I said. 'Then maybe Mammy will see he's well and she'll come back.'

'And we can all be together again,' Tara finished off my thought. Despite everything we still had hope. We didn't belong in this place, we knew that. It was just a temporary home while everything got fixed up.

The next morning we found our new clothes laid out on the bed, ready for us to wear, and after we'd dressed we were shown into the kitchen where we sat with the other children for breakfast of cornflakes and tea. At lunchtime we were given food that came from the main convent and I thought it was lovely – minced meat and mashed potatoes. Half starved as I was, it tasted like the most delicious meal on earth. During the day most of the other children went to school but the nuns said it would take a little time to find us all school places so at first we were left in the house to help out. In the mornings we'd be allowed out to play in the playground and there we'd see children from other sets. We gradually learned that there were three different sets like ours, and of all the staff that patrolled the playground while we were out there it seemed that Teddy and Mona were the nicest. One woman who was in charge of another house was so stern and forbidding that the children in her set played in almost complete silence.

Since we had no school, it was decided we should be put to work instead. Sister Sarah came to our house and asked me and Tara to accompany her to the kitchen. There, standing at the sink, was a small, grey-haired nun, her hands elbow deep in the washing-up.

The sister told us: 'Kathleen and Tara, you're going to be washing up the dishes. I'd like to introduce you to Sister Willie …'

She didn't get any further – Tara and I erupted in howls of laughter. The nun looked horrified.

'What are you doing? Stop that!'

But we couldn't stop laughing and every time we tried to compose ourselves we'd crease up again, helpless to stop the giggles bubbling up out of us.

'Why are you laughing like that?' Sister Sarah asked us, nonplussed.

'Please, Sister,' Tara panted. 'Please tell us. Why does she have a name like that?'

Suddenly the penny dropped. She looked furious.

'That's her name, Wilhelmina, but she likes to be called Willie and it's no reason to be laughing. Now apologise to the nun! You're two filthy-minded, rude little girls!'

And with that she clipped us both around the head.

The poor nun called Willie – she just stood there, very calm and quiet, smiling at us. We were put to work at the sink but for all our efforts we couldn't help crumpling into fits of laughter.

'Stop that!' shrieked Sister Sarah, belting us round the head again. She kept beating me and now it was beginning to smart a lot. My head span, my ears burned and now I started to cry with the pain.

But then I caught Tara's eye and she was laughing and despite the beatings I was getting I couldn't help laughing again.

Then I'd get another wallop to my head.

'Oh, for feck's sake!' I spluttered into the sink.

'Language!' Sister Sarah trilled, and with that I caught another whip round my ear. Seeing this, Tara disintegrated into a heap of giggles once more. The laughter, the beating – it seemed to go on for ever.

But eventually we managed to get through the washing-up – poor old Sister Willie never chided us or beat us. She just stood there smiling the whole time. Only now we couldn't help laughing whenever we were sent to work in the kitchen. And as long as Sister Sarah wasn't around, Sister Willie didn't seem to mind. In fact, because she didn't mind we stopped laughing so much. Only every now and then Tara got it into her head to run by the kitchen shouting: 'Willie in the kitchen!'

I laughed so much I nearly wet myself.

After a couple of weeks, we were sent to school. It was an exciting day for us – none of us had ever been to school before. Mona walked us to the St Jonah's convent school one morning, but when I first got a look at my classroom I was scared. There were stacks of children everywhere, all sitting nicely at their little desks.

It was amazing, fascinating but also very intimidating. I was led in on my own, as Tara was in the older class, and shown to a desk. There I was told to sit quiet and listen to the teacher. That was difficult. I'd never sat quietly anywhere before. I simply didn't know how to behave. The teacher had a hard job just keeping me in my seat at first, let alone trying to teach me my ABC. All the other children were way ahead of me while I couldn't read, write or do sums. I was like a toddler, and to begin with that's how the teacher taught me. She got out the special baby bricks and she started going through the letters with me one by one. I didn't mind – I wanted to learn. I wanted to be like all the other children and know how to read proper books.

The other big change in our lives was the praying. I'd only ever prayed once before and that was when Mammy took us to get our Holy Communion while we were living in the cottage. I'd been taught to say my Hail Mary for that. But I'd never prayed any other time. In the convent we never stopped praying! We had prayers in the morning, when we came home from school for lunch, prayers at tea-time and just before bed. We also had to give thanks to God at mealtimes for our food. It punctuated our whole day. And when a boy in our house got me into trouble, I was made to pray even more.

We were just in the cloakroom one afternoon after coming back from school, taking off our hats and coats, when I suddenly found myself alone with one of the boys called Liam. I thought nothing of it until he stepped in front of me just as I was about to follow the other children into the main house and said: 'What do girls look like?'

'Get away, Liam,' I told him, swatting at him like an irritating fly. But he wouldn't budge.

'I'll show you what boys look like,' he said, and then he pulled his trousers and pants down!

I stood there, staring at him in shock.

Just at that moment Sister Sarah came in the front door, to see Liam completely naked from the waist down, and me standing there, looking at him.

'What is going on here?' she screeched.

'Nothing!' I said hurriedly. 'I was just standing here and Liam pulled his pants down.'

With that she battered me round the head.

'Pull your trousers up!' she demanded, and once Liam had his trousers up again she clobbered him round the head too. Then she grabbed us both by the scruff of our necks and started marching us down the corridor, all the way, shaking us roughly and beating us about the heads.

'You filthy, dirty children!'

Smack!

'You're pure disgusting, the both of you's!'

Thwack!

'You'll be going to hell for this!'

Bam!

She beat us all the way to the chapel and then she told us both to get down on our knees and pray to God for our souls, because we were both dirty little wretches.

Over and over again we had to say the Hail Mary, and by now I was crying with the shock and pain of it all. But also the injustice! I'd never even done anything. And the poor boy Liam, just a little boy, was sobbing like a baby.

When Sister Sarah decided we'd prayed enough, she pulled us up to our feet and beat us all the way back to the house and there we were sent up to the dormitory to pray some more. That night I was sent to bed without supper. For the next few weeks Liam and I were sent to the chapel after school every day for more praying.

On the whole, though, the North Set wasn't too bad – we didn't have a nun with us permanently and Teddy and Mona were kind, protecting us from the nuns when they were about.

So apart from staying out of trouble with the nuns our only real worry was Brian. We hadn't seen him since we'd arrived, and we'd only heard his voice the one time when he came looking for us. I spent a lot of time wandering through the long corridors which linked all the different parts of St Beatrice's, trying to find him. It wasn't really allowed but I was quick and small and could usually get about without getting caught.

One day I walked through the corridor until I came to a fire exit and there were all these green staircases going to different parts of the place. I knew I shouldn't have been there but I was curious. I took the stairs up one flight to a boys' dorm and, once there, I pushed through a door at the back. The door led to another long corridor and I walked down it for a long way until I went through another door and there, to my surprise, I saw a whole load of girls all in their nighties. Some were lying on beds in a large dormitory, others were walking around a lounge area. It was the middle of the day so I thought it was strange they were in their nighties – then I noticed that most of them had very big bellies.

The girls stared at me and I stared back. I knew I shouldn't be there but I was curious. I recognised one of the girls; she'd helped out with the little ones in North Set.

She came rushing over and grabbed my arm.

'What are you doing here?' she hissed.

'I was just looking around,' I said. 'I'm looking for my brother Brian. He's in the big boys' house. Have you seen him?'

I stared into her anxious eyes.

'What is this place?' I asked innocently.

'Never you mind!' she whispered back. 'Listen, you better not be telling a single soul that you've been here and seen us. Do you know what's going to happen to you if you tell? They'll do terrible things to you. You'll get battered like anything!'

'I won't tell,' I promised earnestly. 'I swear, I won't say a word.'

'Good, you better not. Now get out of here. The nuns'll kill you if they find you here.'

And with that she spun me around and shoved me back through the door. I kept my promise – until now I've never told another soul what I saw that day. The truth was, I didn't even know what I was looking at so I really didn't know what to say. It was only later I learned the significance of what I'd seen.

When we finally did find Brian the change in him was shocking.

We met him in the playground one day, and instead of being pleased to see us he seemed angry.

'Oh Brian!' I was so delighted I ran to hug him, but he just pushed me back.

'Get off! What do you want from me?' he said sullenly.

'We're pure happy to find you, Brian. We been looking everywhere for you!' Tara babbled, but Brian cut her short.

'Yeah, well, now you've seen me I don't want you coming here,' he said. 'This here is my house, the big boys' house.' He waved his arm at the house behind him. 'And I don't want you coming anywhere near it, you got that?'

'Why not, Brian?' I asked.

'Just don't feckin' go in there!' he shouted. 'And if I catch any of you's trying to sneak in I swear I'll kill you myself.'

We couldn't understand it. Something had happened to Brian – he wasn't his normal self.

A few months after we'd arrived in the convent, the nun came and told us to get ready because we were going home. Already we'd seen other children in our house coming and going and we were thrilled that Daddy was coming to collect us. Now we could all get back to being a family again. We hugged the other children goodbye – we'd all become good friends in the short time we'd been there and they seemed genuinely happy for us. We assured them it wouldn't be long before their mammies or daddies came for them too. Then we said goodbye to Teddy and Mona and were led back down the corridor to the front gate by the Reverend Mother to wait for Daddy at the gates. Finally, everything was going to be back to normal. Even Brian was smiling as he was led up to join us from the big boys' house.

'At last!' he grinned. 'Anything's better than this feckin' hell hole!'

And with that he got his last clip round the ear before we were released, back to our father.

CHAPTER 10

DESPAIR

'Oh Daddy, it's fantastic!' we enthused, exploring our new home.

We were thrilled to be reunited with our father, who was now all fixed up and back to his old self. He looked healthy and happy when he came to meet us and, best of all, we had a new house in Lockmeet, his home town. It was a sweet little three-bedroom house in the middle of a quiet street, and now we clattered up and down the stairs, poking about into every corner, bouncing up and down on the beds. Me and Tara had a room of our own, Colin and Brian shared a room and Daddy had a room too. It had all been freshly painted and the beds were beautifully made up with clean white linen. It was a relief not to be going back to the cottage again where all the bad memories had tormented our poor father.

Now it was deep winter and we all felt grateful for the heavy coats the convent had given us to take home. Daddy wasn't drinking any more so each morning he'd get up, light the fire in the kitchen and feed us all breakfast before leaving for work while we kids were left to explore our new home and the surrounding streets. It was freedom once again – no more nuns telling us what to do, no more praying and no more beatings. Now we were in the middle of a village we weren't isolated and even Brian started to get back to his old self as we made friends with the neighbourhood children.

One day, not long after we'd arrived in town, we noticed all the kids on the street were bubblier, more excited than usual.

A family of six children lived next door and we overheard them talking about what they had wished for and whether Santa would be delivering their presents under the tree this year. You could see the joy in their faces and the way their eyes lit up as they chatted breathlessly about their 'Christmas presents'.

'What's that you're saying?' Brian asked them, curious.

One of the boys replied: 'It's Christmas, isn't it? What are you getting?'

'What do you mean?' I said. 'What's Christmas?'

The other children stopped talking then and stared at us.

'Don't you know what Christmas is?' the boy replied, clearly flabbergasted.

The other children seemed equally amazed – after all, we weren't little kids. I was nearly nine and Brian was almost 11.

But it was true – we'd never heard about this thing they were talking about. We'd never heard of Christmas or Santa or any of those things.

The boy tried again: 'Don't you lot ever have presents on Christmas Day with loads of food to eat?'

We shook our heads.

'Santa Claus? Reindeer? Christmas trees?'

Again, we shook our heads, ignorant. So the boy went on to explain what Christmas was all about, how it was to celebrate the birth of the Baby Jesus and the Christmas story of how Mary gave birth in a stable with the farmyard animals. He informed us it was a time for children to get presents from Santa, a fat magical man with white hair and black boots who climbed down chimneys and rode about on a flying cart pulled by deer. We listened, entranced, mesmerised.

He went on to describe how all the mammies and daddies celebrate by hanging lights and shiny things from a tree and make a big roast dinner from everyone.

Oh, it sounded wonderful!

We were enthralled by all of this, but now it was getting late and the children were going home. It was going to be a big day tomorrow and they were brimming over with anticipation at all the good things waiting for them.

Gradually everyone disappeared, but I was curious. I wanted to see what the boy was talking about. Now it was dark and the streets were empty. Everyone was indoors, preparing for 'Christmas'.

So I started walking through the streets, peeping in through all the windows of the houses. I saw Christmas trees, all decorated like the boy said with twinkly lights, glistening with white snowflakes while coloured balls hung from the tips of the branches. On top of one tree I saw a glowing white angel. I saw husbands and wives busying themselves about, while some fathers already sat smoking in their armchairs by the windows.

Then I looked into one house and I caught sight of a blonde woman through her front window, folding some clothing while her husband stood nearby. She was slim and very pretty. She reminded me of someone I missed so dearly. For a while I couldn't tear myself away. I was transfixed by this woman, this peaceful family scene. They looked so happy together. After a while they saw me at their window and waved, smiling. I waved back, but still I couldn't move. My mind was racing, my heart pounding in my chest.

Why couldn't my parents be like this? I wondered. Happy together, no fights. Just love and kindness.

More than anything, I wanted my mammy home and for us all to be together again. That would have been my Christmas wish. My eyes filled and I let the tears plop gently down on the windowsill. Then I turned away and walked home.

Nobody said anything about 'Christmas' to our daddy that night – there was nothing to say. It was just an ordinary evening for us. But the next day when we saw all the children playing on the street on their new bicycles, we were thrilled. We dashed outside and the children were so excited, they let us play on their new bikes. We weren't jealous – we'd never known Christmas so we didn't miss it. We were just grateful to be allowed to play with their new toys.

Birthdays and Christmases came and went – I turned nine that January but I didn't know it. It didn't matter. You could have given me all the toys in the whole world – it wouldn't have meant a thing to me. I just wanted my mammy back.

Now Daddy got us into the local school and we settled into a new and comfortable routine. Of an evening Daddy would cook tea and then sit round the fire with us, whittling, while we played. At the weekends he took us on long walks into the countryside, showing us all the places he'd played as a boy, and we even had a family project, to build a big gate at the end of the garden. Daddy wanted a big gate because we were alone a lot of the time when he was at work so he didn't want anybody getting into the house.

'I want the biggest gate in the street!' he declared as he heaved large planks of wood out into the garden. We all helped and it was great fun. Daddy would lift Brian up so he could put the planks down and every day our gate got higher and higher and higher. We all laughed every time we saw it.

'It's Fort Knox we're gonna have here!' Daddy joked.

And it was true – our gate was massive. The biggest in the street.

For a while things were really good. Daddy was loving to us all, we got fed, dressed and washed. But then one day Daddy went to the pub and came home drunk. The next day he did the same. And the day after that. And then it didn't stop. We used to come home to the house at lunchtime because the school didn't feed us and Daddy would usually be there, frying sausages and making our food.

But one day he forgot, and because we didn't have a key we couldn't get in the house – so we just hung around the streets until it was time to go back for our afternoon lessons.

Daddy's routine began to fall apart again. One day he'd be home, the next he wouldn't. Some days we'd have food, other days nothing.

At first it wasn't too bad – the school gave all the kids a currant bun and a glass of milk each morning so we'd usually be okay if Daddy forgot to come home.

But then one day Daddy came back, his arms laden with food – biscuits, bread, beans, sausages and milk.

'I've heard your mother's back in Ireland,' he explained. 'I'm going to go and get her and bring her home.'

We were to feed ourselves while he was gone. We were excited – we really believed our father was going to bring Mammy home.

Over the next three days we managed as best we could on our own while Daddy made the long journey to her home town. Brian fried the sausages for us and we helped ourselves to the bread and biscuits.

We talked about how nice it was going to be once Mammy was back, how pleased she'd be to see us all, and we wondered whether we'd need to move house again, to fit in all the small children.

But when I came home from school on the third day Daddy was slumped in the living room, swigging on a bottle of Guinness. He looked up as I came in, eyes red and bloodshot. I didn't even ask him if he'd found our mother. I knew the answer. From there, things went downhill. Eventually we all stopped going to school because we were so hungry we couldn't concentrate on the lessons, and besides, we were now filthy since Daddy wasn't washing our clothes. It was embarrassing turning up every day in the same stained and ragged dress.

Brian had had enough. He took Tara aside and told her he planned to run away to our grandmother's, the place where he'd been so happy. It was nearly 30 miles away but he didn't seem daunted and he asked Tara if she'd go with him.

'What about the others?' Tara said.

'We can't take everyone,' he told her. 'Just let's get there and then we'll come back for them. It's our only hope.'

But of course Tara told me of their plan and I conspired with Colin to follow them on the day they were due to leave.

For hours they tramped through the fields, me and Colin not far behind, diving into hedges every time they turned around.

Eventually, it was getting dark and we saw the two of them flag down a car. It looked like they were about to get in but I was determined not to let them get away and we ran like crazy to catch them up.

'Don't worry, Colin,' I reassured my little brother. 'They won't get away from us!'

And we jumped out of the bushes just as they were about to speed off.

Poor Brian had the shock of his life.

'If you're getting in this car, you'll have to take us all with you!' I told the driver. 'We're all together.'

Brian was mad as hell and the driver shook his head. There was only room for two.

'Come on,' Brian yelled at Tara as he got into the car. It looked like he was going to leave us there. Then, as he sat in the seat, staring straight ahead, he suddenly let out an exasperated sigh and got out again, slamming the door.

He lent down to speak to the driver: 'No, go on – you're all right. I'll stay here with these.'

And the driver took off. Brian grumbled all the way down the road as we started walking again, this time all four of us together.

'We could have been there by now!' he complained.

'But Brian, we couldn't leave them,' Tara objected.

'I know, I know! Well, now we'll all have to stick together to try and get to our grandmother's house.'

By now darkness had fallen and we hadn't eaten or drunk anything all day. When we came to a river we stopped to drink some water.

This is when we all realised there was something seriously wrong with Brian.

'Now it's dark and it could be miles before we get there,' he fumed. 'I'm not going back to Daddy's. I'm not! And there's no way they're sending me back to the convent. I may as well just jump off this bridge right now and kill myself.'

We were all shocked at what he was saying.

He even clambered up to the top of the bridge, but at that minute we all scrambled to our feet and started shouting and crying: 'Please, Brian. Don't do it! It'll be all right.'

'It won't be all right!' he shouted, angry tears streaming down his face. He wiped them away with the back of his sleeve. 'I can't take it no more!'

But we got to the top then and pulled him down.

He fell back towards us but the anguish and torment was still blazing within him.

'Come on,' Tara urged. 'We got to keep going. There's no point going back.'

It was now pitch black all around and we could barely see the road up ahead. We passed by one cottage and when we couldn't see any more lights up ahead we realised this must be the last one for miles around.

'Colin, you're the littlest,' said Brian to our younger brother. 'Go knock on the door and ask the lady if we can have something to eat.'

Colin, obedient as ever, did as he was told, and when the lady saw him shivering on the doorstep, and us all huddled not far behind, she insisted we come inside.

'What are you doing out here, in the middle of nowhere at night?' she gasped, shocked at the sight of us.

'We're just going to my grandmother's,' Brian replied, as casually as possible. 'She don't live too far away.'

'Well, you look hungry,' she said. 'Do you want something to eat for your journey?'

We all nodded and she sat us in her living room while she went off to the kitchen to make fish fingers. Afterwards we thanked her but said we really must be getting along. The lady seemed eager for us to stay and brought down some dolls for me and Tara. When Brian said it really was time to leave she told us she wanted to make us all some sandwiches for the road and we had to stay till she was done. We should have known she was stalling. We should have guessed they'd be looking for us.

In a short while the police arrived to pick us up.

'What are you lot doing?' chided the sergeant as he bundled us all into the car. 'Don't you realise your father's in a dreadful state? He's been worried sick.'

In the back of the car, none of us spoke. Finally Brian said gloomily: 'I should never have gone to the convent with you lot. I should never have done that.'

It was certainly a disappointment not to get to our grandmother's place. Now Daddy was back to his old self and we were forced to beg and steal for food again. Most days Brian crept into the farmer's fields to thieve anything he could get his hands on – carrots, potatoes, onions – whatever he could steal, we ate. One day we were down at the harbour when we caught sight of a pallet of flat fish that the fishermen had obviously just caught. But there was nobody around so Brian got the idea for us to take the fish. So we walked right up to the pallets and began filling our pockets with fish, folding them into our jumpers when we ran out of room. Then we walked up the road towards our house. We were happy, messing about that day, anticipating the lovely fish we were going to eat when Brian threw one of the flat fish at Tara. It missed her but hit the window of a house we were passing and stuck there, just suspended in mid-air on the window.

We all burst out laughing.

'Imagine the faces of them people when they look out the window and see a fish!' Brian guffawed. 'They'll think it's a bleedin' miracle!'

We all thought this was so hilarious we started throwing all our fish onto the rest of the windows we passed by. We could just imagine the people inside, running to see what was wrong when they heard the soft slap of the wet fish hitting their windows and getting the shock of their lives!

Of course we never stopped to consider that we were throwing away our tea, and when we got to the house we barely had three fish left out of dozens we had stolen.

'God, that was stupid!' I said as we each nibbled on the delicious white flesh later that night which Brian had fried up for us.

'We could have full bellies by now,' Tara agreed.

We never thought about the fishermen who had lost their fish. We didn't think much from one day to the next. We were starving and that was all that mattered. Occasionally the nice lady with the six children next door would take pity on us and give us a loaf of bread, but for the most part we were starving, only staying alive by what we could steal.

Some months after our escape attempt we were playing outside in the street when we saw our brother Aidan walking down the road.

He was carrying a toddler who was obviously Riley while Libby and Lucy walked along next to him. They were bigger than I remembered but I recognised them all in an instant.

My heart leapt – they were coming back!

'Tara! Colin! Brian!' I shouted. 'It's Aidan. And he's got the little ones!'

We all dashed up the street to meet him and see our younger siblings. Riley didn't recognise us at all and neither did Lucy, but Libby knew who we were.

'Aidan! Where's Mammy?' I asked eagerly. I assumed everyone was coming back together.

Aidan looked exhausted and none too pleased.

'Mammy's not here,' he said. I didn't fully understand. I thought she must be coming on later.

We accompanied Aidan into the house and spent the next few hours reacquainting ourselves with our younger sisters and brother.

When Daddy came home from the pub he could hardly believe his eyes. Then he picked up Riley and started kissing and cuddling him.

He tried to hug the two girls too, but they barely knew him and pulled away.

'Aidan, where's your mother?' said Daddy, clearly thinking the same as me, that they were all returning and we'd soon be together as a family again.

'She's not coming,' said Aidan flatly. 'She's just given you the three kids.'

This was obviously news to everyone in the room because at that minute Lucy and Libby started crying and Riley clawed at Aidan to pick him up. Now me and Tara joined in, sobbing.

'We want Mammy,' I wailed. 'Can't you take us all back?'

But Aidan just shook his head: 'I can't do it. She says I'm just to drop the little ones and that's it.'

Aidan tried to leave shortly after but by now the little ones were hysterical and we literally had to rip Riley off him so he could get out the door. Daddy was all confused and upset, surrounded by three bawling children who knew him no better than a stranger and us, broken-hearted and let down once more.

'Kathleen,' he urged. 'Help me here.'

We all did our best to calm the little ones down and I curled up with them in bed that night, holding and cuddling them all, trying to soothe them. They cried themselves to sleep that night. And the next morning it was no better. Poor Daddy was now at his wits' end, and although he treated them kindly and got food for us all to begin with, the arrival of our siblings was to mark the beginning of the end.

Daddy now left us all in the house while he went off, drinking himself stupid all day. He soon stopped bringing food back and we were hungry and neglected all the time. Desperate, we decided to ask the nuns in the local convent for help. We needed to feed the little ones. Now we knew nuns were supposed to be kind and godly so we felt sure they would take pity on us. But they didn't – they just told us to go away.

'That's not very saintly!' I fumed helplessly. 'How can they be turning us away like that?'

Daddy had warned us not to visit our grandfather but we knew where he lived and, with nowhere else to turn, we went to beg his help. We were all excited – we remembered our time with our grandfather fondly and thought he loved us too. Surely he wouldn't let us starve?

But when he came to the door he was angry.

'Get away with you now!' he barked. 'I'm done with the lot of you and your feckin' father. Just be gone and don't ever come back again!'

We were outraged – after all, we had loved our grandfather and now he was turning his back on us. So we grabbed a load of stones and threw them at his windows before running away.

After a while Libby and Lucy got sick – we couldn't get them out of bed in the morning. The place was a filth pit, we were completely malnourished, had sores all over our bodies and there was nothing we could do about it. In the end it was the school that saved us – they told the police that we'd stopped going and they came to check on us.

Seeing the dreadful state we were in, they filed a petition in the court to have us taken away. They told Daddy there would be a hearing and he should get us all ready. For the first time in weeks Daddy made an effort. He got us some bread the night before and on the day of the hearing he was scrabbling around the floor, desperately searching for clean clothes, trying to fix our hair, scrubbing our faces of dirt. But there was no disguising our swollen bellies or pencil-thin arms.

It didn't take the judge very long to decide. Daddy didn't have a lawyer but it didn't matter because he knew all the people in the court from growing up in this town.

'I'm afraid there's nothing I can do, Donal,' the judge told him kindly, as one friend might speak to another in pain. 'I'm awarding all these seven children to the state until they each reach the age of 16.'

'Not all of them!' Daddy wept, wringing his hands as he sat next to us on the bench.

'Yes, all of them, Donal,' said the judge softly. 'Just look at them, won't you? They're half-starved. They're not going to school. You can't do this to them.'

Daddy looked at us then and in that moment I saw it all in his eyes. He loved us so much and he'd tried so hard, but he just couldn't do it.

We were his children, his flesh and blood – he loved us all to death, but he was sick and he simply wasn't capable of giving us what we needed. He looked away then, ashamed. Dreadfully ashamed.

'Won't you, won't you at least let me say goodbye?' he gasped through his tears.

The judge then got up and came towards my father, motioning for the police to stand back. He put his arm on his shoulder.

'You say your goodbyes, Donal. Don't worry. We'll stay with you here till they go.'

Then we were all crying and grabbing onto my daddy. We couldn't bear to see him like this, so broken-hearted. Even the little ones, who were now bonded to my father, clung to him, weeping at his side.

It took a while before they had all the police cars ready for us and then the time came when we had to leave.

'I'll come and see you,' he promised, hugging me tight. 'Once I'm well and I'm out of hospital I'll come and visit you as soon as possible.'

Even the policemen were wiping at their eyes as they led us all to the cars, one by one, and our father broke down then into gut-wrenching sobs. It was too much. I ran into the car, just wanting to get as far away from that sound as possible. When we were finally on our way, I sat back and smiled weakly at Tara. We knew we were going back to the convent at St Beatrice's and we didn't mind. It hadn't seemed that bad the first time.

'It's going to be all right,' she assured me, squeezing my hand as we looked at the road ahead together. 'It's got to be better than this.'

Once we were back at the convent we were taken to the doctor for a medical check while Lucy and Libby were immediately admitted to hospital for treatment. A small, balding doctor with glasses perched on the end of his nose scribbled in his book as he made a note of the lice crawling all over my head, the sores on my arms and legs, and my weight. At the time of admission I was 10 years old and weighed just four stone.

PART III
BETRAYED

CHAPTER 11
WATERSBRIDGE

It didn't take long for me to realise that my return to St Beatrice's was not going to be like the first visit. From the moment we left the doctor's study we were taken to a house two miles down the road from the main convent, which we were told was called Watersbridge. This would be our new home. A small, skinny little nun with a pinched face was standing outside to greet me and Tara while Lucy and Libby recovered in hospital. The boys had been separated from us and placed in another house.

'Children,' the tiny nun announced, 'I am Sister Helen. You will be living here with me in Watersbridge now and I expect you to behave yourselves or there will be consequences.'

She looked at us both sternly, as if we had already offended her, just by being there. Behind her stood a lady who was one of the staff – she was also short but with huge breasts that seemed to drag her even closer to the ground. I was wondering how she managed to stay on her feet without toppling forward when I caught a brisk clip round my ear.

'Jesus Christ!' I exploded angrily. 'What was that for?'

Whumph! The nun hit me again.

'Don't stare!' Sister Helen admonished. 'And don't say those words, taking the Lord's name in vain. This here is your new house mother, Rosie. She'll help you get settled in.'

Tara started giggling next to me and I couldn't help but smile too.

'Don't you start!' Sister Helen warned her as she led us both inside. It was an ordinary-looking house – on one side there was a large living room with comfy-looking sofas, a television and a pile of magazines in the corner. On the other side of the hall was a room, closed off by a glass door, which we could see had nice chairs and an array of little knick-knacks on coffee tables. That was the 'good room', Sister Helen explained. Not for children! We could see the kitchen from across the hall.

By now some of the children had come out to see us, the 'new arrivals', and I recognised a few from our previous stay in North Set.

'Tara! Kathleen!' one little girl called Gina exclaimed, running up, happy to see us. 'What are you doing back here?'

It was nice to see a few familiar faces – Jake, Miles, Victoria and Jessica – but there was no time for catching up.

'Right, you dirty little tinkers!' Rosie addressed us. 'Upstairs for a bath. Now!'

'Don't be calling us that!' I shot back. 'We're not tinkers!'

'You're whatever I say you are, Miss Mouth!' Rosie pulled my hair down towards her, then with her other hand gave me a ringing belt across my head. No, this was not like North Set.

We were bathed and Rosie scrubbed at us both rigorously. I was now nearly 10 and resented being pulled about like a child but Rosie didn't pay me any mind. She yanked my arms, spun me about and pummelled my head with soap. Afterwards we were shown into a small bedroom and told to put on the night-dresses laid out for us.

Unlike North Set we had the nun, Sister Helen, living with us permanently in the house and she seemed far stricter than Teddy and Mona. Clearly, Sister Helen ruled the roost and Rosie was her second in command. Apart from them, there were a few other members of staff whom we were gradually introduced to.

Watersbridge had two floors – all the children's bedrooms were on the upper floor alongside a bathroom, a study and rows and rows of locked cupboards. We learned later this was where all the children's confiscated belongings had been locked away.

The next morning a nurse nun came to attend to our sores, putting cream and oils all over us. When we were finally done we got dressed and ran out of our bedroom, hungry to join the other children for breakfast.

'And where do you think you're going?' Rosie sneered at us as she stood at the top of the stairs, arms folded, blocking our way.

'We just want to get our breakfast,' I told her.

'And you think that leaving your beds in that disgusting mess is acceptable, do you?' She gestured over to where our sheets lay crumpled and tangled up on our beds.

'No, Rosie.'

'No! You two little tramps are going to have to learn to clean up after yourselves in this house,' she said loudly. She seemed to be enjoying herself. 'Now go back in to your rooms and make your beds. Properly. There'll be no breakfast for either of you till you learn how to leave a tidy room.'

So we returned to our room, smarting from her words.

I didn't understand it at all – they were allowed to call us all sorts of bad names like tramps and tinkers but the moment we said flippin' hell or Jesus Christ we got walloped.

'Ah feck this!' Tara spat in frustration as she moved around her bed, tugging at the sheets, trying to pull them straight onto the mattress.

We had looked into all the other rooms to see the beds made perfectly, with neat little corners tucked underneath. Nobody had even shown us how to do it!

We must have been up there struggling for half an hour before Gina bounded into our room.

'Aren't you going to have breakfast?' she asked us.

'We're not allowed till we've done these,' I told her, showing her our poorly made beds.

'Here, I'll show you,' she offered. Then she demonstrated how to lay out the sheets and fold the sides under one by one until the corners were all neat so you couldn't see any creases.

With Gina's help we were soon done and after Rosie's inspection we were finally allowed downstairs for breakfast.

In the kitchen there was a long wooden table lined with plastic chairs. We were given blue plastic bowls and one of the staff ladled out a measly handful of cornflakes while another poured us each a cup of hot, sweet tea from a large silver teapot. I helped myself to a large slosh of milk for my cornflakes.

It was barely enough to fill us up but by now I was used to being hungry and I'd learned to take whatever food I was given, without question. Afterwards we helped to clear up, wash and dry the dishes.

By now most of the other children had set off for school but once again we had to wait to be allocated school places so we spent the day exploring our new home. In the living room there was a TV and two sofas, not enough for the 16 children in our house to sit down.

The 'good room' was filled with nice chairs and a coffee table with pretty china ornaments, but the moment I opened the door to peep inside Rosie shouted at me to close it again.

As the morning dragged on we begged to be allowed to go outside, so one of the staff said we could play in the back garden.

She showed us out the back door into the garden behind the house – it was just a large patch of bare grass. No trees, no toys, just nothing.

The front of the house was far more interesting – it had a couple of large trees and you could see the street and all the people passing by.

But when we asked to be let out the front we were told this wasn't allowed.

By now our mean little bowl of cornflakes was a distant memory and we wandered into the kitchen in search of food. Nothing. There wasn't a scrap of food in the cupboards and the fridge was empty save for a bottle of milk and a slab of butter.

So we waited it out until lunchtime when all the other children returned from school and we were given lunch of a plate of mash and gravy with a pudding of instant whip.

It was pretty awful. The mash was lumpy and watery at the same time, and the instant whip, which I think was meant to be strawberry flavoured because it was bright pink, was so sweet it made my teeth ache. It didn't taste of anything else besides sugar.

It was a relief to see the other children again but there was no laughing and shouting like in North Set; everyone behaved perfectly, quickly clearing their plates and bowls away after lunch and helping to wash and clear up.

By mid-afternoon Rosie was fed up with us hanging round.

'If you two have nothing better to do, I've got some jobs for you.' She smiled nastily. I didn't like Rosie from the first. She seemed to take real delight in making us suffer and in that first day alone I saw her wallop the heads of four other children.

She set us to work then, cleaning, dusting and polishing the hallway, banisters and staircase. Afterwards she took us to the airing cupboard, a gigantic cupboard next to the kitchen on the ground floor.

It was a complete mess of clothes and sheets.

'Right, I presume you know how to fold clothes at least,' she said. 'Get folding.'

So we spent the rest of the afternoon clambering up and down the wooden-slatted shelves in the cupboard, organising and folding all the children's clothes in the house.

To be honest, it was nice to have something to do.

Two days later we were informed we would be going to Our Lady School and given uniforms to wear. We each had a blue skirt, a white shirt, a blue-striped tie, navy jumper and blue knee socks. I felt very smart in my new uniform and hopeful for the fresh start.

That morning I asked Rosie for a new pair of knickers. I wanted to be as smart as possible for meeting all the new teachers and children.

'There's nothing wrong with what you've got now,' she pronounced. 'You'll get a fresh pair of knickers at the beginning of every week, just like everyone else.'

So that morning I stood at the sink in the bathroom and washed my knickers from the day before, squeezing out the water before putting them on still wet so I would have fresh underwear.

The nun walked us to school the first day but after that it would be up to us to get to school every day on time. A couple of miles away, it took half an hour to walk with the nun.

'Now just you mind not to be diddling and daddling on your way back,' she warned us before she left us and we nodded obediently, both a little nervous, a little scared at being thrown into yet another new place. Once again we'd be in separate classes since Tara was a year older.

The nun went on: 'As soon as that bell goes, you move it.'

She snapped her fingers to emphasise her point.

'No talking with other children, no hanging about. It's straight back to the house. Got it?'

Our Lady was a convent school and my teacher introduced herself as Sister Teresa. She was a brisk, no-nonsense person, I could see that. There were no lengthy introductions. I was shown to my seat the moment I arrived and told to sit quietly and pay attention. Though I'd been looking forward to starting classes, my first day was just a painful lesson in humiliation.

'Kathleen!' Sister Teresa trilled midway through the morning. 'Come to the front of the class.'

I hadn't been doing anything naughty. I'd barely got my feet under the desk so I didn't expect anything bad to happen.

'Stand there and put your hands out in front of you,' she instructed. So I did as I was told, not thinking anything of it.

The next thing she took out a metre-long ruler and brought it down hard on both my palms.

After the first hit, I whipped my hands away in shock and pain, grasping them to me.

'Put them back!' she ordered. I didn't know why I was being punished and I felt horrible and humiliated in front of all these other children I didn't know.

Thwack! The ruler came down again on my stinging palms. And again and again. Tears now pricked behind my eyes and I began to cry silently. I don't know if it was the pain or the embarrassment.

Even my tears felt shameful and wrong.

She gave me ten slaps in total before ordering me back to my seat.

'Now mind,' she said. 'That's what you'll get if you misbehave in my classroom.'

I clasped my swollen red hands together under the desk, desperately trying to keep my tears at bay. I stared straight ahead, feeling everyone's eyes on me. My palms throbbed. There was nothing I could do. All these children would be going home to their parents at night. I was going back to the nuns and Rosie. For the rest of the afternoon I struggled to hold my pencil as my hands were so swollen.

As it was, I wouldn't have known what to write anyway. The fact was, at 10 years old I still couldn't read. I'd missed so much school through years of being shunted about that all the other children were miles ahead of me. I just kept my head down and tried not to attract the teacher's attention. I was too afraid to ask for help, too ashamed to admit my problems. When the bell rang at 3 p.m. I dashed out of class to meet Tara at the school gate so we could walk home together.

'How was it?' she asked as we strolled back along the road we'd come from that morning. Grateful for the chance to just relax and be ourselves again, we filled each other in on our day.

'The nun beat me,' I told her and showed her my sore hands.

'What for?'

'I don't know!'

'Ah, they're a right load of shites around here,' Tara said warmly, putting an arm around my shoulder. 'Next time she picks on you just kick her in the shins!'

I smiled then. It was a relief to have a normal conversation where our every word wasn't being scrutinised. We chatted all the way back about our daddy and the other kids in the house.

By the time we breezed back into Watersbridge Sister Helen was waiting for us in the hallway, scowling like she was sucking on a lemon.

'Oh Christ,' Tara whispered under her breath. 'What now?'

'What time do you call this?' Sister Helen addressed us shrilly.

'We don't know, Sister,' Tara replied. 'We don't have any watches.'

'Mind your cheek, madam!' Sister Helen fixed her with a steely stare. 'It is now 4 p.m. – you are late!'

'How can we be late?' I objected. 'We left as soon as school finished and walked all the way back. We didn't talk to anybody or stop for nothing.'

'Yeah,' Tara backed me up. 'How can we be late?'

'You are late because you walked!' Sister Helen explained, as if to a five-year-old. 'You have fifteen minutes to get home every day. If you don't get back in fifteen minutes by walking then you run. You understand? You run!'

'Yes, Sister,' we chorused back. It had only been a few days and we were already sick of this place, sick of all the stupid rules, sick of Sister Helen, the staff, their casual insults and boundless cruelty.

From that very first day we realised the nuns didn't allow you any time to actually get to and from school. It was just about possible to get up in the morning, say our prayers, dress, wolf down breakfast and clear away before we had to run to school to get there on time.

If we were late of a morning we'd get a beating from the nuns there. At lunchtime we had to go back to Watersbridge, which meant running two miles again to the house and another two miles back to school afterwards. At the end of the school day we had to run once more to get back in time. The whole day you could stand in one place and just see a bunch of children running backwards and forwards through the town to avoid punishments. It must have looked funny from the outside, all these children zipping about, but it was exhausting for us. And it meant the food we ate barely touched our stomachs – we were constantly hungry for running all the time!

Once back at Watersbridge we would take off our uniforms, lay them on the end of the bed, ready for the next day, and then put on our play clothes. All the children would then do their homework at the big kitchen table. Once finished we'd be sent into the garden to play until they called tea-time, which was often just some bread with cheese and hot tea. Then we'd be allowed to watch a bit of TV in the living room before bed. I loved this – I'd never watched TV much before so even the boring holy programmes the nuns made us watch were fascinating to me at first. And if we were really lucky we got to see cartoons. Then it was prayers and bedtime.

A week after we arrived in Watersbridge Lucy and Libby were brought back from the hospital. They looked so much better and we were thrilled to be reunited again. They even put us in the same room at first.

That night, Libby called out to me after lights out: 'Kathleen! Kathleen! Can I come in your bed, please?'

'No, Libby. They don't like that. If we get caught we'll be in trouble.'

'Please, Kathleen,' she begged. I could just about make out her silhouette in the darkness, curled up in a ball under the cover, shaking like a leaf. Poor thing! She was only six. Lucy lay on a bed on the other side, sleeping soundly. I reached out to Libby and she jumped into my arms.

'Come on now,' I soothed, giving her a big hug. There was nothing of her – she was skinny as anything and still shaking.

'Stay for now,' I said. 'But in the morning you'll have to go back to your own bed.'

So I wrapped her up like that and she quickly fell asleep. I worried that night I wouldn't wake up in time to get her out of my bed but luckily I woke with the sun that morning and managed to lead her back to her own bed before Sister Helen came round.

Poor Libby, she was so quiet, so intimidated by everything and everyone. The moment she heard a nun she'd jump and just scurry out of the room, making herself small enough so that nobody would notice her.

Each morning they called us at 7 a.m. for those who wanted to go to mass. For everyone else we could get up just before breakfast at 8 a.m.

'Why would you want to go to mass anyways?' I asked Gina one morning.

'They treat you better if you go to mass,' she whispered. 'It makes them think you want to be a good person.'

'But it's too much praying!' I said. 'I've been praying non-stop since I got here anyway.'

Nevertheless, I did try it a few times. Anything for a break from the constant beatings. It seemed that no matter what I did, it was never right. Sister Helen and the staff seemed permanently angry with all of us and it was a sheer miracle if I could get through a day without being walloped. I took myself off to mass in the mornings and nearly fell asleep again during all the Latin prayers. I was bored to holy tears! But it worked for a short while. Sister Helen remarked she was glad to see I was turning to the Lord for guidance, and for a few days I didn't get a beating. It didn't last. One morning I was late for mass and nearly fell in the convent door in my haste.

'Oh feck!' I exclaimed. Sister Helen was so appalled she picked me up by the scruff of my neck and marched me all the way back down the road to our house, beating me all the way.

It was one thing getting beaten myself. But watching my siblings suffer was something I never got used to. And at first, neither Tara or myself could accept it. Although Lucy and Libby had returned to Watersbridge, they were still being treated for their coughs and had to take a medicine every evening before bed.

The little ones were sent to bed earlier than us but when Tara and I came upstairs one night we saw one of the younger members of staff called Elaine trying to force Libby and Lucy to drink their medicine. She had the spoon jammed down Libby's throat and was beating her about the head at the same time so that poor Libby was choking and gagging. She'd obviously just done the same to Lucy, who was spluttering, crying and holding her throat.

'Shut up, you stupid girl!' Elaine was shouting at Libby as she slapped her about. 'Shut up and drink it!'

But of course Libby couldn't swallow it down because she was being pummelled so badly. Without even stopping to think, Tara pounced on Elaine. She grabbed her by the arm and pulled her away from Libby, who had now collapsed on the floor.

'GET OFF MY SISTER!' Tara screamed, beating Elaine about the head with her hands.

Elaine was temporarily stunned as Tara attacked her, smacking her all over her body. But she soon recovered and was now fighting back, beating Tara's hands away. The two of them were scuffling around on the floor, hands and legs flying everywhere. I ran to Libby and Lucy to check they were okay, and though some part of me was willing Tara to give the cow a taste of her own medicine, at the same time I was terrified for Tara.

'Stop it!' I yelled at her. 'You'll make it worse. Come on, Tara!'

Tara dragged herself away from the woman, who was now throwing her arms about blindly to hit back. Elaine then staggered to her feet, breathing hard and staring at Tara, who had now come over to where I was huddled with the two little ones. Tara stood in front of us protectively, defiantly, daring Elaine to come near us.

Elaine looked at us as she adjusted her skirt and jumper.

'Don't take it then!' she spat at Lucy and Libby, now cowering under my arms. 'Just go on being sick! I don't care!'

And with that she stormed out of our room and went back downstairs.

We all stood there, watching after her, our hearts in our mouths, fully expecting Sister Helen to come storming up the stairs any moment.

'You'll get into trouble!' a trembling Lucy whispered to Tara.

'Ah, don't you worry about me. I can take care of meself,' Tara reassured her, but her worried eyes told a different story.

Remarkably, Elaine didn't report Tara to the nuns on that occasion, but it didn't stop the beatings. For some reason, our youngest sister Lucy was always on the receiving end of the worst of them. I caught Rosie giving out to her so bad one time I grabbed her arm to stop her hitting her but then she swung around and walloped me too. Really hard. Then she went back to beating Lucy.

Around the same time Lucy started suffering from nightmares. But they weren't like normal nightmares; it was as if she was fully awake. I'd be fast asleep in my bed when suddenly I'd be woken by a terrible screaming coming from Lucy's room. I'd jump out of bed and run in to see her cowering in the corner, eyes wide open, shaking like a leaf.

'Mammy's here!' she'd tell me earnestly. 'Mammy's here!'

'Ah, Mammy's not here,' I'd say, trying to calm her down.

'No, she is! She is, Kathleen! I seen her. She's under the bed! Look under the bed!'

She was so convincing she'd have me crawling around on the floor, looking under the bed for our mother, who I knew couldn't possibly be in her room. This happened a lot. One time Daddy came back, another time Mammy was there and she jumped out the window. Poor Lucy was haunted every night by the loved ones who'd let her down.

As for me, I couldn't work out what to do. All our lives we'd survived by helping each other, but now, in this new world, we could do nothing to protect one another. In fact, it was the opposite. Our siblings could get into trouble just for being associated with us.

One time I had just come in from playing in the garden when Sister Helen stopped me in the hallway.

'You're filthy, you dirty tinker!' she spat. 'Just look at your skirt, covered in mud.'

'Ah, sure, it's only a bit of dirt, Sister,' I said. 'I'm sure God will forgive me a bit of dirt.'

Lucy was just standing innocently a little way off from me but Sister Helen had her in her sights. She grabbed Lucy and smacked her hard across the head. Lucy howled in surprise and pain.

'What did you do that for?' I asked, shocked.

'That's what happens when you back-chat me!' Sister Helen replied. 'Now go and get cleaned up!'

I was so mad right then I just wanted to run up to her and pull her stupid veil off her head. My fists clenched at my side, fingernails digging into my palms.

'I said go!' Sister Helen barked. 'Get out of here, both of you!'

Lucy had already run upstairs and I followed behind, boiling with impotent rage. For the first time in our lives we could no longer protect each other. In Watersbridge we had to find a whole new way to survive.

CHAPTER 12

GRACE

There was one nice person in our house and that was Grace, our cook.

She joined Watersbridge not long after we arrived, and from the moment she started working there our meals improved no end.

Now the fish that we had on Fridays actually tasted like fish, the sausages weren't burned, the mash was creamy, not lumpy, and the stew was delicious, not just a watery bowl of tough meat and soggy vegetables. Grace was kind – she was an older woman with lovely curly, white hair, and unlike the other staff or the nuns she actually seemed to like us children. So I spent as much time as I could in the kitchen, helping her out and letting her peaceful, loving presence soothe and calm me.

One day, after I'd helped her wash, dry and put away the dishes, I sat at the kitchen table, staring forlornly out the window.

'What's the matter, Kathleen?' she asked gently. 'Don't you want to go out and play with the others?'

I shook my head, scared to say what was on my mind.

'Come on, petal,' she urged. 'Tell Grace. What's wrong?'

'Grace, how am I ever going to learn to read?' I erupted. 'All them other children can read and write and I don't know how. I can't even read the baby books!'

I was desperate to learn how to read and write but nobody at school ever made the effort to help me. The teacher was so fierce and angry the whole time I just tried to keep quiet and stay out of her way. All the while I was falling further and further behind. Now the lessons just drifted by in an incomprehensible blur. If I failed to do my homework I got called a 'lazy tinker' and made to stand outside the headmistress's office. She had beaten me a few times too. Most of the other kids knew I was having problems and sometimes they'd do my work for me or they'd help me out if I was called on in class to give an answer. But it didn't help me improve. I had been in Our Lady School for three months now and I was no better off than when I'd first arrived.

Grace looked at me with real concern.

'I'll teach you to read,' she offered.

'Really?' I couldn't believe my luck.

'Of course,' she said. 'Don't worry. It's not that difficult. We'll just go step by step. First we have to learn how to spell. Let's start here in the kitchen.' She looked around and then went over to the cooker. 'Right, this is a cooker.'

She sounded the word out: 'Coo-ker. Get your pencil out. I'm going to write it down for you.'

So I scurried off to get my pencil and rough book. Bringing it back, she spelled out the word on the page then she pointed at every letter individually and read out each one: 'That's C-O-O-K-E-R. Right, now you try it.'

So I looked at her work and saw the word and looked at the letters. One by one, I copied them out, saying the sounds in my head as I did so. Then Grace made me do it again and again.

Then she pointed to one of the letters.

'What's that one?' she asked.

'It's a K,' I said.

'Good!' she smiled.

Finally, she turned the page over and said: 'Now try spelling it on your own without looking.'

That was my first lesson. The next day we did table, then chair, fridge, floor, door, ceiling, plate and cup. By the end of the first week we'd exhausted all the words in the kitchen so Grace took me outside to the garden and we went through the whole process out there: sky, grass, house, window, boy, run. For weeks Grace put aside an hour every day to helping me learn to read and by the time I turned 11 I was able to keep up in class.

The only other person I liked was my music teacher in school. At first we just learned the recorder but I found very early on that when it came to music I could hear the tune and just pick out the notes afterwards. I suppose that came from my father. The music teacher was a tall, slim English lady called Deirdre and she was one of the only teachers in the whole school who treated me with kindness and respect. Perhaps because I was good at music, perhaps because she knew I got picked on by the other teachers, or maybe because she was simply a nice person, but for whatever reason she was good to me and I lapped it up. Within a short time she'd moved me on to the piano.

'Oh, you've got a fine ear, Kathleen!' she praised me whenever I managed to master a new song.

Twice a week for an hour, I shone. Me, Kathleen, the dirty tinker, the girl from the orphanage. I could be somebody. And I could make music with my own hands. I felt uplifted, I felt happy.

And for much of the rest of the time I just muddled along. By now I could keep up in English and History but my Maths was shocking. So bad in fact that our male teacher gave up almost immediately. I was so far behind he simply refused to teach me, and during lessons I'd either sit at the back, working on something else, or I'd go out and walk around the playground until it was time for a new lesson. The nuns at the orphanage didn't care – there were tests at school and most of the children sat them but they didn't bother with us orphanage kids. We weren't important enough, we were never expected to make anything of our lives so we just got left to sink or swim. If it hadn't been for Grace the cook I would have gone through my whole school life without even being able to read.

Three months into our new life at St Beatrice's we saw Mammy.

Every Wednesday the nuns herded all of the older children into the local swimming baths for an afternoon of swimming. It was fun – there would be about 60 of us all jumping, splashing, shouting and paddling around. There were no lessons so it took me a little while to learn how to swim. In fact, it was Tara that made me. I'd always be clinging to the edge, terrified of letting go. She'd pull me out to the middle of the pool and then swim away, making me doggy-paddle my way back to the edge. Eventually I stopped screaming in terror every time she did it and realised that I was swimming quite well on my own. From then, we had a grand old time, playing and swimming about.

But afterwards, in the changing rooms, it was always a desperate struggle to get back into our clothes without being seen by the staff.

Most of us now were growing and developing and we were embarrassed about our bodies. But there wasn't a towel for everyone so we'd have to share and Tara and I would hold it up for each other like a wall while the other one changed behind it, sometimes clambering into our clothes still dripping wet. There was one member of staff who looked after another house called Winifred. Winifred was a harsh lady and we all hated her. She'd line up her girls in the changing room every Wednesday and insist they change in front of her. They'd all stand there, naked, shivering, wishing the ground would swallow them up. We tried not to look, afraid of being shouted at by Winifred or making the girls' humiliation even worse. One poor girl was more developed than the rest – she had proper breasts and hair down there – and it was always torture for her to stand in front of everyone. This one girl always tried cringing behind a little towel but Winifred would whip it away from her.

'What are you hiding yourself for?' she'd demand to know. 'What have you got that the rest of us don't? Eh? Nothing special about you!'

We were all thankful that Sister Helen and Rosie never felt the need to come into the changing room.

Once changed, we would all be marched across town, set by set, led by a member of the staff from our house. One Wednesday we were just on our way back and Tara and I had fallen behind the others a little way. We were dawdling and messing about when suddenly Tara stopped dead, her face drained of all colour. I followed the path of her gaze towards a blonde woman across the street. It was Mammy!

'Mammy!' I shouted, and we both ran towards her. The woman turned round, alarmed, and in that moment I saw the face I'd been dreaming of for years. The face I'd longed to see so very much. But instead of being full of warmth and love, the face was a mask of fear. And then she ran. She ran as fast as she could and we raced after her, dodging in and out through the crowds of people, still shouting: 'Mammy! Mammy!'

She was so quick and nimble, we couldn't keep track of her, and after a little while weaving between people we lost her. Tara and I stopped, looking all around, but we couldn't see her. Bewildered and hurt, I turned to my sister: 'She ran! Why did she run?'

Tara now was cursing our mother to hell.

'Why? Because she's a stupid bitch! I hate her, Kathleen! I hate the living sight of her. I hate her and I hope that she dies!'

My sister's words were harsh – I could see she was hurting but I couldn't feel the same, I couldn't hate my mother. I was just devastated and baffled. Our mother had come back to Ireland; she'd even managed to find her way to where all her children had been taken. I didn't expect her to come back and get us all – I knew we weren't getting out now till we were 16. There was nothing she could do about that. But she could have stopped to say hello.

After all these years dreaming of a reunion, silently praying for my mother to come and rescue me, to take me in her arms and tell me that she loved me, she had run away from me. Why had she run?

That night in bed, Tara and I whispered to each other.

'That was definitely Mammy,' I told her, as much to reassure myself as her.

'That was definitely her,' she agreed. 'If it wasn't her, she wouldn't have run away. Can you imagine, Kathleen? Running away from your own flesh and blood? Don't you just hate her for it? I won't waste another second thinking or talking about that woman. She's as good as dead to me now. Our daddy was too good for her.'

When it came to our father, we knew one thing for sure: he loved us and he would never have run from us, no matter what. In fact, as soon as he was released from hospital he came to see us in Watersbridge. It was the biggest surprise when he just wandered into the kitchen one day, whistling away and beaming from ear to ear. We jumped up and all raced towards him. He picked us all up one by one, swinging us around.

'What are you doing here?' Rosie said when she came in to investigate the hullabaloo.

Daddy smiled at her pleasantly: 'I've come to see my little girls, haven't I?'

'No, you're not supposed to be here,' she replied primly, pulling her black woollen cardigan over her gigantic breasts.

Daddy towered over her.

'And who says I'm not? No reason I can't see my kids – and take them out to get sweets!'

And with that me, Tara, Lucy and Libby started cheering enthusiastically.

'Won't be long!' he called back to Rosie, now utterly stunned and stammering with unconcealed fury.

'But, but …'

Daddy plonked Lucy on his shoulders, took Libby by the hand and Tara and I skipped gaily out the front door by his side.

It was so wonderful to see our father – he looked well again, and all the way to the sweet shop he asked us about our new life.

'Yes, they treat us good, Daddy,' Tara told him happily.

'We like it here!' I agreed. 'There's nice children and I'm going to school now.'

None of us told him the truth – what was the point? He couldn't do anything about it now. We were all wards of the state until we turned 16. It would only have brought him anguish and more guilt.

'We thought we saw our mammy in town,' Tara confided later as we sat sharing a bag of toffees on the park bench.

'Yes, I heard she was in town too but I ain't seen her,' he nodded sadly.

When he dropped us back at Watersbridge an hour later the police were there, and Rosie was standing next to them, shrieking and pointing at my father: 'There he is, officer! That's the man who abducted the children.'

'What seems to be the problem, Officer?' My Daddy turned on his famous charm. 'These are my children and surely you won't begrudge a man coming to visit his kids or taking them out for a toffee once in a while?'

'Mr O'Shea,' the officer said, nodding respectfully at my father. 'According to our records you only have a twice-yearly visiting permit for these children. And that's got to be at appointed visiting times.'

Rosie's little head was bobbing along as he spoke.

'That's right!' she announced triumphantly, jabbing her fat little finger at my daddy's chest. 'Twice yearly. And appointed times. You can't just swan in here without asking and take the children away.'

Sister Helen was standing on the other side of Rosie, smiling coldly at us all. I could see she was acting a part to the police officers. The caring, saintly nun. You'd never believe for a moment that this kindly-looking woman, who'd dedicated her life to the Lord, spent most of her day walloping the heads of little children.

'Come along now.' She put on her posh voice as she bundled us inside. 'Let the officers sort this out with your father. It's tea-time.'

Daddy winked at us all as we looked back at him longingly.

'See you next week!' he called out after us, and we laughed as Rosie exploded at him again.

Nothing on this earth would have kept my father from us. It's true he only had visitation rights twice a year but he ignored that as much as he ignored Rosie and the nuns. Every two or three weeks he'd come wandering into the house, wherever we'd happen to be, and he'd take us out for toffees. The nuns called the police on him again and again, but only succeeded in annoying the police.

The last time the officer came round, he looked thoroughly fed up.

'He's just sitting there with his children,' he reasoned. 'Now what is wrong with that? He's not going to take them away, he knows he's not getting the kids back. Just let him see them. It's not doing anyone any harm, and frankly, Sister, we have other work.'

So that was that. Daddy visited whenever he liked, and sometimes, when the weather was too bad to walk out, we'd sit in the living room and he'd take out his mouth organ and play for us and all the other children. Some of the little ones got so used to seeing him there they started calling him Daddy too! We didn't mind – they were like our brothers and sisters anyway and since they didn't have their own daddies visiting them we were only too happy to share ours. There was so little love and affection in that miserable place that the tiny shreds of light that shone into our lives had to be shared to be truly enjoyed.

'Play us "Wild Rover"!' they'd shout.

'All right, all right!' he'd call back, genially. 'Give me a minute now!'

He'd think for a bit, then he'd put the instrument to his mouth and play the song perfectly, note for note. Sometimes we'd sing along with him but if it was a fast song we'd grab each other's hands and spin each other about, stomping round the room, clapping and dancing in time. It was so good to hear music in that house, and to hear it coming from my father. We hadn't heard him play since Mammy left. As soon as one song was finished all the children would shout out for the next one:

'Play "Jug of Punch"!'

'Play "Molly Malone"!'

'Play "Dick Darby"!'

One after the other he played the children's requests. For a short while we could all forget ourselves and let the music take us away.

Daddy gave us that. Whatever else he'd failed to give us as a parent, he never stopped giving us love.

CHAPTER 13

LOSING TARA

I was so excited I could hardly keep still for a minute. My legs jiggled up and down, my hands flew all over the place and I kept jumping out of my seat to run to the window.

Come on, come on, come on!

I scanned the driveway impatiently, searching for signs of activity. We'd all of us been away for the summer – each farmed out to a different family while St Beatrice's closed down and the nuns all got themselves a nice holiday.

I'd been sent to Cork to stay with an older couple and though it was a relief to get away from the nuns and the cruel staff at St Beatrice's I missed my brothers and sisters, especially Tara.

Tara and me had hardly ever spent any time apart so sleeping in a strange bed in an unfamiliar house without her for weeks on end was torturous. In the daytime I was left outside to play with the neighbourhood children, and though the couple were kind to me it was lonely and confusing trying to fit in with a new family. I couldn't wait to be reunited with Tara.

Now, one by one, we were all returned to Watersbridge, where we kissed and cuddled each other like mad, babbling about what we'd done and where we'd been for the summer. As the doorbell rang, we all leapt up and rushed to the front door to see which one of the 16 or so children was standing on the other side. 'Who's it going to be?' we all said to one other. It was so thrilling seeing my family again; I was like a jack in the box, bouncing up and down every two minutes.

I clasped Lucy and Libby to me, squeezing them both tight. Just seeing their faces again made me well up. I marvelled at how much they'd both grown over the summer without me.

Have you been good girls? I drilled them. Have you missed me? Hasn't your hair got long! Have you been brushing it twice a day? Were you polite to your family?

Now I was just waiting for Tara to get back and it felt like time was dragging by so slowly she was never going arrive. Finally, the doorbell rang and I raced to the entrance, my heart pounding. It was her! I flung my arms around her, laughing and kissing her face all over. But Tara seemed quiet, reserved, not her usual self at all. She hugged me back but as she did so she whispered: 'Kathleen, I've got something to tell you. Not now. Later.'

I nodded, then took her hand and led her into the kitchen for tea.

Grace was there, a big smile for us all. Tonight we had bread with a slice of cheese and a slice of beetroot each.

'I missed you all,' she said, as she put the food down in front of us.

'I missed you too, Grace,' I said. 'Nobody cooks like you!'

'Course they don't!' she chided warmly.

We wolfed down our food, then returned to the living room to play with the little ones until the nuns called bedtime.

All of us in Watersbridge had different bedtimes according to our ages – the little ones had to be tucked up by 7 p.m. so they'd say their prayers in the hallway before we helped them change out of their clothes, folding them up neatly at the end of the bed, then took them to the bathroom to go to the toilet and put them to sleep. By now Libby and Lucy were in a room by themselves and Tara and I had our own room too. The next group went up at 8 p.m. and our bedtime was 8.30 p.m. But by the time we'd finished with the little ones it was usually time to start doing our Rosary as it took an hour to get through.

As I was clicking through the beads, my knees killing me as usual, my mind churned and I felt sick with anticipation. What was the matter? Tara didn't seem herself. She was usually so happy and bubbly but now she stared down at the floor, lost in thought. All my excitement of being reunited with my family had vanished, overshadowed by Tara's dark mood.

In our bedroom upstairs I undressed slowly, taking off my clothes and carefully folding them on the bed. I slipped my long orange nightie over my head then took off my knickers just before getting under the sheets. I hated going without underwear in bed but the nuns wouldn't let us keep them on so I always did this last.

We lay there side by side waiting for the nuns to turn the lights out and leave.

It wasn't until past 10, when Sister Helen stopped patrolling the corridors, that Tara turned onto her side and whispered: 'Kathleen, my holiday was horrible.'

'Why Tara? What happened?'

'The daddy, he came into my room every single night and he'd kneel down by my bed and put his hands under the cover and start touching me, touching me all over. Even down there!

'And then while he was doing that he'd be touching himself too. It was disgusting. I was frozen solid with fear. I didn't know what to do. It happened every night. Every single night!'

A wretched little sob escaped her but now that she was talking she didn't want to stop.

'Sometimes I'd go upstairs to bed and then I'd wake up and he'd be doing it to me. One time I tried to put my legs together and push his hand away but he just pushed my hands back and I couldn't stop him.

'The mammy, she caught him one time. He was doing it to me and she came in and saw and whacked him over the head with the brush. Then they both went out and there was a fight in the house. But it didn't stop.

'Kathleen, this went on and on … for the whole holiday!'

I was numb with shock. It was disgusting. Disgusting! I could hardly believe it. Poor Tara! She was crying properly now – big, heaving, snotty sobs, and I flung my arms around her.

We lay like that for a while, her crying; me, too appalled to speak.

After a while I said the only thing that occurred to me: 'Tara, you have to tell somebody!'

'No! I can't tell anybody. What would they do to me?'

'But Tara, they'll be sending us back to these homes at Christmas time and he'll just carry on doing it. It's not right.'

Tara was crying even harder now.

'No one will believe me! Who would believe such a disgusting thing? It's too bad to even mention – it's a sin. And then God knows what they'll do to me! They'll call me a liar and … and worse!'

'Let me say something.'

'No – you mustn't,' she insisted. 'Then they'll punish us both.'

Tara put her head in her hands and wept like a baby. I felt dreadful for her and helpless to do anything.

Suddenly my own loneliness at being separated from my family over the summer seemed like nothing compared to her suffering. I couldn't imagine how bad she'd felt all this time, with no one to talk to and this evil man doing awful things to her every night.

'Well, what can we do?' I said in a small voice.

'Nothing. We can't do anything. Just let it be,' she replied, sighing. But she cried long into the night.

The next day and for many days afterwards I caught Tara staring into the distance, lost in thought. Now, instead of sharing a joke and teasing each other occasionally, I found my sister was trapped in a world of her own, cut off from me in a way I could never imagine before. I wanted to tell the nuns what had happened to her, to stop it happening again, but she'd sworn me to silence so I didn't say a word. Tara withdrew into herself and at night she said she was thinking about running away.

'If you're running away, I'm going with you,' I told her.

'Well, first we've got to know how to do it and where we'll go,' she said. 'We can't go back to Daddy.'

'No,' I agreed. 'We can't go back to Daddy.'

But I hoped she wouldn't run away because I didn't want to leave the little ones to the mercy of these nuns on their own. Plus, we really didn't have anywhere to go.

Of course, when we got back to St Beatrice's our life was as bad as it had been before. Sister Helen still ruled Watersbridge with an iron fist.

Now we had a new nickname for her: Scald Fingers, as she had these long, skinny fingers which she whipped so hard across your face they left red marks like a scald.

The day after we got back to the house I swore in front of her.

'How many times have I told you not to take the Lord's name in vain!' she reprimanded. 'That's a sin, Kathleen. You need to ask God for forgiveness. Go to your room and say four Hail Marys, three Our Fathers and five Acts of Contrition.'

I ran upstairs to my room and I was down on my knees praying in a flash:

'Hail Mary, full of grace. The Lord is with thee.
Blessed art though amongst women,
And blessed is the fruit of thy womb, Jesus.
Holy Mary, Mother of God,
Play for us sinners,
Now and at the hour of our death. Amen.'

I hated it but I always did as she said. After all, she was a nun and she knew better. And I really didn't want to be sinful.

But it was so confusing to me, this place – it seemed like everything was a sin. Being late was a sin, swearing was a sin, talking with your mouth full of food was a sin. During one prayer time, when Sister Helen was looking particularly holy, something occurred to me.

'Sister, if God is good, why do you punish people so much? Is that in the Bible?'

I got a good slap for that. I should have kept my mouth shut. That was always my problem.

At Christmas we were sent off to the same families again and this time Tara came back even more distraught. I listened to her crying every night in bed. She tried to stop him this time by wearing tons of clothes, she told me, but he just pulled them off her. Every single night he went into her room and abused her in silence.

Now, back in St Beatrice's Tara was sullen and angry much of the time. She didn't sleep well at night so she couldn't concentrate in school and started to get into trouble.

It was so unlike her – Tara was always good at her lessons. She was a fast learner and had caught up with the other children quicker than me. Now she dragged herself into her classes and I could tell at the end of the day that barely anything had penetrated the whole day. Every night, I begged her to tell the nuns, believing they'd stop sending her there if they knew what was happening, but she wouldn't agree.

'They'll send me away to the reformatory,' she wailed.

We were terrified of being sent to the reformatory – we knew it was a kind of prison where the bad girls were sent and forced to work long hours every day in the laundries. They were locked in their rooms at night and never allowed out. One girl from Watersbridge was sent away there a few months before. They came to get her in a car and she fought so much she broke the kitchen window. She never came back.

But in the weeks leading up to the next holiday Tara became even more morose. She hated the nuns, she hated school – she hated everything. Still only 12, the light had gone from her eyes, her head was down all the time and she rarely smiled any more. She was bitter and depressed. I was the only one who knew and I couldn't bear this to go on any longer. I couldn't bear to hear her night after night crying in the bed next to me, her hands clasped to her chest in despair. All I wanted was to stop the pain.

So one day I plucked up the courage.

I waited until Tara was out of the house on an errand and I searched out Sister Helen, who was in the lounge.

'Sister Helen, I want to tell you something,' I started nervously.

'Yes, Kathleen? What do you want to tell me?'

'It's about Tara, about her holiday.'

She took me into her room, a place I'd never been in before. There was a bed, a sink with a mirror and built-in wardrobes all the way round the walls. There was no other furniture but the room was stuffed floor to ceiling with all the toys, games, dolls and clothes Sister had confiscated from the children over the years. With nothing to sit on, we stood opposite each other in the middle of the room. Now I was growing up I was almost as tall as Sister Helen, and we looked at each other, eye to eye.

'Yes, Kathleen?' she asked impatiently.

'Yes, erm, well, you see Sister, there's wrong things being done to Tara on her holidays. Very bad things,' and then it all poured out of me.

Sister Helen just listened in silence, a serious expression on her face, wincing only occasionally when I touched on the most unpleasant details. It wasn't easy but I told her everything, even though I cringed with shame describing what the daddy had done to my sister.

When I'd finished she said: 'Okay, you can go now, Kathleen.'

The whole time I'd been speaking she hadn't said a word – it felt good to tell someone, someone important who could stop Tara's nightly horrors. As I closed the door a wave of relief washed over me.

At least Tara wouldn't be sent back there any more, I thought. Sister Helen is going to stop it. She's a nun – she's surely not going to let that happen again. For the first time in months I felt light and happy – I'd felt weighed down by Tara's appalling secret, unable to help, depressed at the knowledge that it would just go on and on without end. Now I couldn't wait to tell Tara.

But when I broke the news to my sister, her reaction wasn't what I'd hoped.

'Oh my God, oh my God!' she screamed. 'Why did you tell her? You shouldn't have said anything. Oh God, Kathleen! I shouldn't have told you!'

'Tara – I had to tell her,' I insisted. 'She's going to stop it.'

'No she's not. I'm going to get punished. Oh Jesus!'

Her fear was infectious – suddenly my heart raced and I was consumed with terror. I was so certain before that this would make things better, but now I wasn't sure. Had I done the right thing? I was scared and totally confused.

'Tara.' Sister Helen approached us a week later at breakfast. 'Tara, can you go and see Sister Dorothea after you've finished here, please.'

Sister Dorothea? The Reverend Mother? Why would Tara need to go and see the nun in charge of the whole of St Beatrice's? We exchanged anxious looks and my heart began to thump in my chest. We both had an idea what this was about. I couldn't think straight that whole morning at school and kept getting stuff wrong. Sister Teresa rapped me on the hand twice for not being able to answer her questions. I raced back home for lunch and found Tara in the lounge, smiling. It was a good sign. We went upstairs to our bedroom to talk privately. As soon as the door was shut behind us I demanded to know what had happened.

'She asked me about it, you know, the holidays!' she whispered. 'So I told her, I told her everything and she was really nice and when I'd finished she said: "That's enough, you can go home now." And that was it.'

It didn't seem so bad – Tara actually looked relaxed for the first time in months.

'Ah, that's great,' I said, breaking out into a massive grin. I took her in my arms and we hugged. I was so relieved. Surely that would be the end of it now. They couldn't send her back again, not after telling the Reverend Mother all about that evil man.

That night we stayed up late, chatting and laughing away, so much so that we got a telling off from Sister Helen.

'That's enough with you two blatherers!' she admonished. 'I've had it listening to your twittering. Just get to sleep!'

We giggled into our pillows. Then something occurred to me: 'Maybe they'll send him to prison!'

'I hope so,' Tara said. 'I hope he rots there for ever!'

One morning, two weeks later, we were getting dressed for school when Rosie put her head round the door to tell Tara not to bother getting dressed because she wasn't going to school that day. We wanted to ask her why but she waddled away before we got the chance.

'You're so lucky!' I teased as we skipped downstairs to breakfast a few minutes later, me in my blue uniform, Tara in her nightie.

Nobody was ever allowed to come to breakfast in their nightclothes. It was a real novelty. Suddenly we spotted a group of strange people gathered in the 'good room' – the Reverend Mother, another nun we'd not seen before and Jim Duffy, a man we recognised as the social worker. As soon as they caught sight of the two of us, they stopped talking.

Tara froze. She realised at once why they were there.

In that instant I saw a look of utter terror cross her face and she bolted, running up the corridor towards the stairs.

But Jim lunged and made a grab for her. It all happened so quickly we were too shocked to move, but then, in a second, all hell broke loose.

'What do you want?' I screamed at Jim.

'All of you, get out and get to school!' Sister Helen stood in front of us, blocking our way, ushering us out the door as Jim picked up Tara, who was now kicking and screaming, and shut her into a side room.

I was terrified. I didn't know what was happening.

'Tara! Tara!' I screamed over and over. But Sister Helen had now taken my arm and was physically dragging me out of the house.

'Get to school now!' she barked, literally pushing me out of the door.

I hadn't even had my breakfast.

Tara never did get dressed that day. She was taken in her nightie straight to the reformatory. That was the hardest day of my life – all day long I was in pieces, worried and frightened, just waiting to go home so I could see Tara again.

But when I returned that afternoon, she wasn't there.

'What's happened to my sister?' I asked Sister Helen.

'Tara has been sent away to the reformatory and she isn't coming back,' she replied coldly.

I started to cry: 'But why? Why is she there? Why did you send her away?'

Not a flicker of emotion passed over that heartless woman's face. 'She's just gone and that's that. And you'll be going there too if you don't behave yourself.'

I knew straight away why they'd sent her there – it was because we'd told them about the abuse. It was because *I'd* told them. It was *my* fault Tara was gone. I tried everything to get her back, to make it right again. Week after week I went to the Reverend Mother and begged her to let me see my sister but her reply was always the same: 'Next week, maybe next week.'

But of course next week never came.

'Please, please let her come back,' I wept over and over again. 'I'll be so good, I promise, Sister. I'll be the best girl in the whole world. Just let her come back.'

But they never even let me have a phone call with her.

When Daddy came to visit next I ran into his arms, distraught.

'Tara's gone,' I told him.

'I know, my love,' he said sadly. 'I know. They told me.'

Without Tara, I felt lost. I couldn't eat, I couldn't sleep and I cried constantly. In all the turmoil and upheaval of our childhood I'd never been separated from Tara before. She was everything to me, the person I'd clung to as our lives had disintegrated around us.

Now she was gone and it was all my fault. The nuns put my sisters Lucy and Libby in my room in place of Tara but I was still a mess. I felt such a horrific guilt nothing could make me feel any better. And to make matters worse, I was scared of being sent away myself so I was afraid to do or say anything.

That's when the panic attacks started – I'd be just sat in the middle of the class and suddenly I felt I couldn't breathe. I'd be gasping for air and crying uncontrollably.

I had no idea then but it was to be many years until I would see my sister again and learn the terrible truth about what happened to her at the reformatory.

It would take a lot longer to forgive myself for putting her there.

CHAPTER 14

ABUSE

I lay in the big comfy bed and wriggled my toes contentedly. It was early one morning in July and I'd been at Fiona's house now for two weeks. During the summer holidays St Beatrice's closed down for seven weeks and all us children were once again farmed out to various Catholic families across the country. I'd spent so many months missing Tara that it was a relief to finally get away from St Beatrice's, away from those horrible nuns and the daily reminders of my sister. This time I'd really got lucky, I thought to myself, as I snuggled further down under the thick soft duvet in Fiona's bedroom. She was a lovely lady – short, heavy-set with dark hair pulled back in a bun and glasses. She made clothes for Irish dancers and she was one of the nicest people I'd ever met. Her face was so warm and friendly, you couldn't help but like her just by looking at her. She had a big heart, a big laugh and a gentle way about her. Fiona was married to an older man, James, an ex-soldier, now retired, and they had three boys – an 18-year-old called Jim, and two younger boys, Lachlan, seven, and Dominic, five. But secretly Fiona had always longed for a girl and she treated me like the daughter she'd never had. So for me, an orphan in search of a mother, it was bliss. I missed my family and the children at the convent, of course, but I didn't miss the harsh convent life, the endless praying, the cold corridors and spiteful nuns. I basked in the warmth of Fiona's care.

Each morning, James rose early and went for a walk – a hangover from his military past – and I would go in to Fiona's room and lie in her bed as she bustled about, getting herself ready for the day. I'd watch her twirl her long hair round and round into a tight little bun, occasionally helping up the little wisps that escaped from underneath. Then we'd go downstairs and eat a breakfast of warm bread rolls with tea on one end of the long wooden table that took up the whole of the downstairs. After we'd cleared away, we'd move over to the other half of the kitchen table which was laid out with all of Fiona's dressmaking things and she'd let me help her cut and sew the costumes while the two little boys played outside. I loved it.

'Why don't you call me Auntie Fi?' she suggested very early on. I wanted to, I would have loved to – she was more loving than most of the aunties I'd met in my own family – but it didn't feel right. Not at first. As the day progressed Fiona would inevitably get a call from a client and she'd take me out on her visits, always introducing me as her 'niece'. Everyone seemed to love her and she took such care and pride in her costumes that she brought smiles and happiness wherever we visited. In the evenings we'd watch TV, sew and talk. It was lovely, perfect. So I should have known it was too good to last.

I awoke early that morning, three weeks after my arrival at Fiona's house. I could tell by the dim light outside that it was early, too early to go into Fiona's room. So instead I crept downstairs to the living room in my nightie to watch cartoons on TV.

James was already seated in his armchair, fully dressed and watching the news.

'Do you want me to change channels?' he asked genially, his round eyes crinkling at the corners.

'Yes please,' I replied.

'Ah, you do it,' he said. 'You're nearer the TV.'

So I walked over to the television set and flipped the channels until I saw Tom and Jerry chasing each other wildly about.

'Sure, that's better now,' he smiled, nudging the glasses on his nose to get a better view. 'Why don't you sit here with me and we'll watch together?'

So I went over to the armchair – I was really too big to sit on someone's lap. Now 12, I was already quite tall for my age and developing at an alarming rate. Instead, I perched gingerly on the chair's arm, but James put his arms around my waist and pulled me on top of him. I was too surprised to say anything.

The next thing I knew he was holding me tightly with one arm while the other hand crept up my leg, pushing away my nightie.

I struggled, trying to get off, but James pinned me to him, now putting his hand right up between my legs.

I didn't have any knickers on, because the nuns had trained me out of sleeping in my knickers, so his hands went to my most private place.

Oh God!

I was shocked. His other hand was now wandering all over my chest. Still I struggled.

I couldn't believe this kindly elderly man was doing something so horrific. He had me locked in a tight grip and all I could hear was his heavy breathing behind me as he moved himself against me.

I didn't know what to do – I wanted to scream 'STOP' but I was afraid of waking up the whole household. James didn't say anything. He just held me there as he touched me everywhere. It felt like it would never end. I could hear the music from the cartoon now but it felt like it was coming from miles away.

Eventually he let me go. I stood up, horrified. I couldn't even look at him. He didn't say a word. I quickly pulled my nightie back down and bolted up the stairs towards Fiona's room. I didn't care what time it was or if she was still asleep, I had to tell her what happened!

But as I pushed the door of her room open, my hands shaking, my mouth dry, she turned over in bed and smiled dreamily at me.

'Morning, sunshine!' she beamed.

Her face! She seemed so happy, so content.

In that moment I saw everything that would happen to this lovely lady if I told her what her husband had done to me downstairs. She would believe me, I knew that. She wouldn't be able to live with her husband any more. She would leave him. The children would be brought up in a broken home. Their lives would be torn to shreds.

Could I do that to them? To her? I wanted to tell her so much. I was dying to say something, but did I want to ruin her life?

'Morning,' I stammered back.

'You're up early – hungry already?'

'Yes.' I couldn't do it. I just couldn't.

'Good. Let's get breakfast on the go then, shall we?'

From that moment on I knew I would have to be on my guard. I couldn't tell Fiona what was going on, so I would have to find ways to avoid being alone with James. Of course from then on I wore my knickers in bed – luckily James never came into my room. Fiona had made that clear right from the start – it was my room alone and none of the boys were allowed in there. But to begin with I didn't know when James would attack me again so I took to sleeping in the little boys' bedroom. Fiona didn't mind. I told her it helped me to sleep because I was used to being with other children. I also stopped going downstairs in the morning. Most of the time I stuck close by Fiona, following her around everywhere like a lost puppy. But I couldn't avoid him altogether. There were times Fiona was called out to measure up a child or do a fitting and she refused to take me with her. I'd beg her to let me accompany her but she told me it really wasn't her choice and sometimes the families didn't appreciate someone tagging along, even if she told them I was family.

'Just stay here and mind the boys,' she said. 'I won't be long. I promise.'

So then I'd be trying to stay as close to the little boys as possible while she was away. But it didn't always work. Again and again James got me alone, and then, without speaking a word, he'd grab me from behind and start trying to put his hands under my clothes, all the while rubbing himself up against me. His own children could be upstairs in their room or playing in the garden but that wouldn't stop him. And each time it happened I felt my cheeks flush with embarrassment and shame.

James attacked me four more times before I was sent back to the convent and I knew one thing for sure, I wasn't going to tell any of the nuns. After losing Tara I knew that it wouldn't do me any good to confide in them. I didn't even confide in Grace, though I wanted to. What could she do? It would only make her feel bad for me, and then, if she felt bad enough, she might be tempted to tell one of the nuns herself and I'd be sent away. No, I would just have to find a way out of this.

Fiona cried when I left at the end of August.

'You'll come back soon,' she smiled through her tears. 'Won't you? I'm going to miss you so much but we'll have a wonderful time at Christmas.'

It broke my heart – all I could do was hug her and thank her for all her kindnesses. Now, back in the convent, in the quiet of the night I confided in Gina. Ever since Tara had left Gina and I had become best friends. She was a small, dark-haired girl with a quick smile and a wacky sense of humour. Originally from Ulster she was one of 13 children who had all got split up and sent to different places. We got along famously.

'You're not the only one, you know,' Gina said, sighing, when I told her about James. 'There's far worse going on at some of these houses.'

'I know,' I replied. 'I'm just going to have to deal with it, aren't I?'

'You'll have to kick him in the bollocks,' Gina said, wide-eyed. 'Men don't like that. Makes them go all funny.'

'Really?' I didn't know very much about boys. 'I don't think I could hurt him. He's an old man.'

'Well, you'll have to do something unless you want it to get worse. Did he tell you not to tell?'

'He never says anything to me.'

'Bastard.'

This gave me food for thought. It was true – all us children talked to one another. We knew there was terrible abuse going on in some houses. One of the boys in Watersbridge called Jake was sent to a farm during the holidays where he was forced to sleep with the mammy. And the daddy and sons were sleeping with the daughter.

'It's pure disgusting!' Jake spat as we spoke about it one day. 'She won't let me out of the feckin' bed! *They* are the animals,

Kathleen. Them! Not the pigs or the sheep. I'd rather sleep with the bloody pigs!'

As the weeks went by I spoke to others who told me about their own experiences of being attacked and assaulted at the homes they were sent to. We all felt the same – there was no one to tell. If you told a nun, you'd be locked up. So we just told each other and patted each other on the back and said it would be all right, never really knowing how it would be all right.

There was just one little fella who wouldn't tell me what was going on. His name was Shay and he was the sweetest little boy you could ever hope to meet. He was seven and small with it, and whenever we were sent out into the garden he'd sit on the ground, digging in the dirt with a twig or just staring at the others. He had jet black hair and an impish little face – us girls loved to baby him and cuddle him loads and he always had a smile for us children, though he got sore picked on by the nuns. As usual, we were all due to leave the convent again at Christmas and of course I was going to be sent back to Fiona's house, though my bus was one of the last to leave that day. One by one all of the children were either picked up by their families or sent away to catch buses.

I was sat in the kitchen that afternoon, just talking with Grace, when I heard Sister Helen's voice shrieking across the corridor: 'Catch him! Kathleen, catch him!'

At that moment I saw Shay streak across the corridor and bolt out the back door to the garden. I leapt up and darted out after him.

All over the garden he ran and ran as I chased him. I couldn't believe a little boy could move so fast. By now Sister Helen had come outside and was standing, staring at us as I chased him all over the place. Next to her was a burly-looking man and a well-dressed woman, obviously Shay's host family.

'Get him, Kathleen!' Sister Helen yelled at me.

'Why's the boy running away?' I overheard the woman say to her husband.

'Beats me. Maybe he's soft in the head.' He shrugged. But Shay's face was pure white with fear.

'The boy's frightened,' the woman insisted. 'You tell me. Why's he frightened?'

The man didn't say anything. At that moment I made a lunge towards Shay and tackled him down to the ground. I felt his tiny heart galloping along through his feeble chest under his clothes as I held him down.

'Shay, why don't you want to go with the man?' I whispered, so the others couldn't hear.

'Kathleen, please! Please don't let me go,' he begged. And in that instant I knew. I knew straight away what was happening. I looked in that poor boy's eyes and there was no mistaking it – there was sheer terror there. He was fighting for his life.

Meanwhile a full-scale row had erupted behind us.

'Why is this child so scared of you?' The wife was insistent.

Sister Helen was trying to smooth things over: 'Well, it's all done with now. She's got the boy. He'll be fine.'

'I don't think so,' the woman replied and spun about on her smart heels. 'I think we'll just leave it for now, Sister.'

And with that, they left, much to Shay's relief and Sister Helen's fury.

She turned too, to show them out, as I sat back on the grass, now completely breathless from all the chasing. Shay threw his head back onto the grass and closed his eyes, a small smile on his thin lips.

But as soon as Sister Helen returned she hauled him up by the scruff of his neck and gave him the worst hiding I'd ever seen.

That poor lad – she dragged him by the hair, all the way out of the garden, beating him about the face at the same time. She did this all the way down the corridor and then ripped his clothes off him, demanding he go to bed.

As soon as the coast was clear I went up to take him a glass of water. He was curled up under his cover in his pyjamas, sobbing, and when he looked up I saw his whole face was covered in fresh red marks.

Scald fingers.

I sat down on his bed and said softly: 'Shay, why didn't you go? Now you'll have to be in bed all this time.'

He was tearful but defiant: 'I don't care, Kathleen. I don't care. I'm happy here. I'd rather stay in bed.'

But he wouldn't say anything more so I just cuddled him and let him cry as I rocked him back and forth.

As much as I hated James and returning to his and Fiona's house at Christmas that year, I felt I could protect myself. I wasn't a helpless child like Shay and this wasn't a household that knew no shame like the farm. It was just him. And as long as I could avoid being left alone with him I felt it would all be okay.

Fiona was overjoyed to see me.

'We're going to have such a lovely holiday,' she enthused when she met me at the bus station. 'You must tell me what you want for Christmas.'

'I don't want anything,' I replied. And it was true. I didn't want anything from them. Christmas, birthdays, presents, they didn't mean anything to me. But she kept pestering me on and on until eventually I just told her I wanted the *Beano* album, just to shut her up really.

And at the beginning it really was a lovely holiday. I managed pretty well to avoid being alone with James, mainly by putting the boys between him and me. But then one night James and Fiona went out to a Christmas party, leaving me alone with all her sons.

Usually Jim was out performing or rehearsing since he was a trophy-wining Irish dancer. I'd seen him in competitions with Fiona and he really was excellent – his feet flew around so fast and he kicked so high in the air he almost looked superhuman. It took hours of training to get so good and that meant Jim was fit and strong. This night we were just sat on the sofa, me and the three lads, when Jim started messing around with me.

'Come here and give me a kiss!' he teased.

'Don't be stupid,' I replied, laughing at first. The other two boys were laughing too – it was all a big joke.

'Tell your daft older brother to behave, will you?' I asked the two younger lads and they started yanking on his arms and telling him to behave or they'd call the Garda.

But then Jim's mood changed.

'I said give me a bloody kiss, won't you?' he snarled. He seemed angry now and made to grab me. When I saw the strange, fierce look in his eyes, I jumped up and ran upstairs to the bathroom. I heard him thundering after me and then, before I could get the bolt across, he yanked the door wide open and pulled me out.

'I'm going to kiss you,' he insisted viciously.

'Lachlan! Dominic!' I screamed desperately. 'Come up here, would you?'

Just then, Jim cupped his hand round my mouth.

'Stay where you are, lads!' he called out. 'Just stay there and watch TV!'

Then he whispered nastily: 'You bloody slut! I'm going to rape you right here and now!'

He had me pinned down on the floor in the upstairs hallway, and under his weight I could barely move. He was so strong from all that dancing, I couldn't for the life of me get away. He started kissing my face, my neck and lips and pumping up and down on top of me, though we both had clothes on. I squirmed and tried to get up, but he'd pinned my arms to my side. I was disgusted but scared too – he was so tall and strong, I knew he could have raped me right then if he'd wanted to. He had transformed from the easy-going boy I'd known all this time into a complete maniac.

'Don't bloody struggle, you bitch!' he spat in my face. 'Just let me do it. Just lie here and let me do it.'

He was like a man possessed, pistoning up and down on me until after a while he grunted, sighed and stopped moving. Then he rolled himself off me and stood up.

'Just come downstairs now,' he said coldly, looking at me with contempt as I lay there sobbing with shame. I scrambled up and ran into the bathroom, this time managing to get the bolt across, and there I crouched into a ball and screamed silently into my hands, crying like a baby.

By the time Fiona and James came back that night I was already tucked up with the two little ones. I wasn't going to tell her this either. How could I? She worshipped Jim. She was so proud of him – he was her everything and he was nuts about his mother. Only now I had the two of them to contend with, neither one knowing what the other was up to. I was so ashamed and embarrassed the whole time. We'd all be sitting in the living room at night and I knew the two of them were staring at me and I couldn't say or do anything except shift uneasily in my seat, crossing my arms and legs defensively.

I even took to going to bed at the same time as the little ones, just to ensure nobody could get me alone.

Christmas arrived and Fiona presented me with my *Beano* annual, which was nice, but, even better, she'd secretly made me a maxi dress because she knew I was mad to get one. I was thrilled with my dress – for ages I'd seen other girls on the streets wearing them and I'd wanted one of my own. The maxi dress Fiona made me was gorgeous – orange with little flowers, half-length sleeves and a ribbon under the breasts from which the pleated dress flowed. But even as I tried it on for the first time, my happiness was dimmed by the thought of the two men in the same house.

Christmas dinner was amazing with turkey, roast potatoes and all sorts of meats. We drank lemonade and afterwards played out into the snow. In the evening Fiona and James took us all to their club where we met all the other kids from the village and Fiona introduced me to all her friends as her 'dear niece'. But from then on I had to always be on my guard – James attacked me a couple more times but it was Jim who proved to be the worst. His attacks got more and more vicious; now he was shoving his hand up my jumper and putting it between my legs too, squeezing me there till it hurt. I tried to do what Gina suggested but I barely got a chance to put my knee in his bollocks because he usually had the full weight of his body on both my legs. If I had a hand free then I'd punch him but it only made him angrier. It was such a relief to leave after New Year and return to the convent but, once again, Fiona was a flood of tears as I left.

Back at St Beatrice's life went on in the same way. Sister Helen was as cruel as ever, swinging at us children all the time. She was fast with her hands, like it was second nature to her. Sometimes I watched helplessly as she beat the little ones. Other times I couldn't help myself. I caught her in the hallway one day with a little girl, Pippa. She'd been brushing her hair so hard Pippa had pulled her head away to escape and in that second Sister Helen cracked her over the head with the brush. It was so hard I heard it bang off the poor child's skull.

'Stop it!' I exclaimed. 'What did you do that for?'

'Kathleen, get out of the hallway!' Sister ordered.

But I wouldn't leave. Instead, I called her a name.

'You spiteful little witch! What do you need to be hitting on the child like that for?'

At that, Sister Helen spun around and started beating me on the head. Now provoked, I lifted up my arms and tried to make a grab for the brush to stop it coming down on my head, but instead I got hold of Sister Helen's veil from behind.

I yanked hard and in one smooth movement it slid off the back of her head to reveal her hair. I was shocked – instead of a neat haircut, Sister Helen wore her short grey hair all chopped up and uneven, like she'd just hacked at it herself with a pair of scissors.

I'd never seen a nun's head before. None of us had. Sister Helen looked horrified – she grabbed the veil herself to stop it slipping off any further and ran into her room, still holding it over her head. But it was too late. We'd seen her hair. In that moment I saw Sister Helen for the person she was – just a nasty, evil little woman abusing her position to make little children miserable. Without her habit, she was human, just like the rest of us. She re-emerged from her room a few minutes later, her habit restored to her head, but she was fuming. I'd humiliated her in the worst way possible and that month I lost all my pocket money.

As Easter approached that year, I realised with a sinking heart that once again I would be sent back to Fiona's house in the holidays. I couldn't face it. So when I was put on the coach at Easter I did something really stupid. I got off halfway.

I was just sat brooding on the bus when the driver announced we were in a village I'd never heard of before. Suddenly I found myself standing up.

'This is me,' I announced merrily and took my case and jumped off the bus. By the time the bus had driven away I'd forgotten even the name of the village I was in. I had no idea where I was, no money and no way of getting out. I wandered into the centre of the village and sat on a bench in the park, listening to the birds and admiring the budding trees. What to do next? If I knocked on someone's door, they'd soon work out I was running away and send me back to the convent. I thought I could try getting a lift but there didn't seem to be any cars around. The place was empty – it was the smallest village in the world.

Right, you're free now. I told myself. Come on, what next?

I never did come up with an answer, so finally, after hours of wandering aimlessly, I took myself to the small police station and told them I'd got off the bus at the wrong stop, asking if I could call the convent.

They put me through to Sister Dorothea.

'Just wait for another coach and the police will put you on,' she advised. 'Kathleen, how can you make a mistake like that?'

'I just did. I got off at the wrong stop.'

'And why did it take so long before you rang? What were you doing?'

'I didn't know what to do. I was just sitting, waiting for another bus.'

I knew it was a daft thing to do but at that moment I just couldn't face going back to the house again. I wanted to run away for ever. But how can you run away with no money? I had no choice but to go, and when I got there things were worse than ever.

Jim's attacks were becoming more violent and insistent. He tried every which way to put his hand in my knickers, though I fought him as best I could.

'You know, I am going to have sex with you,' he told me that time. 'You should just stop fighting. It's going to happen, Kathleen, whether you like it or not.'

I knew he was right too. There would come a time when he would just rape me and there would be nothing I could do. So when I left the house after the Easter holidays I resolved never to go back again.

When I returned to the convent I just went straight up to Sister Helen and told her: 'I'm not going back to that place again. You'll have to find somewhere else to send me next time.'

'Why not, Kathleen?' Sister Helen said sternly.

'I'm just not going and there's no way you're going to make me go.'

'Why?'

'I'm just not going.'

I wouldn't tell her the reason. I didn't want to be locked up. But I wasn't going and that was all there was to it. Fiona took it badly. She wrote and called numerous times, begging for me to return.

I read her letters with tears in my eyes: 'I'm completely broken-hearted. I never had a girl and I wanted you to be my little girl. I felt we had bonded and now you are tearing my heart to pieces. But the worst part is that I don't understand why. Why won't you come back, Kathleen? Something must have happened. You can tell me. Whatever it is, we can fix it.'

She always signed off the same: 'Your adoring Auntie Fi.'

After a while it was too hard; I ripped up the letters and refused to take her calls. The nuns went mental at me but there was nothing they could do.

It took a lot of courage to say that I wouldn't go back, knowing I risked being sent away. But I was stronger than most and I knew that if I didn't stand up for myself there was nobody that would do it for me. Yet there were so many like me. And none of us could tell the truth – there was no one who listened or really cared what happened to us. Whatever abuse went on in St Beatrice's or in the places they sent us will never truly be known. We children were forced to keep our shameful, dirty secrets all to ourselves. All the while the nuns drilled home the idea that sex and fornication was sinful and anyone who did these things would go straight to hell. So we felt tainted, sinful and wrong, even though none of us had wanted these things in the first place. We couldn't even take confession and cleanse ourselves of our sins because telling *anybody*, even the priest, could be dangerous. No wonder, then, that so many couldn't live with what was done to them as children. No wonder that so many secrets like these were taken to the grave.

CHAPTER 15
DRUGGED

'You're to go upstairs, Kathleen,' Grace mumbled when I raced in from school that lunchtime. I knew we were having chips that day so hoped I wasn't going to be gone long before I could get down for my lunch. I should have stopped to notice that Grace didn't look at me when she spoke, but I didn't. I should have picked up the strain in her voice, but I didn't. No, my mind was on my stomach and just filling it up.

'Okay,' I shouted back, taking the stairs two at a time. When I got upstairs and went to my room I was surprised to see three staff members there – Sara, Colleen and Jane – alongside Sister Helen, who had a very serious expression on her face. I stopped dead, trying to assess the situation.

What was going on? Why were they all standing there, just staring at me? It was very strange. But before I could say a word the three staff members dived on me, pinning me to the floor by my arms and legs.

Laying on the floor, helpless and unable to move, I felt like a trapped animal. Panic started to rise in my throat.

'You're going to take this pill,' said the oldest staffer Colleen, producing a small white pill with a black dot in the centre. If they had just given me this pill with my lunch and asked me to take it, I probably would have done. But they'd attacked me first, which made me scared. What in the hell was in this pill?

'No!' I said vehemently. 'I'm not taking it. Now let me up!'

But the staff wouldn't let me get up. I was on the floor kicking out and punching but they held me firm.

'You're going to open your mouth and take this pill,' Colleen said again.

'Why?' I said. 'What's the pill for?'

'Just take it.'

Sister Helen then walked out of the room and by the look on her face I knew something really serious was happening to me. She hadn't said a word the whole time.

'We're just going to stay here, however long it takes,' Colleen said evenly. 'And then if you don't take it we're going to force you to take it.'

I shook my head again and shouted: 'No, I won't take it.'

So Jane pulled my hair back, opening my mouth wide while Colleen squashed my cheeks together and forced the pill into the back of my throat. Then she clamped my mouth shut and held my jaws together with both hands, ordering me: 'Swallow it! Swallow it!'

But I wouldn't for ages and ages. Why did they want me to take the pill? Were they drugging me to take me away to the Reformatory? If I swallowed the pill and lost consciousness, I wouldn't be able to fight them off. So I held out a long time – but eventually I had no choice. Saliva dribbled out the corners of my mouth as I tried to keep the pill on my tongue and not swallow, but it was becoming too much. So finally, I gulped it down.

Colleen made me open my mouth to show her it was gone then she said: 'Get up, get ready and get back to school.'

I clambered to my feet; my uniform was a mess, my hair all scruffed up. They left and I straightened myself out but by the time I came back downstairs again lunch was over and I had to go back to the school. I caught Grace's eye and she shook her head. She knew what they had done to me.

I went back to school that day, petrified I was going to pass out at any minute, but I didn't really feel much different. That night I managed to get Grace to myself.

'What is it, Grace? What did they make me take?'

'I don't know,' she said. 'I don't know what it is, Kathleen, but you're not the only one. What they're doing to the children in this house isn't right.'

'Is it vitamins?' I asked hopefully.

'No, it's not vitamins.'

The next day Colleen came up to me during lunch and handed me the pill again.

'You either take this now, the calm way,' she said quietly, 'or we do it the other way.' So I took it. And again she made me open my mouth to show her it was gone. After a week of this I started to feel heavy and detached from the world, like nothing seemed to matter. I would just sit there, sapped of energy, not bothering with anything. I asked Grace over and over what they were giving me but she genuinely didn't seem to know.

'I don't want to feel like this,' I said to her one day as I lay slumped over the kitchen table. 'I want to feel myself again, just normal.'

'I hate it,' Grace fussed. 'I can't bear to see what these nuns are doing.'

'Can't you do something about it?' I asked.

'Kathleen, I would love to do something about it,' she replied, sighing. 'I would love to. But if I did, then they'd get rid of me and you wouldn't have anyone. It's just … it's just so very hard to fight the nuns.'

But Grace did find a way to help me.

'Get their trust,' she advised. 'Let them think you're taking it willingly, then they'll stop checking on you and I'll help you get rid of it.'

So that's what I did. Before Colleen approached me the next day I asked for my pill, as if I wanted to take it.

I let her think I was her puppy dog.

Then I put it in my mouth, pushed it to the side of my cheek with my tongue and took a swig of water so it looked like I'd taken it.

When she wasn't looking I spat it into my hand and snuck it to Grace to throw away. We did the same again the next day, and the next. If Grace didn't get a chance to come round my side of the table, I just hid the pill in my sock and then threw it in the toilet after lunch. Within just a few days of this I started to feel normal again, all my energy returned and, with it, an unbelievable rage.

What were these people doing to us? I wanted to shout and scream and tell the world. We were being drugged like laboratory mice for no reason whatsoever. I'd asked some of the other children who also got the drugs if they knew what they were but no one had a clue. I knew why I'd been given the drugs – it was to make me pliant and docile. But by now I was 13 and I was growing older and stronger every day. One day, I promised myself, one day I'll be out of this hell-hole for ever and then no one will control me.

For my next summer holiday I was sent to live with a wealthy family in Cork. The father John was a tall, handsome man but his wife Irene was a horrible person who ordered everybody around and got into angry tempers for no good reason. They had two small boys – David was one and Nick, three – lovely little lads. But from the word go it was clear that I was there to look after the children, cook and clean.

After Irene and John had finished work for the summer we moved up to their holiday home in Galway and there I was made to clean the house from top to bottom.

Irene seemed permanently cross. First thing in the morning she'd order me to give the children their breakfast, then she'd say: 'Kathleen, it's time to get the kitchen ready.'

And she'd make me pull everything out and clean like crazy. I was scrubbing for hours and hours – inside fridges, behind the cooker, inside cabinets and drawers. When I was done with that I'd be set to work on the floor, then the windows. And when we were finally done with the kitchen she moved me on to the rest of the house.

All throughout the summer the family held long, lavish dinner parties for their friends, for which Irene employed a cook to help her prepare the food. But I was the official pot-washer. During the day I would be cleaning up after Irene and her cook, then she would send the cook home for the evening and I'd have to wash up the plates and dishes while she hosted the dinner party. I wouldn't have minded but she always had three or four courses and at least 20 people round so I spent my whole summer with my hands in the sink.

It was pure slave labour as far as I could see. Even if I had a little time off she didn't allow me to watch television. I'd just be sent to my room. The one good thing was that nobody tried to assault me. It was better than that. Also, I adored her two children. Probably more than she did. Poor little Nick. He copped it badly from her. I would often be in charge of giving the children their tea at night but sometimes she would try and make him eat afterwards, and he, completely full up, couldn't eat, so she'd wallop him round the head.

She was angry a lot of the time, often shouting at me for being too slow doing the cleaning or yelling at her husband in front of everyone for disturbing her while she was getting ready. A plain lady, she had dark brown hair and wide hips. But every night she would plaster on the make-up and adorn herself with heavy, clunking jewellery. She had a wardrobe full of beautiful clothes but somehow they never looked very beautiful on her.

'GET OUT OF THE ROOM, I'M GETTING READY!' we'd hear her scream from upstairs, and sometimes you didn't know if her husband or one of the children was going to come scampering out. She gave it out to everybody, regardless.

The children were kept away from her guests and she barely gave them any attention, always desperate to put them to bed at night as quickly as possible. She couldn't wait to get away from them. So they clung to me and I didn't mind. I had always been around younger children and I knew how to look after them. It was second nature. A couple of times me and John took the children out to the beach on our own, just to get out of Irene's hair, while she was on one of her rampages. John was just as glad to be away from Irene as us and on those days you could see everybody visibly relax. It was just about the only time that the man smiled. We'd walk the beach for hours, delaying the moment of our return for as long as possible. Sometimes we'd get an ice cream or help the boys find crabs in the rock pools. This was what a real summer holiday was all about! To me, those lazy, loungy days on the beach were glorious but far too short. Going back to Irene was always unpleasant.

At least the food was in plentiful supply, and because I was around the children I got to try all the nice things they ate like fish fingers and burgers. The one thing I found difficult was undercooked steak with all the blood dripping out of it, which is how Irene dished it up to everybody, whatever their preference. One night I was given a bloody steak and I couldn't bear to even look at it, let alone taste it. I kept moving my mash and peas away from the oozing blood with my fork.

'You're not leaving that,' Irene commanded from the head of the table as she pointed regally at my meat with her fork. It was not a question, it was an order.

I shook my head. 'I can't eat that. That's just a plateful of blood.'

'Kathleen,' she said in her posh voice. 'You eat it. Do you hear? That is very expensive steak. You're not wasting food, not in my house.'

But I just looked down and shook my head. On and on she railed at me, as if I was a criminal at her table. Could she have guessed how terrible she made me feel? All those references to being 'ignorant', 'uneducated' or 'utterly without class'. That evening I excused myself early, claiming I had a headache, and raced up to my room.

I was fuming. Mad as hell. I didn't know what to do with myself. I was so angry I wanted to scream but I couldn't. I was too angry even to cry. I was depressed, lonely and humiliated. Just then I spotted a green notebook I'd been given at the end of the last day of term. All the children at our school had been given a small green journal for taking part in sports day. I grabbed a pen and started scribbling down everything that had happened. Without realising it, I started talking to the diary like a friend would. I told the diary about the abuse, the nuns drugging me, how much I was missing Tara and my fears for my other brothers and sisters. It was such a relief. When I finally finished writing an hour later I felt a million times better.

From that moment I realised that writing down my feelings helped me greatly. Now I had an outlet for all the pent-up rage and frustration I'd kept inside for so long, and my diary became vital to me. I felt I could have all my secrets there and nobody was going to question me about it. Of course I was terrified somebody would find it, so once back at the convent I hid it under my mattress. The other children knew it was there, of course, but none of them would tell on me. None of us had much in life. We had a pair of day shoes bought once a year – which meant that by the end of every year most of us were cramming our painful toes into shoes at least a size too small, we had our Sunday shoes and Sunday clothes. My only other real possession was a tiny fluffy yellow chicken like the kind you get at Easter. I would sit it on my bed every day and I always warned the others not to touch my chicken. One day I found my chicken dismembered and scattered round my bed – head on the pillow, legs at the end of the bed, fluff and feathers everywhere. Lucy was giggling guiltily. I was genuinely surprised. Lucy wasn't normally naughty like that and I didn't see why she thought it was so funny, especially since none of us had much.

'What did you do that for? Destroy my chicken like that?' I asked, hurt.

'It's because you're giving it out to me all the time about clearing up the room,' she pouted. 'I'm sick of you bossing me about.'

It was infuriating! I only bossed them about because the nuns insisted we keep our rooms tidy. If we didn't then we'd all get it from them. That's what it was like in there – they made you do their dirty work.

'I only do it to stop us all getting into trouble,' I insisted. 'Would you rather get a beating from the Sister?'

'Ah! Blow it out yer arse!' she shouted and ran out.

I looked forlornly at my poor chicken. I'd been trying to protect them from the nuns and this is how I got repaid?

The only other thing I owned was a pair of tiny stud earrings. We weren't allowed to have pierced ears but one of the other girls called Megan did it for me, just after she did her own. She got a darn needle, put a thread on it and then pushed it through my ear. At first we didn't have any earrings so we just had thread coming out of our ears, which we hid from the nuns by keeping our hair over our ears.

By now I was 13 and I refused to have my hair cut into a bowl shape the way they'd done every year since I'd arrived at Watersbridge.

Whoever needed a haircut would get marched into town by one of the staff and sit in the barber's chair to receive the same dreary little bob every time. We all looked the same. But now I refused.

'I don't want my hair like a boy any more,' I told them.

So that was that – I started growing my hair back again, the way it was when I was younger.

Yes, I was 13 now, a teenager, and I was starting to assert myself more and more. Seven months after starting me on the drugs, and six months after I secretly stopped taking them, they stopped giving them to me. They obviously wondered if they were working the way they were supposed to since I'd recovered back to my normal self after just a month.

Now, when I caught the staff giving out to the younger ones, I found it impossible not to say something. I was sick of the beatings, the non-stop abuse. One afternoon I came into the hallway to find the staff member Sara brushing little Pippa's hair. But she wasn't just brushing it, she was ripping the brush down her head so hard it was pulling out her lovely curls. Pippa was crying silently in pain so I said: 'Will you stop it? Can't you see you're hurting her?'

Sara turned savagely on me and tried to beat me about the head but now I was too big and quick for her. I dodged her blow and started swinging my arms back at her till we were brawling in the corridor. It was then that two other staff members got involved. Colleen, thc older member of staff, dived onto me and pulled me backwards by the hair while another one, Martha, pinned my arms to my sides. Now I was incapable of moving Sara boxed me on the arms and legs. Three against one – that's the kind of people they were. It was never a fair fight in Watersbridge.

I hated them. They were spiteful and cruel, especially Colleen. Colleen seemed to reserve a special kind of nastiness for me. She never spoke to me, only to shout, and seemed to take real wicked delight in knocking me about. She didn't like Grace either so she resented the fact that I was close to her. She got her own back in horrible ways, like telling the nuns I'd done things which I hadn't. There were many times I lost my pocket money because of Colleen.

But every day I was getting bigger and stronger. I'd even been given my first bra and knickers set and started my period. Though I knew what it was from the other girls I was reluctant to reveal anything to the nuns. And I was right; when I eventually told Sister Helen so that she could give me the pads, she asked to look in my knickers! There was no way that was going to happen. I refused.

'I just want to check you've got the bleeding,' she admonished.

'Sister, I'm sorry. It's not happening.'

And off she went in a huff.

They were small victories, little acts of defiance. At the time I didn't think of them like that. I just had limits, that was all. I could only take so much and then, at some point, I couldn't go any further. That was what the nuns saw in me – wilfulness, disobedience, something wild and untameable. And in the end, all the drugs in the world weren't going to change that.

CHAPTER 16

ATTACKED

Every Sunday we had to go to church – all dressed up in our Sunday clothes, the nun from each house would lead us down the road and, once in, we were bunched in our house sets and ordered to be on our best behaviour because this was one time of the week the townspeople saw us orphan children all together. It was about the most boring time of the whole week and I usually occupied myself during the sermons by trying to spot my brothers. I hadn't had any contact with Colin, Riley or Brian since we'd been sent into St Beatrice's but occasionally, on a Sunday, if I was sat in the right place, I'd catch sight of one of them and we'd exchange sneaky waves across the pews. I only saw Riley very occasionally and Brian was so lost to me now he barely acknowledged me even when we did see each other. But Colin always waved back. Whenever we saw each other his whole body would jerk upright, his face would come alive and I could see he was just as happy as I was to find me. It was so bittersweet – just a fleeting smile, a quick, furtive wave and that was it.

Until one day, on my way back from school, I saw Colin loitering on the road.

'Kathleen!' He came bounding up to me and gave me a massive hug. He looked so grown-up in his school uniform and his smart hair combed to one side. I could hardly believe it was the same little boy who had held my hand unquestioningly as we roamed through the fields as children – the boy who had curled up in my arms as we lay down to sleep each night, not knowing what would happen to us the next day, but comforted by each other's presence.

'Colin! You're so tall. Look at you! I hardly recognise you now. But I can't speak long. I've got to be back in five minutes or the nuns'll kill me.'

'I know, me too. But I had to see you, Kathleen! What about on Saturday? Can you meet me on Saturday?'

The boys always had more freedom than us girls and they were usually allowed out on a weekend, but recently I'd started working for a family downtown on Saturdays and it crossed my mind that I might be able to get my work done quickly and go to meet him. They had two older children – Aimee, 10, and Aidan, nine – and a little baby. I'd wanted to take the kids to the park before but the mammy had always said no. It meant I had to handle the children inside the house, which wasn't easy. Since I was only a few years older than the boy Aidan, he was difficult when I was in charge. I'd had to cajole him down from the roof on more than one occasion when he took it into his head to go climbing. Petrified he'd fall and break his leg, I'd called up to him, pleading and bribing him down with promises of treats and TV. But the parents always went out on a Saturday – if I was alone with the kids, what would stop me from taking them to the park?

I nodded.

'I'll try. If I can get away I'll meet you in the park at 3 p.m. Wait for me. If I don't make it this Saturday, try next Saturday.'

'Try, Kathleen. Really try. I've missed you.'

'I've missed you too.' I smiled. He was still the sweetest boy you could ever hope to meet.

That Saturday I went to the family as usual. It was an hour to walk to their home and once there the parents left me with the three children and instructions to tidy up the bedroom, lounge and kitchen.

Once I'd got through with my chores it was only 2 p.m. and I knew that if I could convince the kids to keep quiet then we could go to the park and I could see Colin.

'Look,' I told them. 'This is a special treat. I'm going to take you to the park. But your mammy and daddy say it's not allowed so you can't tell them. If you tell on me then we won't be allowed out any more. Okay?'

Aidan and Aimee quickly agreed so I strapped the baby into the stroller and we set off to the big communal park in the centre of town.

Colin was sat on a bench near the swings when we arrived and my heart soared to see him.

'Is that your boyfriend?' Aimee asked suspiciously as she noted the boy staring at us and my goofy smile.

'No, it's my brother,' I replied proudly.

Colin got up when he saw us, and after I'd shooed the kids off to the swings we sat on the bench together.

'How you been?' I asked him.

The brave smile and the dismissive shrug told me more than he could ever say.

'I've missed you all,' he said.

'Yeah, I've missed you too. What about the others? Brian? Riley? Do you see them?'

'Brian is in a different house and he doesn't want to see me anyway. Riley's in my house but it's split so we don't see each other very much.'

Just then Colin grabbed my arm and leant in to whisper: 'Kathleen, there's bad things happen in my house. Riley … Riley … he's not having a very good time of it.'

I looked into his eyes, wide and urgent. I felt the tears well up in my own.

'What is it, Colin? What's happening?'

'It's the staff, the older boys. They do things to the younger ones. Everyone knows. Everyone! We just can't say anything about it.'

My eyes closed in despair. I couldn't take it in. When I opened them again Colin had pushed himself back against the bench and was turned away from me, to hide the tears that threatened to break through.

Just then I noticed his right ear was swollen and red.

'Colin, what happened to your ear?'

'My ears got boxed. There's a man in my house, Mr Booth, he ain't very nice. I don't hear too well in that ear now.'

We talked for a good 20 minutes. It was such a relief to see my brother, and as sad and lonely as I knew he was, at least he was still the same loving boy I'd known before. Just before we left I promised we'd meet again the next week.

And so it went. Every Saturday, after I'd finished my chores, I'd bundle up the children and take them to the park where they played happily on the swings and I talked with my brother. For the most part we chatted about what was going on in our houses – I told him about Tara being taken away and all the different homes we were sent to for the holidays. He told me about the evil Mr Booth and how he hurt all the boys. I wanted so much to see Riley but he was too young to be let out at weekends. Colin knew he was suffering, though, and, like all us children, was powerless to do anything about it.

Poor Riley – he was just a baby when he was sent to live in St Beatrice's. He never stood a chance.

'Will we ever be together again?' Colin asked me one day as we explored the wood behind the park. We loved being in the woods more than anything. Among the trees and nature we felt free again, just as we'd been as youngsters.

'I hope so, Colin. I really hope so. Once we're 16 we can get out of here, then we'll all get together again and no one will be able to do anything about it.'

The days were shorter now – winter crept up behind us and shocked us all with her chilly blasts every time we stepped outside the house. I spent Christmas with the rich family again, and though I couldn't bear Irene's bossiness and the constant work I loved being with her children. I turned 14 just after the holidays and it was then a new friend, Dara, came to our house. I'd seen Dara over the years and knew she was from the house run by the nasty Winifred. It was never explained why she just suddenly turned up at Watersbridge but I was so glad of a new friend. Dara was a pretty and caring girl. She confided in me that she'd hated it at Winifred's.

'They're all terrified of her in there,' she said. 'The kids are afraid to do anything. They've got all these dolls lined up in the house so anybody that goes there thinks we're so lucky because we have dolls to play with. But you know what, Kathleen, we're not allowed to touch them dolls. They're just for show. The kids don't have anything in that house. And at nights she gets little ones up out of their beds and she does stuff to them.'

'No!' I couldn't believe what I was hearing. She was a woman. Women don't do that sort of stuff. No way!

'I swear, Kathleen. I know. I seen it for myself. I spied on her one night. The nun doesn't sleep in the house with us, it's just Winifred. And she gets the small ones up and she makes them do stuff. It's terrible, Kathleen. Just terrible. Everyone in our house knows it too.'

I lay in bed that night and shivered at the thought of what might be going on that very night. I knew Dara was telling the truth. I recalled how much we all hated Winifred for the way she whipped your towel away from you at the swimming pool. The way she made her girls line up naked in front of everyone, till they were shivering and pink with embarrassment. It seemed that no matter where you were in St Beatrice's, you weren't safe. Here we were, lonely and abandoned children in need of a place of safety, in need of a stable, loving home, and what did we get? Nothing but battering and abuse at every turn. It seemed so wrong, so topsy-turvy. And the worst part was that it was all going on in a place run by nuns and priests, the very people who were meant to be good and kind. The anger swelled up in my chest again. No matter how bad things had got with Daddy, at least we were never sexually abused in his care. How could the judges and police say we were better off in this place, where a child couldn't even sleep safely in their bed at night?

A few weeks later I was walking back from the main convent with Dara. We were doing one of our stupid plays, where all the children in the convent had to sing and dance for the entertainment of our host families. We were made to do it every year, and every year I hated it. This year we were part of the chorus for *Oklahoma!* Each house would rehearse separately in the big hall in the convent and then, at the end of term, they'd invite these families to our concert. I suppose it was a way of saying thank you for taking all us poor orphans in, but by now I had nothing but contempt for the people who homed us when St Beatrice's was shut. Why did they take us in? Mainly to abuse us or work us like slaves. Sure, there were a few good souls about like Fiona, but even in her family the men saw me as a plaything for their own sick desires. In their minds we were the lowest of the low, so they did what they liked, thinking nobody would ever believe us if we told. And even when we were believed, we were blamed for causing the trouble to begin with.

It was late in the afternoon on a gloomy day in February and it had been dark from the moment we'd got up that morning. Now the wind whipped up my hair and I could feel the first tell-tale drip of the thunderstorm which had been threatening to break all day. I'd been dawdling but now I broke into a trot to catch up with Dara, who was just a little way ahead of me.

Just then, a boy jumped out of the ditch at the side of the road. It was Daniel. I recognised him as an older boy who had left St Beatrice's two years before, now a full-grown lad of 18. Daniel grabbed me round the middle and dragged me straight into the ditch. He rolled on top of me then and started clawing at my clothes like a madman.

'What the feck are you doing?' I gasped.

'I'm going to rape you, Kathleen,' he panted, tugging at my jeans and kissing at my throat. He was like a man possessed, savage and violent. At that moment I started to scream: 'Dara! Dara!'

But Daniel grabbed my hair and bashed my head back against the earth, so hard it made my teeth clunk together and my head ring. He ripped at my top and fumbled inexpertly with the zip on my jeans, yanking them down again and again

– thank God they were tight on my hips and refused to come off. I wriggled and squirmed beneath him, pushing at his face as he tried to shove his tongue down my throat, his spit drooling all over my cheeks.

Now I was fighting for my life, tight fists punching out at anything I could, hoping to hurt him enough that he would get off me.

At that moment I heard Dara scream above us: 'Oh my God! Get off her!'

Daniel jumped up and leapt out of the ditch. He didn't even look at Dara, who was standing over us both, horrified. He just ran.

'Are you okay?' Dara asked as she offered me a hand and pulled me out of the ditch. I was shaking, my head was pounding and my clothes and hair were a state. All I wanted to do was get back to Watersbridge.

'Sister! Sister, you have to call the police,' I blurted as soon as I was through the door. We'd run all the way home.

Sister Helen caught my state of alarm, my hair full of dirt and leaves, and the ripped clothes now just hanging off me.

'Kathleen, calm down,' she soothed, putting out a palm to my shoulder, but I jumped back, evading her comforting gesture.

'Sister, you have to call the police,' I repeated urgently. 'Daniel, the boy that left here two years ago, he jumped me from the ditch on the way home and he tried to rape me.'

All the staff and children were now gathered in the hallway, silently watching the spectacle.

'Now, now,' she said. 'Let's just calm down first, Kathleen. Hmmm?'

'But you have to …'

'I think you better get a glass of water and calm down before we do anything rash.'

'Don't you understand?' I was enraged now, hysterical. 'That boy tried to rape me! If Dara here hadn't saved me, he would have done it too!'

'It's true,' Dara nodded. 'He was like an animal!'

There was silence. I just stood there, looking at Sister Helen, waiting for her to do something. But she didn't move.

Instead she turned to Colleen: 'I think we better get the children's tea now. Why don't you all go through to the kitchen?'

'Sister!' I exploded again. 'Call the feckin' police now or so help me I'll do it myself!'

'I think you better watch your language, young lady,' Sister Helen snipped. I glowered back.

She tried a different tack: 'Look, you've obviously had an upsetting experience. I don't know what the boy did but we'll look into it. We'll get to the bottom of it and sort it all out. Okay?'

I couldn't understand it. I'd been attacked in the street, there was a witness, the boy had clearly planned this. He'd been waiting in the ditch for me. What exactly was there to sort out?

I stood there, breathing hard.

'Give me the phone,' I demanded in a low voice. I knew there was a phone in Sister Helen's little room.

'I don't think that's a good idea, Kathleen. Not in the state you're in.'

'I'm calm, Sister, but this here is a crime. And I want to report it. Let me use the phone.'

'No, Kathleen. Not right now.'

'When my father comes, I'm going to tell him what happened. I'm going to tell him everything. And that you did not call the police.'

By now one of the other staff had put her arm around my shoulder and was leading me towards the stairs. I crumpled in her arms, despairing. The shock of the attack finally unravelled me.

'Come on now,' she urged. 'Let's get you cleaned up. You've had a fright. Best to try and calm down.'

The staff cleaned me up and got me into my nightie. I was too upset to eat that night so I just went straight to bed. I lay there wondering what it would take for a nun to help a child in this place. Why wouldn't they help me? Why did they treat us like we were nothing? Not worth bothering the police for when we were attacked?

What's the point? I wondered. What's the point of telling them anything? They just don't care. This is a major thing that's happened and yet a nun, a *holy nun*, just lets the criminal get away with it.

The incident was never spoken about again. It was almost as if I had done something embarrassing that was best left alone. I never called the police. Without the backing of the nuns I felt they wouldn't believe me. And I never told my father either – I knew how he would react. He'd be so angry he'd go after the boy himself and then Daddy would wind up in prison. No, the whole thing was hushed up. Just like so much in St Beatrice's. There was a wall of silence around our lives, and the evils that were done to us, which it seemed nothing could penetrate.

CHAPTER 17

LOVE

It could have gone on for me like this – being lonely and miserable all the time. But it didn't. Life changed completely when I met Shane, and I fell in love. One day I stopped to talk to Colin outside his school, which was on my route home from my school. Before now we'd never managed to speak during the week because all our schools let the children out at different times. But after we started meeting at the park we worked out that if Colin hung around then I could catch him for a short while when I got out half an hour later. This time when I saw Colin I noticed that, standing a little way off, watching me intensely, was a tall, handsome boy with shoulder-length blond hair and beautiful blue eyes.

I caught him looking at me but didn't say a word.

The next day he was there again in the same spot as I ran home – he watched me as I went past and I thought he was going to stop me but he didn't. The next day he was in the same place again. This went on for a few days until one day he plucked up the courage to stop me.

'You're Kathleen, ain't you?' he called out as I hurried by. I turned around to face him. He really was the most handsome boy I'd ever seen in my life and wearing a long black jacket and jeans with holes in the knees, just like the cool kids in my school.

'Yeah,' I replied. 'Why you askin'?'

'I just seen you with your brother Colin, that's all,' he said. 'And I wanted to say hello. You sure don't hang around, though. I thought I was gonna need a net to catch you.'

I laughed then. This boy was obviously from a normal home where there weren't nuns waiting round every corner, ready to give you a hiding for the smallest thing.

'My name's Seamus,' he smiled broadly. 'But you can call me Shane. Everyone does. Why don't you let me walk you back?'

I liked Shane immediately. He was the same age as me, 14, and he was kind and sweet. He told me all about his family, his dad the greyhound race trainer and his brothers and sisters. I told him about my family too – for the first time I felt something stirring in me that I'd never felt before. I wanted to tell Shane about my life, I wanted to share my secrets with him instead of my diary. For the first time I felt a connection with a person which went beyond anything I'd known before.

'You better stop here,' I told him that first time he walked me home. We were only halfway back to Watersbridge but I knew the nature of this town. The nuns had spies everywhere and if I was caught talking to a boy it could only mean trouble for us both. I was about to turn away when Shane bent down and gave me a soft kiss on my cheek. It took my breath away!

'Thanks for letting me walk you back, Kathleen,' he said, holding my gaze in his baby blue eyes. 'Can we do this again tomorrow?'

My cheeks flamed red. I was totally caught off guard.

'Tomorrow? Okay. Bye then,' and with that I ran off, my heart thumping like mad in my chest, an irrepressible smile on my lips.

The whole of the rest of the night I caught my mind wandering back to that quick, innocent peck on the cheek and the intense look in Shane's eyes. Nobody had ever looked at me like that before. It was all so new and exciting.

We met up the next day and for many days afterwards. Sometimes he'd greet me with a present he'd bought – a little box of chocolates, a drink or a pack of biscuits. I had to hide these gifts under my clothes when I got into the house, just in case a nun saw me and questioned me. After a while we started to meet in the park on Saturdays, when Colin wasn't around. We'd walk round and round the park while Shane pushed the baby in the pram, talking about everything under the sun. When we sat on the bench, Shane took my hand, holding it for a few seconds before I pulled it away, frightened that someone might see and get me into trouble.

'What are you so scared of?' Shane asked me, troubled.

'You don't know what they're like.' I sighed, frustrated and full of sorrow that I couldn't show Shane how I really felt.

'What do you think they'd do if they found out? It's not a crime to be friends with a boy, you know.'

'It is in their eyes!' I scoffed. 'It's all one big sin. Just … just trust me. Okay? I like you Shane but it's too risky.'

I was in love. For the first time in my life I felt happiness, true happiness. Life seemed to have a new meaning for me. I leapt out of bed every morning, excited to go to school because I knew that afterwards I would see Shane. I wolfed down my breakfast and lunch, barely tasting the food. My mind was just on Shane. Constantly. Everything about him was perfect – from the flyaway blond hair to his slouching coolness. I didn't know I could feel this way – I wanted to blurt it out to the world, to share my overwhelming joy. It was bubbling out of me, and if I hadn't confided in Gina I would have literally burst with ecstasy. I could live again! He gave me that. He opened my eyes to the possibility of being a person one day, someone who meant something to another being. Someone who was cared about, thought about, loved.

All day long I'd daydream about Shane and then when I saw him waiting at the end of the road for me my heart would leap in my chest and I'd melt at just catching sight of his shy smile. He was so gentle, so kind. He just wanted to show me affection, and I wanted the same.

One day I managed to sneak out of school early and we went wandering over the fields behind the town. We walked for ages and ages through the long, tall grass until I was absolutely sure nobody would see us and then I let Shane hold my hand for as long as he liked.

'I'd like you to meet my family,' Shane told me that day as I sat on a wall next to the field and he stood, leaning in towards me.

'They can't tell anybody,' I said, worried still.

'It's okay – I'll let them know all about the nuns,' he reassured me. 'They won't say nothing. I'd just like it if they met you.'

'Okay,' I agreed. Silence. Then Shane bent down and slowly, gently, put his lips on mine. He tasted salty and hot. Then he took my head in his hands and I wrapped my arms around his neck. My whole body thrilled. We kissed like that for ages, tangled together like a rose climbing up a tree. I felt his heart beating through his thin white shirt and smelt the clean, lemon scent from his clothes. Out there, in the fields, we were free, we could be ourselves. And all I wanted was to stay there for ever with him, never go back to the convent again.

And so it went. For six months Shane and I were blissfully happy. Most Saturdays we met in the park and, when it was safe, we'd go out to the fields together, just kissing and cuddling. In the times I felt low and sad, Shane would just put his arms around me and hold me like that, not talking. I had already told him everything about my life till that point, about my family disintegrating, the way my mother had abandoned us and losing Tara to the reformatory. He listened, always, with a concerned look on his face, then he'd tell me: 'I won't leave you. I ain't going nowhere, Kathleen. Not without you.'

I still saw Daddy on a regular basis and he noticed I was happier. Once he took me to the pub for lunch and I was that lovesick I couldn't eat a thing.

'What's up with you?' Daddy asked. 'What ails you, child? Why aren't you eating your dinner?'

'I'm just not that hungry, Daddy,' I said. I couldn't tell him the truth. Daddy would have gone mad if he knew I had a boyfriend but he was looking at me with a twinkly smile and I guessed he knew something was up.

Shane had plans to take me to meet his parents and we knew that one day we would be together for ever.

'When you're 16,' he'd say, stroking my hair. 'Then we can do what we want. We'll run away to England together and get married and nobody will be able to say any different.'

I held onto this dream of ours like a prize, hugging it close to me at night, imagining the idyllic life we'd have together, our children, our home.

One day after school Shane met me as usual at his school gate. And almost instinctively he took my hand as we walked.

'Don't do that.' I pulled it back sharply. 'We'll get caught.'

'But Kathleen, I love you,' he implored. 'I love you and no one's going to find out. Please. Please, I just want to show you off.'

'You can't. You never know who's looking, who might tell. These people in the street, the shop folk, they may tell the nuns.'

'Nobody's looking at us,' he argued. 'Just let me hold your hand today. Just this once.'

And so I did, much against my better judgement. I trusted him and I held his hand, and, of course, it wasn't long before the report went back.

That night I was called to see the Reverend Mother. My heart sank as I entered her room in the convent to see her sitting behind her desk, a stern look in her eye, with Jim Duffy standing at her shoulder.

'Kathleen, come in, please.' She motioned for me to sit on the chair opposite from her. I did as I was told.

'Kathleen,' she peered at me over her half-moon spectacles. 'Let me get straight to the point here. You've been seen today holding hands with a boy.'

I couldn't deny it because it was true. I'd been caught.

'He's just a friend,' I mumbled, defensively.

'That's fine, Kathleen,' the Reverend Mother said, smiling winningly. 'We understand. Perhaps you would be able to bring your friend here for a meeting?'

'Why?' I was immediately on my guard. What did they want to meet Shane for?

'Oh,' the Reverend Mother went on, still smiling. 'We just want to talk to him and talk to you.'

Even Jim Duffy was smiling at me now but I didn't trust them for a minute.

'I'm not sure it's a good idea,' I said, squirming. My eyes darted around the room, taking in the large silver crucifix, the candlesticks on the wooden chest and the brightly painted pictures of biblical scenes on the walls.

'Don't be frightened, Kathleen,' the Reverend Mother said gently. 'Nothing bad is going to happen. He can still be your friend. We just want to talk to you both and sort everything out so it's all out in the open. No sneaking around. Hmm?'

I was 15 now, growing into a woman, and I listened to the Reverend Mother's new, softer tone. She was talking to me kindly, as if I was a grown-up and not a child. Perhaps they wanted to meet the boy I was in love with, just as I was planning to meet Shane's parents.

Nothing bad was going to happen, she'd said. Perhaps my age meant I was now allowed to be friends with a boy? So I agreed, and the next day, as arranged, Shane and I presented ourselves to the Reverend Mother after school at 4 p.m.

Once again Jim Duffy was standing next to the Reverend Mother – this time I thought I could detect a malevolent glint in his smile when we walked in. He coughed and shook Shane's hand, then offered us both seats opposite them. The Reverend Mother's smile had vanished now. She gestured for Jim to speak.

'Shane,' he started. 'Thank you for coming here today. We understand from Kathleen that you two are friends and she's admitted you have been holding hands in the town.'

Shane looked nervously at me. I bit my lip and looked down.

'Now, Shane,' Jim went on, 'can you tell us what else you and Kathleen have been doing?'

'I don't understand. What do you mean?' Shane looked confused. I'd assured him of the Reverend Mother's promise that nothing bad would happen to us. But Jim's voice had an interrogatory edge to it.

'We'd like to know,' Jim spoke louder now, crossing his arms together and raising his chin up, 'what you've been doing with this good Catholic girl? A girl who is only a child after all, just 15, and who has been entrusted to the good nuns for her care.'

'I … I … we haven't done nothing,' Shane stammered.

'How long have you been friends then?'

'About six months.'

'Have you kissed her?'

'No!' I jumped in. 'No, we haven't kissed.'

I looked pleadingly at Shane. Suddenly I knew we'd been tricked. This was not what the Reverend Mother said it was and I knew we had to ensure we didn't make things any worse.

'We're just friends,' I insisted again. 'What's wrong with that?'

But by now Jim wasn't listening to me at all. He glared at Shane, one eyebrow raised, as if awaiting an answer.

'No, we haven't kissed,' Shane repeated. 'We haven't done anything else. We just held hands, that's all.'

Jim now strode out from behind the desk to face Shane, who was still seated, and towering over him he started very quietly: 'I'm going to say this once. Just once. Do you understand?'

Shane nodded, fear in his eyes. An oppressive silence settled in the room between us all.

Then Jim spoke: 'You are *forbidden* ever to see Kathleen again. If you do, we have the power to lock you up. Do you understand? You will go to prison. And you, Kathleen – you'll be sent away and you won't be able to see your friends or your family. Do you hear what I'm saying? You are never to see this boy ever again.'

Shane was now shaking with terror.

'I won't see her again,' he promised, his voice quivering.

Jim looked at me. I was so angry, I could have screamed. Shane was the one tiny piece of happiness in my life and these damn nuns were taking him away from me.

'I said – do you understand, Kathleen?' Jim fixed me with his hard stare.

Now the Reverend Mother got up from behind the desk, sighed and drifted over to stand next to Jim.

'I'm afraid this is very serious, Kathleen,' she said in her softer tone. 'You have risked enough already just by associating with this boy. Now you don't want to be sent away, do you? Like your sister? If this boy really is your friend and you care what happens to him then you won't see him ever again. You could get him into an awful lot of trouble and ruin the poor boy's life. You don't want that now, do you?'

'No, Sister.'

'No, you don't. So will you make the solemn pledge right now, in the sight of God, not to see the boy again?'

They were shredding my heart to pieces but they didn't care one bit. Well, I wasn't going to take this. They could threaten us all they liked. I wasn't giving up Shane for all the nuns in the world!

I breathed deeply, calming myself down. *Don't give anything away*, I told myself. *Just let them think you are compliant*. I'd dealt with these bullies for so long now I knew how best to handle things.

I had to stay calm, composed.

'No, I won't see him again,' I said quietly. 'I promise.'

'Good,' she seemed satisfied. 'Now you can both go. And don't forget what we have said here today. The consequences of ignoring our advice will be very serious for you both.'

I almost ran out of there, I was so desperate to get away from them. Shane and I walked quickly through the corridors together, not saying a word, not even daring to look at one another. I listened as the soft patter of our shoes sang out and echoed against the hard brick walls on every side.

Forget those nuns, I thought. *We'll just have to be more careful from now on*.

Once outside and away from the convent walls, I whispered to him: 'I'm so sorry, Shane, they lied to me. They said it would be okay.'

Shane's eyes were full of tears: 'Kathleen, I can't see you again.'

My heart stopped a beat. What did he mean?

'You can't be serious,' I said quickly. 'You can't do what them nuns say. We love each other!'

'I know, Kathleen, but they'll lock me up!'

I was desperate now, pleading: 'There's no way you can listen to them. How can you not want to see me again?'

'I'm going to be locked up and you are too. We have no choice. There's no other way.'

Angry tears now blurred my vision – he was getting away from me. I couldn't let him go, not this easily.

'You can't let them win, Shane!' I nearly shouted at him. 'They've taken everything away from me. Everything! Please don't do this. I won't be able to stand it.'

'I'm sorry,' was all he could say, wiping at his own tears with the back of his sleeve. 'I'm sorry. I don't know what else to do.'

'Not this! Don't do this! I love you, Shane. I've never loved anybody before. Please don't make this the end.'

'I'm sorry, Kathleen.'

We stood there for a moment, each of us trembling with emotion. I wanted to fling myself into his arms and never let go. I wanted to take off right then, run away someplace they could never find us. We'd go into the woods, live off the land.

My mind flitted through a thousand improbable scenarios before landing back here, outside the convent.

I felt my soul shrinking then, my world collapsing in on itself. It was hopeless! They would find us, they would lock us up and then our lives would be ruined.

They had destroyed the one good thing in my life, and now I was heartbroken.

'Goodbye Kathleen.'

'Goodbye Shane.'

He bent down and kissed me one last time on the cheek – it was more than I could bear. I turned and fled.

I wanted to run and run and run. I just couldn't go back to my home, my life, my world without Shane. It didn't seem possible.

But there was nowhere for me to go. Instead, I burst into Watersbridge, flew up the stairs and collapsed onto my bed, crying. I cried and cried and cried. That night I didn't even have supper. I couldn't eat a thing.

By now it was late spring and school was almost at an end. True to his word, Shane stopped showing up at his school gates on my way home. Every day I looked for him but he was nowhere to be seen. Gina did her best to comfort me but I was devastated beyond reason.

'Kathleen, he'll wait for you,' she reassured me. 'He'll wait until you're 16 and then you can both go away together, like you planned.'

'I should never have trusted that bloody nun!' I was barely listening to her. 'I shouldn't have taken him back to the Reverend Mother. I should have just lied, denied everything from the start. The holiest nun told me a damn lie. What does that say about these people?'

'You can't change it now,' she said. 'But Shane loves you. You'll see him again soon.'

'When is soon?' I wailed. 'Every day without him feels like a year. It's worse than torture. I had one nice thing in my life, I had some hope. And now I've got nothing again.'

Being in school probably made things worse because, once the summer arrived and I was sent away with my friend Tess to work in a children's orphanage on the coast, I found I was finally able to put Shane out of my mind. All the places where we used to meet were far away now – and the fresh air, new environment and constant work kept my mind occupied, during the day at least.

For the first time since I'd been sent to St Beatrice's I wasn't given to a family over the holidays. This time I was allowed to work in the summer orphanage for the little ones.

All the babies and toddlers who couldn't be placed in families in the holidays were looked after in this orphanage and, because I adored children, I was allowed to go with them. Tess and I were pure excited to be going – but it wasn't at all how we imagined. The two staff and one nun who ran the place did next to no work – they just smoked fags and drank tea while me and Tess did everything for the kids. And there was *a lot* of work. I was in charge of the 20 older children from two to five years old in the upstairs of the house, while Tess had responsibility for the dozen babies, who were aged eight months to two.

It was a full-on day which started first thing in the morning when I had to put all the children on their potties. For the ones that weren't toilet trained, we had to change their nappies, which were made of terry towelling. First we'd take off the towelling nappies, flushing all the poo into the toilet, throw the nappies into the buckets for washing, then we'd have to change them into new towelling nappies, making sure we didn't poke the little ones with the giant safety pins we used to secure them. That was always a worry for me, ever since I'd accidentally nicked one little boy on my first day. Once all the children and babies were changed, clothed and fed, we had to rinse out all the nappies before sticking them in the washing machine.

The staff were surly, bored women, unsuitable to be looking after children.

'Don't use too much cream!' they'd shout at me whenever they caught me plastering the babies' bottoms with Sudocrem to stop them getting rashes. If I was out, I'd always come back to find at least three children screaming and crying hysterically, with the staff nowhere to be seen.

I felt sorry for the poor children. They were so young but they'd lost their family, their mammies and daddies, just like I had. One little girl was just a year old and she was constantly crying: 'Mammy! Mammy! Mammy!'

It broke my heart. Another little boy, James, was a real cuddly little fella. Just eight months, he had a kidney problem which meant he had to stay in his cot most of the day. I used to shower him with kisses and cuddles. The children loved us; they were so upset when Tess and I had to return to St Beatrice's in early September. And I too was sad to leave them. I worried for them all. What would happen to these children? They never got cuddles from the staff or the nun. And it was all they really wanted.

I wasn't back at school longer than a week when Colin stopped me on the way back from school.

'I've got a message for you,' he said, smiling coyly. 'It's from Shane. He says to meet him in the park on Saturday. The usual place.'

I nodded quickly, a serious expression on my face, but inside I was singing: *Yes, yes, yes!*

CHAPTER 18

LOSING IT

'We'll do this!' Shane held both my hands in his and locked me in his beautiful blue stare. It was like gazing into a crystal clear lake on a sunny day.

'We only have to wait a few more months then you'll be 16 and we can go to England. I'll get the tickets – I'll borrow some money from my da. I can't let them take you away from me.'

It was everything I'd longed to hear. Just seeing Shane again sent my spirits soaring. He looked more handsome than ever, his long, lean body now taller, his hair fine and wild around his wind-stung cheeks and full lips.

We met that rainy Saturday in September and both fell into each other's arms. Now sheltering in the woods, we planned our escape. For two hours we talked about how much we'd missed each other and renewed our vows to stay true to one another.

I went home that night, content and comforted that my future happiness was now assured. Shane had been terrified of Jim and his dark threats, but after talking it over with his parents they'd agreed to help us get away. All I had to do was hang on until January, for my birthday, and then everything would be okay. Everything would be fine.

For the next two months I kept my head low at Watersbridge, did everything the nuns and staff asked of me and still met Shane in secret on a Saturday when I looked after the kids. One afternoon he sneaked me back to his home on the outskirts of town where I met his family – a kindly grey-haired lady introduced herself as Shane's mammy, his daddy was similarly tall like Shane and had a playful, jaunty way about him, while his older brother, Alan, was serious and bookish. They all treated me with respect and promised they wouldn't get us into trouble. An excitable, yappy white dog jumped up at my knees while Shane did the introductions.

'Don't mind Poppy,' he laughed. 'She's just jealous because you stole me away from her.'

I wandered through their cosy home, family photographs lining the hallway, surprised to see the pictures of Shane at various ages grinning out at me from his childhood. Here he was on a beach in a pair of tiny red shorts holding up a crab, here he was blowing out candles on a birthday cake surrounded by beaming children in colourful paper hats, here was one of the whole family in their best outfits, stiffly arranged around the mammy who was seated in a chair. Shane seemed so happy in them all.

'Kathleen, you're always welcome in our home,' said Shane's mammy, as she served up tea and biscuits at her kitchen table. 'We know how you and Shane feel and we've told him there's no way he could get sent to prison by anyone for that. Not while we're around.'

I was thankful for her support and admired the way they stuck together so firmly. A whisper of envy struck me then. I longed for a family of my own to show off to Shane, a family that took pictures, that put them on the walls. A family that even had walls! But we'd all become unstuck many years before.

It was November now and I wrapped up warm against the biting wind on my way back to Watersbridge. Stomping out my numb toes on the front porch, I was relieved to get inside our home, which was always warm. Once I'd peeled off all my warm layers, I ran straight upstairs, keen to find Gina so I could tell her all about meeting Shane's parents.

But when I got into my room I was horrified to see the oldest and meanest staff member, Colleen, beating my sister Lucy about the head.

Colleen was a wizened, skinny old woman, the one who'd forced me to take the pills. She was a nasty cow, always taking great delight in dealing out punishment. I'd seen Colleen beat my siblings any number of times but there was something different about the way she was doing it today. There was real spite in her face, hate even. She had Lucy by the hair with one hand and was slapping her hard with the other. Poor Lucy was cowering underneath her, powerless to stop any of the blows. Next to her were Libby, Megan and Gina. I didn't stop to think. It was too degrading to watch.

So I spoke up: 'Colleen, stop beating Lucy.'

The others all jumped back in surprise. Nobody ever talked like this to the staff. But today I was angry. Lucy was 12 now, yet she was being made to cower like a little girl. It was humiliating and demeaning. But before I could say anything more, Colleen turned around and walloped me around the face as hard as anything. I stood there for a second, my cheek burning with the sudden pain. And then I jumped on her. Without any warning and without really knowing what I was doing, I just went for her like a dog on the attack.

I'd had enough. Enough of their brutality, enough of their bullying and their abuse. I was a grown woman now and I wasn't going to take it any more. I dived on top of her and I started punching and kicking her with all the strength I could muster. I heard my voice, as if coming from far away, yet I never felt more like myself than at this moment. Years of suppressed rage came flooding out of me: 'YOU THINK YOU CAN JUST GO AROUND HITTING EVERYONE YOU FEEL LIKE? YOU AIN'T EVER GOING TO HIT MY SISTER EVER AGAIN! AND YOU'RE NEVER, EVER GOING TO HIT ME.'

Once on the ground, I grabbed Colleen by the hair and started to drag her out of the room. She was too shocked to say anything, but worse, she was too weak to put up a fight. I was the stronger one now and I felt the blood surging round my body as I finally felt the power I'd been denied all these years.

'YOU NASTY, EVIL LITTLE BITCH!' I spat at her, yanking on her head with my full force, taking out clumps of curly brown hair. When I couldn't hold onto her hair any longer I spun her round and grabbed her by the feet, pulling her harder and harder along the corridor.

'YOU'RE ALL EVIL IN THIS PLACE. EVIL! I HOPE YOU ALL DIE AND ROT IN HELL.'

Now I was half-dragging her, half-kicking her towards the staircase.

Somewhere, a long way off, I could vaguely make out the screams of my sisters and friend as they begged me to stop. But I couldn't stop. I'd crossed a line somewhere and couldn't go back. I'd lost all control of myself. I just wanted to hurt this evil cow, hurt her like they had been hurting us all for so long.

I kicked her on the head, I kicked her on the stomach, I kicked her legs, her shins and her back. Everywhere I could find. And I did it hard. Hard. Hard. HARD. Her glasses spun off her head at some point but I didn't care. She was screaming now, screaming for her life, but it only fuelled my burning anger.

'You don't like it, do you?' I fumed, disgusted by the quivering body beneath me. I bounced her now against one wall then the other. When her feet slipped out of my grasp I dragged her by her hands, her body swinging this way and that. Her clothes ripped, her shoes fell off. Now at the top of the stairs, I hoisted her skinny frame over the banisters and shoved her over, so I just had her by the legs and her body dangled head first over the long drop beneath. She was whimpering now, like a frightened animal.

'I'M GOING TO KILL YOU, YOU BITCH!' I thundered as I held onto her legs. 'I'M GOING TO THROW YOU DOWN THE STAIRS AND KILL YOU BECAUSE THAT'S ALL YOU DESERVE FOR YOUR CRUELTY AND YOUR BEATINGS.'

The banisters on our floor were 20 foot off the ground floor. Curls of hair hung limply upside down and I struggled to keep my grip on her trouser legs, wanting so much to just let go.

Oh God, I wanted to kill her. Right then, I knew I could do it. I could let her go and that would have made me so happy. She would fall head first onto the polished wooden floors and die. I'd had enough. I'd finally, finally had enough and though I knew all the bad things that could happen to me afterwards, in that moment, in that pure exquisite moment of revenge, I just wanted to hurt her. Hurt all of them for the years of hurt they had put me and my family through.

But I didn't. I didn't let go. Through the crimson mists of my rage, a sound came as if carried by a wave, a sound like a shriek of fear, and I knew it was my sister's voice. The sound came louder and louder.

'Please stop, Kathleen, Please stop,' Lucy was sobbing. 'Please don't throw her over. You'll kill her!'

And suddenly I came back to myself. I came back and found myself holding a grown woman over a banister, threatening to kill her.

I was listening to the girls crying – and I was holding this woman. And right then I fought myself to try and stop. Because I knew I shouldn't do it. I had to stop because some part of my mind was out of control. I was confused. My head felt like it was going to explode.

Come back, Kathleen, I said to myself. *Come back. Don't do this!*

It was a struggle and I don't know how long it went on for because in the turmoil of my inner battle I was oblivious to what was going on around me. And then, suddenly, as quickly as the anger had come, it went away. It left me completely and I pulled Colleen back to the landing, shuddering and breathing hard. I set her down safely but her legs collapsed under her and she fell to the floor. Drained and shaking myself, the adrenalin surge now over, I felt empty. I left her there, turned and walked back to my room like a zombie. As I went to close the door behind me I saw the other girls rush to help her. She was so battered and shaken up she was burbling like a baby.

Still numb, I sat down on the bed.

Gradually, gradually, the shock left me, my hands and legs stopped shaking and my breathing returned to normal.

Oh my God, what have I done?

It was only now the enormity of my actions hit me.

I'm done for! They're not even going to send me to the reformatory for this. I'll go to prison and it will be much, much worse than anything else.

The fear washed over me bit by bit. I'd sit on the bed, wringing my hands, then, unable to sit still, I'd get up and walk around the room for a bit. After a while I'd sit down on the bed again and hold my head in despair.

Oh God, oh God, oh God. What have I done? I've ruined everything. There won't be any running away with Shane now. I doubt he'll even be able to find me, wherever they send me.

As time went on the reality of my situation became bleaker and bleaker. Gina, Libby and Lucy crept into my room – they were all crying.

'Oh Gina!' I cried. 'I'm going to be locked up for this, for sure.'

'Kathleen!' she wept. 'I don't know how you're going to get out of this. This is terrible. This is the worst thing ever. They're going to put you in prison.'

That night I didn't go downstairs for tea. Instead, I listened to the sounds of the house and waited for the inevitable reckoning that I knew was coming. I heard Sister Helen come in, I heard her hushed tones as she conferred with the other staff. Then I listened as she opened up Colleen's room.

What should I do? Shall I run away before they come and get me? But I don't know where to go. I have to make a plan! Think of something, Kathleen! Think!

But my mind was blank – what could I do? Any moment I expected the door to open on a group of staff and police to take me to prison.

I didn't sleep a wink that night. My stomach was riddled with nerves and anxiety. I was sorry for what I'd done then. I wanted to take it all back but there was nothing I could do to change it.

At some point in the night I resigned myself to my fate. *Oh, just let them take me. Whatever happens, I'll just have to face it, accept my punishment.*

The next morning I dressed myself for breakfast. Gina and my sisters were looking anxious and worried. There was one thing I knew I had to do before they took me away. I went out of my room and walked down the corridor and opened the door of Colleen's bedroom.

There she was, lying in bed, her legs full of lumps and her head and face purple and black from where I'd kicked her. She was such a sorry sight, I felt wretched for causing her such pain.

'Colleen, I'm sorry for what I did,' I told her.

She didn't say a word, just looked at me.

'I'm sorry,' I went on, and it was there I should have stopped.

But still she didn't respond and the silence gaped wide open, just ready for me to fill. I twisted my skirt in my hands and looked at her, now remembering the many times I'd seen her beat other children. Remembering all the times she'd beaten me.

'I am sorry. I am … but, but I couldn't help it. It's what you did all this time, you see – beating people. How does it feel like to beat people the way you do? It ain't fair. You don't like getting hurt and we don't like getting hurt. And you do it so freely like it's nothing. But we have feelings too. But at the same time I'm very sorry, I really didn't mean it.'

She could barely meet my gaze. After a while she said: 'It's okay, Kathleen.'

And then I felt it, I felt her humiliation. She didn't say anything horrible to me – I suppose there was nothing horrible she could say. She'd been well and truly beaten and perhaps now she knew how it felt. Yes, I was sorry for hurting her but some part of me felt like a tiny piece of justice had finally been done in this place. For once the weak had fought back.

Still, I was terrified for what the nuns would do to me now. I slunk downstairs and placed myself at the table for breakfast, fully expecting to be hauled out to see the Reverend Mother or to meet Jim Duffy in the hallway, just waiting to take me away.

But nothing. Nobody said anything to me. Sister Helen was there, going about her business, but she didn't speak to me at all.

It was bizarre, incomprehensible. When would the punishment come?

I walked to school that morning, still confused and anxious. Lucy walked along beside me, brooding and miserable.

'I wish you hadn't come in and seen me like that,' she said. 'It didn't have to happen like that.'

'It's not your fault,' I told her. 'You didn't do anything.'

'We tried to stop you,' she went on.

'I know, I know,' I tried to reassure her. 'I just snapped. I don't know, Lucy. I couldn't hear anything. All I wanted was to hurt her real bad. I didn't even know I could be like that.'

'What will they do to you, Kathleen?'

'I don't know, Lucy. I really don't know.'

All day long it preyed on my mind and when I got home at dinner-time I was braced, ready for whatever they had in store. But still, nothing! Everyone was just going about as normal, like nothing had happened. I took Grace aside and told her everything that had happened. She'd clearly heard about it already – how could she not know? Colleen was still in bed – she wasn't going to be able to walk for days. They were taking her meals in bed.

'They're really going to put me in prison, Grace,' I whispered, and now, for the first time since the incident, I broke down crying.

All this time I'd been too shocked and worried to cry but now the fear and regret finally caught up with me and I collapsed into tears as Grace put her motherly arms around me.

'Kathleen, Kathleen, hush now,' she soothed, patting my back. 'Don't worry. They won't put you in prison.'

'Did you see Colleen's legs?' I asked her.

'Yes, I did.'

'They're bad, ain't they?'

Grace was quiet – I could almost hear her thoughts: she deserved it. Grace had always hated Colleen and her cruel ways.

Instead she told me: 'Look, the situation is bad. But we don't think you're going to get sent away. We'll see.'

She didn't know herself, and though she was doing her best she couldn't fully reassure me that I wasn't going to get a dreadful punishment.

So I waited and waited and waited. Still nothing. All this time I was full of anxiety and remorse. The longer it went on, the worse I felt about beating Colleen and threatening to kill her. I didn't know where it had come from, this sudden burst of anger. Was I like my father? A violent person who couldn't control their temper? Would I be taken to a mental hospital for electric shock treatment? I was so grateful I'd come to my senses before I dropped her down the stairs. Thank God I didn't kill her. I would never have been able to live with myself if I had.

Every day now I went to see Colleen and brought her water and sometimes her meals. I pitied her, her legs were terrible sore and she became very withdrawn. Every day I spoke to Grace, asking her what was going on. I just didn't understand it. Why wasn't I getting punished? Why had no one mentioned anything to me?

Grace could see I was getting more and more stressed. I couldn't eat, barely slept at night and my stomach was in knots all the time, killing me with the pain.

One day after tea she pulled me aside and said: 'Kathleen, sit down. Let me do your tea leaves.'

I didn't know Grace could read tea leaves so I was intrigued when I saw her get a cup ready, draining it of water before turning it up onto my hand so the leaves fell onto my palm.

'Right.' She pulled my hand closer to her now. 'Ah, okay. I see you're going to travel.'

'Am I?' I was astonished. I didn't know Grace even believed in all this hocus-pocus stuff. 'Where am I going to travel?'

'I see you're going to England.'

What? I couldn't believe it.

'Grace, this is not really true,' I objected. 'Do you really believe in tea leaves?'

'Yes,' she said firmly. 'I do. And you're definitely going to England. But don't you say that to anyone. This is me telling your fortune. Got it?'

I nodded. Something was a bit funny about this but I trusted Grace and I knew she wouldn't be doing this for no reason.

'Now don't cry and don't worry any more,' she went on. 'You're definitely going to England. You're not going to be sent away.'

It was the most comforting words I'd heard in weeks. Some of my family were in England still, so I knew that if I was going there I would be seeing them.

I was nervous and scared still, but partly relieved.

'Am I really going to England, Grace?' I asked her again, desperate for reassurance.

'You are! You are! So don't be scared.'

I smiled then and Grace smiled back at me. We cuddled – then she pulled me back to face her.

'But you mustn't tell anyone I said so,' she repeated. 'This is our secret. Okay?'

I nodded. England! Away from here! That night, and for the first time in a fortnight, I slept long and well.

PART IV
SURVIVORS

CHAPTER 19

ESCAPE

It was two weeks before Christmas when I got up the courage to ask Sister Helen where I was being sent for the holidays.

'You're spending the Christmas holidays in England,' she replied coolly. 'With your sister Bridget.'

Oh my God! Grace was right. I ran straight downstairs into the kitchen, brimming over with excitement.

'Grace! Grace!' I beckoned for her to come closer so I could talk to her quietly. 'Grace, you were right. I'm going to England for the holidays.'

'You see,' she smiled, her beautiful blue eyes crinkling in the corners. 'I told you, Kathleen!'

The days flew past now and I was in a tumult of emotion. I was thrilled to be going to see my family of course, but nervous as hell. I would see my mother, I knew that. What would she be like? What would I say to her? Two days before I was due to leave Bridget called me on the phone.

'Fergal will come to pick you up and take you over on the boat,' she instructed. I remembered Fergal from all those years before.

'We can't wait to see you, Kathleen,' she said before she rang off. 'It's going to be lovely having you here.'

On the day we all left most of the children were sent away before me. The house was very quiet. That morning I'd asked Sister Helen what I should pack in my small travelling case.

'Just a few things,' she said. 'Don't pack everything. After all, you'll be back here in a few weeks.'

Yes, that was true. I wouldn't be gone long so I only took a couple of pairs of trousers, a dress, a jumper and some underwear.

Now I went downstairs to find Grace, who was clearing the kitchen in preparation for the winter break.

'I've got something for you,' she said as I wandered in. She went to her large black bag that she kept in the corner and took out a white envelope.

'It's a Christmas card,' she said slowly and deliberately. 'So you're not to open it until Christmas Day. Okay?'

'Oh thank you, Grace!' I said, jittery with excitement.

She looked at me long and hard then, tears filling her eyes.

'Come here.' She put her arms out to me and enveloped me in a long, warm cuddle. I hugged her back, but when I tried to pull back she kept me tight in her embrace. I started to laugh.

'All right, you can let go now, Grace!'

Grace let me go and started dabbing at her eyes with her apron.

'Don't cry. I'm coming back, Grace!' I told her.

'I know, baby. I know,' she sighed, turning away from me. 'You will be coming back.'

With most of the children gone now, the house felt empty. I strolled into the garden where I saw Lucy still sitting on the wall. Any moment now Fergal would be here to pick me up.

'I'm going soon,' I told her as I approached. 'Wanted to say goodbye and wish you a happy Christmas.'

Lucy was joining a family she'd been to many times before and so far everything had been okay there. But it still didn't stop me worrying about her during the holidays. She was so fragile – she needed her family so much.

But Lucy didn't say a word; she wouldn't even look at me. She just kicked her legs against the wall and pursed her lips.

'What's wrong?' I asked.

'You're going to see Mammy and all the others,' she sulked. 'It's not fair. I don't know why we can't all go with you.'

'Well, it ain't my decision, Lucy.' I shrugged. 'Anyway, I'll tell them all about you and maybe we can all go together for the Easter holidays.'

'That's *if* you come back at all,' she shot me an accusatory stare.

'What do you mean?' I said. 'Of course I'll be back. Come on, give us a kiss goodbye.'

But she wouldn't. So I quickly stood on tiptoe and planted a small kiss on the side of her cheek and left her like that. I didn't know why she was so upset with me. It wasn't my fault I was being sent away. Ah well, I was sure she'd be fine again when I saw her after the holidays.

The one person I hadn't managed to see in the whole time since the incident with Colleen was Shane. There just hadn't been a chance. Since we weren't even supposed to be meeting up he no longer waited for me at the school gates and I hadn't had the opportunity to get away on a Saturday to see him in the park. But word must have got to him about the beating, I reasoned. The children from the orphanage all talked to each other and I was sure he would have found out and understood why I wasn't coming to see him. Never mind, I told myself. I'll come back from the holidays and fix everything. After all, once I was back in St Beatrice's it was only a matter of weeks before I turned 16 and then we could put our plan of running away together into action. Being sent to England now was even better for us – I would meet my family, have a chance to see them first and find out where me and Shane could live once we came over together. I was sad not to see him before Christmas of course, but for now I had enough to deal with. I was about to meet the family I hadn't seen in years. I was about to meet my mother again, the woman I'd dreamed about and cried over for so long.

Fergal came to get me late in the afternoon and by then the only people left to say goodbye to were Sister Helen and Colleen. It was an unremarkable farewell with them both. Each of them simply said: 'Goodbye, Kathleen.' And that was that. Fergal picked up my case and led me out of St Beatrice's. From the moment we stepped outside the front door, I felt a surge of freedom welling up inside me. I didn't even give the place a backward glance. No, I was leaving for England where nobody would tell me what to do. I was free again!

But the long trip took its toll on my nerves. With every hour that passed I became more and more scared of what was going to meet me at the other end. What would they all look like? How would they treat me? On the boat I didn't talk much. Fergal kept trying to start conversations but they all petered out into silence. I couldn't speak at all. There was such a storm of emotion raging in me I couldn't express a single thought. Some part of me felt inexplicably sad, though I couldn't for the life of me work out why. I didn't even ask him many questions – I would soon see the truth for myself.

It was early morning when our train pulled into Paddington, and the shock of my new surroundings was truly overwhelming. We were in London, a city I'd only seen in postcards or on TV. The place was swarming with people, busy people, smart people, all dressed up and click-clacking about with places to go in a big hurry. The buildings were vast, tall enough to obscure the sky. I saw the cinema, a beautiful ornate building in the middle of the street. And the lights! Oh, the lights were magical. The noise of the people, the cars, the buses and the general din came at me from every angle. It was truly an assault on all my senses.

By now Fergal was more excited than me, eager to be reunited with his family. He flagged down a big black taxi – a massive car that I'd only ever seen before in pictures.

'Not long now,' he grinned as we climbed in and gave the driver our address. 'Our house is just ten minutes from here.'

I tugged at my long brown coat, suddenly self-conscious at my plain clothes. My nerves had now reached a critical point. I shook as we pulled alongside a small house with a black front door on a quiet street.

Stay calm, I told myself over and over. *Just stay calm*.

But it was near impossible. I knew that today I would meet my mother. *What will I say to her? What do I call her? Will she like me?* All these thoughts raced through my mind and I felt my head buzzing with confusion and fear. I was trying my hardest, but how could I possibly stay calm?

Bridget opened the door before we'd even walked up the small path to the house. She looked different from how I remembered her; older, like a fully grown woman.

'Kathleen!' she sang, opening her arms wide. She must have heard the cab pulling up. I hugged her shyly, awkwardly. She was my sister, my family, yes, but also a complete stranger. She welcomed me into her home and took my coat before leading me through the hallway to a small, perfectly neat and clean living room. Bridget always was a clean freak, I thought, noting the spotless carpet, the plumped-up cushions on the sofas and freshly polished cabinets.

Fergal gave her a big hug too and then, in a moment, a small girl appeared at my elbow, her shy, anxious smile matching my own.

'This is Annie,' Bridget said proudly. 'My daughter.'

'Pleased to meet you,' I said formally. But Annie, who was five and cute as anything, didn't stand on ceremony. She threw her arms around my waist and buried her head into my hip. Then she looked up, curious.

'Are you my aunt?' she asked inquisitively, her nose wrinkling at the tip. 'You don't look old enough to be my aunt. Are you from Ireland too?'

It was funny, she had an English accent and I couldn't quite believe that she was Bridget's own daughter. A child cried from somewhere upstairs. Bridget bustled out, reappearing a few minutes later with a bewildered little boy with dark hair sticking straight up on his head who had clearly been asleep just moments before. He was clutching a well-chewed blue toy elephant and leaning into his mother's shoulder.

'My son, Alfie,' said Bridget. 'He's only just two.'

It was still very early, just gone eight in the morning, and Bridget offered us both tea and toast. Fergal tucked in, famished. We'd only had one meal since leaving St Beatrice's – a soggy ham sandwich on the boat. But I refused the toast, I couldn't eat a thing. Bridget showed me round her home – it had two bedrooms upstairs and I would be sharing with Annie. There was a living room divided by a pair of sliding doors and a kitchen leading to a small garden in the back.

Just as it was coming up to nine o'clock, the phone rang.

Bridget went to answer it.

'Yes, they're back,' she spoke. I knew in that second it was my mother on the other end of the line.

'You're at the school now? Then you're coming over? Okay, no problem.'

Bridget put the phone down and turned to me. 'Your mother's on her way over.'

I felt sick. I didn't say anything. My heart was beating at a million miles a minute.

'She has another family now,' Bridget went on, putting me in the picture. 'She met another fella and they've had two kids.'

I could barely take it in for the roaring in my ears. The time just seemed to fly by so quickly that the next thing I knew there was a knock on the door.

Oh my God! I felt light-headed. Maybe I was going to faint? My stomach dropped to my toes and I started to tremble.

In a second Bridget had opened it and I heard greetings at the door, my mother's voice! I expected then to see the same woman I remembered from five years before walk in. But she didn't. Another woman did.

This woman had my mother's slim body and the same long blonde hair but there was something different about the face. She looked harder than my mother. She was pushing a child in a buggy who looked to be about a year old. I sat, rooted to the spot, unable to move.

'Oh hello, Kathleen,' my mother said, very casually, as if I'd only popped out for half an hour. 'Did you have a nice journey over?'

'It was fine,' I managed to mumble. There were no big hugs, no kisses, no warm words or greeting, love or remorse. Nothing. It was as if I was a pleasant but completely irrelevant stranger.

Mammy plonked herself down on an armchair in the other corner of the room, next to Bridget, and began chatting away to her.

I was sat, hunched up on one corner of the sofa where there was clearly room for another.

Was that it? Nothing more? I'd waited all these years to see her, cried over her so many times, and that was all she had to say to me!

In that moment, in that very instant, my feelings for my mother evaporated. It was as if I had never loved her.

While she chattered away to Bridget, I surveyed her – the faded blue jeans, red chunky knit jumper and black pumps. She wore no make-up and looked far older than I remembered but I could see that people would think she was still slim and pretty.

During a lull in their conversation my mother turned to me. 'Was the crossing all right?' she asked coldly. 'Was it rough?'

'It was okay,' I told her. God, this was awful. Awful!

I knew then that the mother I had lost all those years ago was dead, and this was a new one. One who didn't seem to care for me or her children back in Ireland. They're still there! They're still your kids! I wanted to shout. Six more of your children locked up in dreadful institutions, being beaten, bullied and abused. In my mind I pulled up an image of each of my brothers and sisters in turn: Brian, Colin, Tara, Libby, Lucy, Riley. Your kids, Mammy! But I didn't say it and she didn't ask me anything about them. And I knew too that if I hadn't been there, sitting right in front of her, she wouldn't have given me a second thought either. I knew that now. I looked at her bored-looking child sucking mindlessly on a dummy in its buggy. Mammy had another family now. We didn't matter.

Mammy stayed about an hour and a half that first day, not saying much to me at all, only occasionally looking in my direction. When she left she just waved me goodbye like she didn't care if she ever saw me again. No kisses, no cuddles; we were strangers. I wanted her out as soon as possible. My feelings for her had been destroyed and all that was left was the bitter aftertaste of those long wasted years, wanting her back. When she'd gone I knew Bridget sensed something was wrong but she didn't know what to say.

So I spoke: 'That's my mother then.'

'Yeah, that's your mother.'

And we just left it at that.

I played with Annie for a while in the garden and then Bridget told me something that made my heart leap with joy.

'Tara's on her way down,' she told me. Until this moment I hadn't even known Tara was in the country. I was so excited and happy at that moment. My sister! My beloved sister! It had been four years since I'd seen Tara and now I was giddy at the thought of being reunited.

When she walked in the house I could hardly believe this tiny, slim girl with long, long hair down to her hips was my sister. She was beautiful! We kissed and cuddled like mad. She had a baby too!

'I've got so much to tell you,' Tara babbled. 'Oh Kathleen, I've missed you like crazy.'

Now I was the happiest person in the world. Tara lived a few streets away in temporary accommodation, a hotel, she told me. The baby was still just a few months old but you could never tell Tara was a mother – she was such a young girl herself and thin beyond belief. I had so many questions for her; we had so much to catch up on, but now was not the time. That day all my older brothers and sisters came to see, and each of them had kids, so the whole time we were surrounded by children. Liam and Aidan seemed happy to see me, so did Claire, who I hadn't seen in ten years. She told me she had been in Dublin until she was 19 and then came to London to be with Bridget. She now worked in a hospice and had a boyfriend in London. It was lovely to catch up with everyone but all I wanted was to be alone with Tara. As she left that day she clasped my hands in hers and urged me: 'Come to stay with me. Please come.'

Though I was to spend that first night at Bridget's house, I knew it was only a matter of time before I would go to Tara's. We had so much to catch up on, so much to say to each other. She had been smiling like mad all day long, but behind the smile I could tell something was terribly wrong. The way her eyes kept drifting off to stare into the distance, the way, every now and then, I'd catch her shaking her head as if shooing a bad thought out of her mind. And her body was thin, so painfully thin.

It had been overwhelming seeing everyone again and, despite my delight at being reunited with my family, they were still virtual strangers. Kind strangers, people who treated me like family, but they didn't have a clue who I was any more. And I knew them even less. It would take time before we were all comfortable in each other's presence again. So much had happened in the time we'd been separated. But I knew Tara. I knew my sister. And I knew for a fact something wasn't right.

CHAPTER 20

A CHILD IN LONDON

'Tara? What's wrong, Tara?' I'd been sent round to see my sister the day after my arrival. But when I got to the hotel where she was staying I found her sitting on the end of her bed, in her nightgown, her long dark hair hanging limply around her face, sodden and puffy from crying.

'I don't know,' she said in a quiet voice, thick with tears. Her baby Sam was snoozing in his cot, peaceful and content.

I'd never seen such a beautiful baby!

'It's just all too much,' she managed before collapsing back onto her bed and wrapping the sheets around her. I looked about me, the clothes everywhere, empty food packets strewn about the floor, unwashed dishes. I decided to set to work. So I started tidying up and cleaning their small room while Tara lay in her bed, occasionally letting out little whimpers as she cried.

Gradually, over the course of that first day, I found out that Tara had been in London just a few months before meeting the father of her child at a restaurant where they both worked. She had fallen pregnant so quickly it had been a shock to them both and they were trying to make a go of things – but Tara now seemed adamant she no longer wanted him in her life.

'I don't love him,' she confided later that day. 'I love the baby but I'm finding it so hard, Kathleen. It was all I could manage to come and see you yesterday but nothing could have stopped me. Nothing in the world. I've missed you so much, Kathleen. Stay with me? Please?'

I went back to Bridget's that night and told her everything. She nodded and replied: 'She's got the baby blues. It's probably best if you do stay with her for now. She needs someone to help her out.'

And that was that. I packed my small bag and moved into Tara's room, sleeping with her at night, curled up together as we used to do as children.

To begin with, Tara barely spoke and hardly ate a thing. For the first few days she just lay in bed, occasionally getting up to feed or change Sam. I could see she adored her little boy, but it seemed everything was a struggle. At first Sam's dad was living with us too but Tara told him two days after I arrived that she didn't want him back again. He was shaking with emotion when he stood at the door, one hand on the handle.

'Tell your sister that if I leave now I ain't ever coming back!'

I looked over at Tara and she whispered: 'Go! Just tell him to go!'

And hearing this, he turned around and left. From then on it was just me, Tara and the baby, and we soon got ourselves into a little routine, each taking turns to look after Sam. Gradually, Tara started to come back to herself, and one evening, while we were both sat watching TV, I managed to get up the courage to talk about what happened.

'Tara, what did you do all them years?'

'Oh, Kathleen, it was terrible,' she started. 'That morning they grabbed me they threw me in the car. I was screaming and crying. I didn't know what was happening to me. When we arrived at the reformatory about 45 minutes later, a sister came out the front door and they brought me into this old building and said this was where I was going to be staying now. The Reverend Mother was there and I was just left in a room on my own, crying. I kept saying I wanted to go back to St Beatrice's but they never listened. I didn't understand it. I kept asking why I was there but nobody would tell me. The place was run like a prison.

'From the moment we got up at 7 a.m. till bedtime it was the same. Get up, get dressed, go to church, back to the breakfast room, then cleaning up. Then it was school lessons for two hours and lunch. Then another couple of hours school and then I worked in the bakery for four hours every day, except on Saturdays when it was six hours, and the rest of the time it was cleaning, praying or eating meals. There was no time for anything else. Once a week we had to wash our own clothes by hand – even though there was a laundry right next door.

'We did everything – we prepared our food, cleaned up after lunch, cleaned the dorms and the whole of the place. I used to cry over doing so much cleaning. In the house there were these glass doors and it was my job to clean them. I hated it. It was work, work, work all the time and no time to go out and play. Once a week on a Saturday they'd let us go into town with £1 pocket money but you didn't get your pocket money if you didn't clean your things right. And the worst part, the worst part was that we were locked in the whole time.

'There were 12 of us girls there, and wherever we went they locked the doors behind us. In the dining room they locked us in, in the bakery we were locked in – everywhere. Even if we wanted to go to the bathroom they locked us in. In the whole time I was there I never opened a door for myself. Not once.

All I kept doing was crying and thinking of you and the others. I missed you all like mad. I had bars on my window and at night I'd look through the bars to the sky and moon and think about you all endlessly.

'Eventually, I realised they weren't never going to let me out so I tried to escape. The second time I ran away it was me and four other girls and we went to Cork, but it didn't take them long to find us. The third time I finally got away for good. I thumbed a lift all the way to Daddy's, and when I got to the house Aidan and Liam were there too. Even Brian – I think he had been let out just a few weeks before.

'I was there two weeks before the police came looking for me and when I opened the door I became frantic, hysterical and I was hanging onto the door and crying and screaming: "I'm never going back there. You can't make me go back!"

'Well, the police were shocked and I think they felt sorry for me because they said they wouldn't take me in such a state. They said a social worker would come the following day to talk to me. So that night Aidan and Liam brought me over to England, and that's how I escaped. I don't know what I would have done if they'd sent me back there, Kathleen. It was awful.'

By now I was crying too – I felt so dreadful for my sister.

'God, Tara. I'm so sorry!' I wept. 'It's all my fault. If only I hadn't told Sister Helen about what the daddy was doing to you all that time, maybe they wouldn't have taken you away.'

'Kathleen, I know it wasn't your fault,' she sighed. 'Don't blame yourself. It was them nuns – they were evil. They should have locked that daddy up in prison, not me. They don't care about the children at all. I hate them. Hate them!'

She spat these last words with such vehemence I was taken aback.

She turned to me, her eyes burning with passion: 'I don't ever want to be locked up or told what to do ever again by nobody.'

'Me too!'

'We'll stick together from now, Kathleen! They can't keep us apart ever again and nobody will stop us doing exactly what we want!'

My heart soared – this is exactly how I felt too. Tara had clearly been through much worse than me in the years we'd been apart but we'd both come out with exactly the same feeling. It was only a matter of time now before I was free too and then Shane and I would come back here and live with Tara.

Tara was still battling her depression over Christmas at Bridget's but I helped her as much as I could and every day she got a little better. By early January my thoughts had returned to the convent. I was back at Bridget's house one afternoon and, as I helped her wash and dry teacups in the kitchen, I said: 'It's been lovely being over here with you and the others, but I suppose it's time I should be going back soon.'

Bridget put her head to one side and looked at me, quizzically.

Then she said slowly: 'But Kathleen, you're not going back.'

'What do you mean? Why am I not going back?'

'The nuns didn't send you here for a holiday, they sent you for good.'

I was shocked. It never occurred to me that I wasn't going back to the convent, that I wouldn't see Lucy, Colin and Libby again.

I had to be certain: 'Are you sure, Bridget? Are you really sure I'm not going back?'

'Positive.'

Some part of me wanted to be happy – this was what I'd dreamt of for so long: freedom. But I couldn't be happy. This wasn't how it was meant to be! I couldn't bear the thought of leaving my siblings alone in that awful place. And now I knew I'd never see Shane again. I ran upstairs to Annie's room and locked the door behind me before bursting into tears. Why hadn't anybody told me? Why had they pretended it was just a holiday? I didn't understand – I hadn't had a chance to make any plans, to say goodbye even to my own sisters!

If only I'd known, I could have fixed everything. Now I realised why I'd never been punished for beating up Colleen – this was my punishment. Maybe they'd planned to send me away all along, but, in choosing not to tell me, they denied me the chance to make things right with the ones I was leaving behind. It was so cruel, so cold.

Suddenly, something occurred to me. I went to my bag and dug out the card Grace had given me. I'd forgotten it was there but now I tore open the white envelope. The picture on the front was a posy of violets and roses. As I opened it up, £40 fell out. I stared, disbelieving, at the money in my hand. English pounds! She had changed her own money into pounds!

'To my dearest little Kathleen,' the card read. 'I hope you find happiness in your life and may all your dreams come true. I love you very much. Goodbye for now but I hope we will see each other again one day. Your ever adoring Grace.'

Even Grace had known I wasn't going back there. Now I started to sob great big, snotty, heaving sobs. I would never see my beloved Grace again!

For a few days afterwards I felt low and sad. My mind kept returning to the ones I'd left behind in St Beatrice's. Now it was Tara's turn to cheer me up.

'Don't worry, Kathleen. It will be Colin next and then after that the others will come. It won't be long and then we'll all be together again.'

It was true – this was a new life for me now and I had to get used to it. Of course it didn't stop me missing them, or Shane, but for now I had to adjust to a new world. There was too much to think about here for now – for one thing, we had to find a way to support ourselves.

At first I lived off Tara's social security money and the small amount that Sam's father gave to us. But after a while that money stopped coming and one day Tara said: 'We need to work. I can go back to the restaurant I was at before if you look after the baby. That way we'll have our own money and we won't have to rely on anyone else.'

So that's what we did – at first it was just Tara cleaning for the Chinese restaurant up the road while I took care of Sam. But after a while I started working there too. I was 16 now, living in London and earning my own money.

Picking up my first pay packet was amazing. Handling the money carefully in the small brown envelope I started to imagine all the things I could buy – my own food, my own clothes! It was a revelation. Tara and I used to love going to the shops, picking out clothes for ourselves and the baby too. We were like two mothers with one child. For the first time I didn't have to wonder how I was going to get fed or ask someone to give me something. It was mine! The cleaning work was easy and looking after babies was second nature – after all, I'd been doing it all my life. A few months after I arrived, Colin came over to join us too and that's when the fun really began.

We all lived in the one room in the hotel, me and Tara sharing the double bed while Colin had the single, and we got

Colin a job in the same restaurant as a kitchen assistant. Now we all took it in turns working, looking after the baby and going out exploring London, taking the baby too. We were just children ourselves and, locked up for so long, we cherished our freedom. On pay days we'd all go to the cinema, a beautiful old building in Paddington, and spent the whole day there, diving in and out of the different screening rooms, watching film after film after film. We became such regulars the manager got to know us and he'd sneak us in the back for free. We'd spend hours roaming the city streets or exploring the capital's many parks, running wild and screaming through the wooded areas, playing, just as we used to do as young children.

Tara was now waitressing and I saw what good tips she was earning. I wanted to waitress too but I found the long bills difficult to add up. My maths education had been so poor I struggled with the very basics of calculating money and change. One of the waiters at the restaurant, a man called Alex, offered to help and he taught me how to count up the orders, how to add VAT and how to give change quickly. He was a kind man, though at 22 he was a little older than the rest of us.

'Why don't you all come down to the West End with me?' he asked one day. 'You'd love it there.'

We quickly agreed and it was there, in Oxford Street and Piccadilly Circus, that our eyes were truly opened to the delights of London.

It was pure magical!

We'd spend hours at the amusements, playing all the slot machines, wandering through the cool shops in Carnaby Street or exploring the massive department stores like Selfridges. My favourite shop of all though was the giant toy shop Hamleys, spread out over seven floors of endless fun. We were good friends and, despite being up all day cleaning and out all night playing, we were happy as can be.

My whole world was opening up now – the three of us were having the time of our lives and, because we were always up for playing and messing around, others joined us too. Alex became part of our little group, as did Monica, an English girl who also worked at the restaurant. On the weekends when Sam was away at his grandparents we'd stay out all night long. Since Alex lived above a shop we often went back to his place, keeping him up till the early hours playing tag or hide and seek among the aisles.

But in all the fun I never forgot my family still in St Beatrice's. I wrote to them a few times but I never heard back. I thought of writing to Shane too, but I didn't know what to say. In my mind I had another plan. I would save up enough money to go back to Ireland and then I'd find him and we'd get married. But despite earning good money from the tips, I never managed to save very much, and every week, after splurging on a night out or a new dress, I'd tell myself – next week. Next week I'll start saving.

I saw Bridget and her family on occasion and often when I went round there our mammy would be there too. There was so much I wanted to ask her, so much I wanted to know – but more than that I just wanted her to rescue my younger brothers and sister from St Beatrice's. She was the only one who could do it.

One afternoon, we were sat in Bridget's front room and when Bridget went into the kitchen I blurted it out: 'You know, Mammy, by you leaving Lucy and Libby and Riley, they were tortured.'

It was like her whole body had been electrocuted – she shot out of her chair and started screaming at me: 'I don't want to hear this. Get out! Get the hell out!'

Shocked and terrified, I scrambled to my feet and ran out the front door, without even saying goodbye to Bridget. I couldn't believe how she reacted. It was terrible. I had so much more I'd wanted to say – I wanted to tell her what happened, about the beatings and the abuse, but she wouldn't hear any of it. As I walked back to the hotel that day I fumed at her in my head: Why don't you go and get your children? Why do you act like they don't even exist? They could be suffering there and you're sitting here all nice and happy.

As soon as I was back at the hotel I told Tara everything. She was dismissive: 'Mammy is wicked. I hate her. I don't know why you even bother. She's never ever going to let you say anything.'

But I couldn't hate our mother. It's true my feelings for her had gone but I still wanted *her* to show *me* love, try to resurrect some bond between us. I couldn't be like Tara and just cut her out of my life completely. Surely there was a way through to her, a way to reach the mammy I had known all those years before. So occasionally I'd drop in to see her at her house, help her out with the kids or the cleaning.

One time I tried to jog her memory.

'Mammy, do you remember the day we saw you? You ran away from us, from me and Tara.'

'I don't know what you're talking about,' she replied gruffly. 'I wasn't even there. I've never even been back to Ireland.'

'We saw you, and when we called you, you ran away. Why did you run?'

'It must have been someone else,' she insisted, and I left it at that.

Time after time she rejected me, and yet I still went back for more. I know now it was foolish of me, but I was a child still. I needed love, a mother's guiding hand. But one occasion put the final nail in the coffin of our relationship. I was over at hers, cleaning her house as usual for her new husband Jack's family who were coming from Ireland to visit. I scrubbed her bathroom, kitchen and hallway till they gleamed, then I turned out all the beds and made them up beautifully, turning down the corners in neat folds, just how I'd done at Watersbridge. Afterwards, as we sat in the living room, watching the children play, Mammy spoke: 'Jack's family doesn't know I've had children before. So when they come, don't tell them who you are. Just say you're the babysitter.'

I blinked a couple of times then nodded: 'Okay, I'll say that.'

But inside a little part of me died that day. How could she let me clean her whole house and then deny that I was even her daughter? I would have preferred it if she'd told me to leave before they came.

I sat, rooted to the spot, too devastated to move, but I didn't want to show her how much she had hurt me with her casual dismissiveness.

When the doorbell rang 20 minutes later, I got up and simply walked out, not even looking or talking to the guests. I didn't see Mammy for a long time after that. It was too much. I was trying to find my feet in a new world but every time I saw her I felt myself stumble a little. No, I was better off without her.

It was around this time that I started to develop feelings for Alex. He was so kind and caring and I knew that he had liked me for a long time. By now Tara had met another fella, and when we went out she'd sometimes have him back to stay. So I would end up at Alex's, just the two of us. We got close, talking late into the night, and I confided in him about Shane.

'We can only be friends,' I told him firmly. 'Nothing more.'

And he graciously accepted that. Still, he was so good to me, buying me clothes and taking care of me. I fought my feelings for so long until one night it happened.

'You know, Kathleen,' he said as we sat together on his sofa. 'I like you, and I'm the one who is here. Now.'

'I know.' I bit down on my lip.

'You like me too, don't you?'

I nodded. And then in a second he bent down towards me and we were kissing like crazy. All those feelings I'd buried for so long, determined that one day I'd return to Ireland, came pouring out of me. We kissed madly, passionately, like nothing I'd ever experienced before.

After that, there was no holding me back. I'd tasted passion and now I wanted more. Night after night I went back to his, our kissing sessions becoming ever more steamy and desperate, until eventually we were without our clothes. And then, though shaking and scared at first, we made love. Now I was blissfully happy, working, going out and falling deeply in love. The one thing I didn't think about, the one thing that never occurred to me, was the possibility that I too might fall pregnant. So I didn't think twice when my period refused to come the next month, or the month after that. It didn't dawn on me for a second that I could possibly have a baby at my age!

It was Bridget in fact who noticed the change in me a few months later: 'Kathleen, your belly's getting big.'

'Oh, that's because I'm eating a lot,' I replied.

It's laughable now but even when the morning sickness came I was completely ignorant. Finally, Bridget took matters into her own hands and made me an appointment to see the doctor. Inevitably, the test result came back positive. I was pregnant.

Sitting there, in that doctor's surgery, I suddenly felt guilty and disgusted with myself. Bridget, on the other hand, looked triumphant.

'Thought so,' she said. I felt like I'd suddenly been caught out – now everyone would know I'd been having sex! Even though I'd decided I would never pray or go to church again, I'd never truly shaken off the nuns' harsh lessons. They'd literally been beaten into us that sex and fornication was a sin. I felt dirty and ashamed of myself. Even then it didn't really sink in that I was expecting a baby. My overriding feeling was that I'd done something very bad and that was humiliating. It was only when they took me to the clinic for a scan that the truth finally hit me. I was five months pregnant. Five months! I would be having a baby very very soon. Suddenly, I broke down into tears – what was I going to do?

I called Alex immediately and told him everything. He was so shocked he could barely speak at first. Then he asked me if I was sure, if there wasn't some mistake?

'Of course I'm sure!' I erupted, angry now. 'I saw the head and legs and the little heart beating on the scan. What the hell are we going to do?'

Alex was calm.

'Well, we'll just have the baby and we'll be a family,' he said in his soothing tones. 'Don't worry, Kathleen. It's going to be fine. In fact it will be better than fine. We'll be a happy family, the three of us.'

I turned over this thought in my mind – a husband, a baby? It was all happening so fast.

'It sounds so easy,' I said, sniffing, comforted at least that Alex was standing by me. 'But I'm still scared.'

And it was true – I was 17, five months pregnant and very, very scared.

CHAPTER 21

MOVING ON

I felt the button pop before I saw it go flying across the room.

'Oh damn!' I exclaimed and Tara fell about laughing. It was my wedding day and I'd bought the white cotton dress two weeks before. But now I was bursting out of it. In the space of a fortnight I'd gone from looking slightly round across my middle to full-on pregnant. It seemed like it almost happened overnight. Now I barely fitted into my dress. As a last-minute fix, Tara sewed me up at the back.

Life seemed to be zipping along at lightning speed. The moment we'd agreed to be a family, I'd booked us in at a registrar – the last thing I wanted was a child out of wedlock. The idea terrified me. Now, a month after finding out about the baby, I was getting married. It seemed strange, unreal. I couldn't quite get my head around it. Even as we stood at the little table in the town hall, taking our vows, I couldn't stop myself from giggling. This couldn't be real! This couldn't be me.

Alex looked cross: 'Shhhh! This is serious.'

'I know, I know.' I tried to compose myself. Then I apologised to the registrar and asked her to carry on.

I knew I was meant to feel excited, elated even, but I didn't. I felt weirdly detached, even a little sad. I loved Alex and I wanted to be with him but I knew I was also saying goodbye once and for all to my childhood and my fantasy of being with Shane one day. That part of my life was over and I had to put him out of my mind for ever. It wasn't a big ceremony – my brothers Colin and Aidan stood as witnesses and Bridget and Tara were there too. I didn't invite my mother. I didn't want her anywhere near me.

I didn't enjoy my pregnancy at all. There hadn't been any time to get used to the idea so I spent most of the remaining months worried and scared about what was happening to me and my body. I couldn't imagine having another human life inside me, and the fear of the birth kept me up at nights. And I was right to worry – when I went into labour in November 1983 the pains were unbelievable. And they didn't stop! I was three days labouring and during that time I couldn't eat or sleep or do anything. I must have put the fear of God into every woman on the maternity ward because I screamed the place down day and night. Eventually the doctors became worried about the baby and, fearing the baby's heart rate was dropping, they sliced me open.

By then I was in such agony I didn't care what they did – I just wanted that baby out of me. I felt a little sting down below and the next thing I knew they placed a tiny baby on my chest.

'It's a girl!' the doctor announced.

She was all wriggly and pink, and the relief was so overwhelming I fell asleep almost immediately.

It was only when I awoke the next morning in a clean bed on the ward that I finally got a good look at my baby. Lying asleep next to me in her see-through cot I saw this gorgeous, tiny child with slanted eyes and a mass of dark hair. I fell in love right there. How could she be mine, I marvelled. She's so beautiful and so dark! I was completely besotted. I lay next to her, looking at her for ages. I didn't even want the nurses to pick her up – I could have just lain there, staring at her all day. And then when her little eyes flickered open, I swear to God she looked at me too and, in that instant, we bonded. Later, they told me that newborn babies can't see but I didn't care. My little girl and I definitely found each other that day.

'Maya,' I told Alex when he came to see us. 'I want to call her Maya.'

I didn't have any problem loving Maya – she was the perfect baby, in my eyes. My only problem at first was being too protective. I didn't want anybody to touch her or pick her up and I was determined that no one else would give her the bottle, except for me. My fear raged inside me. What if she chokes? What if she stops breathing? I was everything that my mother wasn't – fiercely protective, over-cautious and loving beyond reason. I just wanted to kiss and cuddle her all day long. The only person I would let near her was Tara – I trusted Tara with my life. Even poor Alex had a hard time in the beginning because I didn't want him holding or touching her. It took a long while for me to relax enough to trust others with my treasured child.

Maya was just a few months old when I fell pregnant again. This time I knew the signs, and my heart lifted when I realised I would be having another child. We really were becoming a proper little family. It was true that Alex now had to work hard to support us all and didn't get to enjoy as much family time as we both would have liked, but we were happy. Alan was born in February 1985. They were just over a year apart and I was pure delighted to have a boy.

I loved my two children and I yearned for them to meet my father. But by now Daddy was on the drink again, and though we occasionally spoke on the phone I didn't want to visit him while he was unwell. By now Riley, Libby and Lucy were also over in England. They had all been sent over together because we heard St Beatrice's was shutting the orphanage so Riley was just 12 when he came over, Lucy, 13, and Libby, 14. While Riley went to live with my brothers, Libby and Lucy stayed with us. It was wonderful to be reunited at last – it was everything I'd ever dreamed of. I always felt terrible for the kids left in Ireland, worrying and fretting about them constantly. I couldn't wait for them to come over. But I also knew the struggles they faced when they arrived. They weren't exactly going to be thrilled to be reunited with our mother, a woman hardly capable of being a mother. It was a big transition and now they weren't little girls any more, they were teenagers.

Lucy had a lot of anger in her, and though I understood why, it wasn't fair that she took it out on me. For days everything would be fine, then suddenly she'd blow up at me for no reason. She demanded so much attention it became a huge strain on the whole family. Eventually she decided to move into her own place and live independently. It was for the best – Lucy was hurting just as much as any of us but her rage was hard to live with. Maybe she never forgave me for not coming back to the orphanage, or maybe it was the rejection from our mother that hurt her so much. Either way, things were better between us the moment she moved away. Meanwhile, Riley found it very hard to settle down. We didn't know where he was from one week to the next. He went to live with each of my brothers and then started staying with friends. From the age of 12 he was like a butterfly, flitting around, unable to rest or relax. Libby, easy-going and carefree, stayed with us until she fell in love herself and went to live with her husband.

* * *

We were all still as close as ever and all my sisters helped out when they could, though by now Tara had two more of her own. If I occasionally bumped into Mammy, it wasn't through choice, it was because I was visiting Bridget and she happened to be around. I always found our meetings so difficult and uncomfortable. Now I had children of my own it seemed remarkable that Mammy sent us away like she did. I wanted so much to ask her why she did that, but I couldn't, afraid that I knew the answer already. She didn't even make an effort with my kids, her own grandchildren. It irked me slightly but by now I really didn't care all that much.

The one person who cared deeply what Mammy thought was Riley. Riley had been the last of us to come over, and judging by how he skitted about from Mammy's to Bridget's to Aidan's place, he found it difficult to settle down. He was a lovely boy, and grown pure handsome, just like Patrick Swayze. The girls all adored him, but the one person he wanted love from simply couldn't give it to him.

He hit the drink hard. And sometimes drugs too.

'Did you ever love us?' I heard him wail once to our Mammy, clearly pissed out of his head. 'Do you love me now? Could you love me, Mammy?'

'Don't be so stupid!' she'd retort. 'You're drunk out of your mind.'

Then he'd disappear for weeks or months at a time, flitting from one friend's couch to another. We never knew where or when he was going to turn up next.

Riley had endured a bad time in St Beatrice's, I remember Colin telling me that. I know he'd been abused by older boys and the staff. Poor boy. He didn't even have the happy memories of a family life to sustain him, the way we older ones did. He'd been a baby when everything fell to pieces. His attempts to win our mother's love became ever more desperate and extreme. One time I was in the room when he told our mother he had cancer. My stomach plummeted. I felt my head go light.

'Did you hear that, Mammy?' he repeated. 'I said I've got cancer. And it's really bad. They say I'm dying. Are you going to cry, Mammy? Are you not going to give me a cuddle?'

Reluctantly, she put her arms out to him and patted him mechanically on the back. One. Two. Three pats. That's all he got. He fell into her embrace, a happy, child-like expression on his face.

When we left that day I told him: 'Riley, I'm so sorry about the cancer.'

'Ah, don't worry,' he replied. 'It's not true. I just said that to Mammy to see what she'd do.'

'WHAT? YOU STUPID FECKIN' EEJIT!' I exploded at him. 'What do you go around saying a stupid thing like that for?'

But Riley just shrugged. I was mad at him at first but later I saw how tragic and sad it was. The man had to tell his own mother he was dying of cancer, just to get a cuddle.

Everyone was getting on with their lives and occasionally I'd catch up with Brian too, who had moved over to London when Tara came and now had a wife and children of his own. But I couldn't stay around Brian for long – he was too full of anger, too wound up with rage. You'd be sitting there drinking tea together one minute and the next he'd be at you, shouting his head off. I knew something wasn't right with Brian. I knew bad things had happened to him. I'd heard him say the name of the staff in charge of his house so many times in anger.

'Feckin' Tim Healey!' he'd yell, punching the air. He was never violent to any of us, but Brian was difficult to be around.

He'd grown into a beautiful man with pure blond hair, gorgeous green eyes and a strong, muscular body from working the building sites. But all the good looks in the world couldn't make up for his volcanic tempers and, gradually, we drifted apart.

Over time we started to hear about other children from the orphanage, others who had not made it. Jake and Victoria had become drug addicts – they were found dead one day on the floor of the flat they shared. The police said it was death by misadventure but we all knew the truth – it was a suicide pact. One little girl, Anne, had fallen down the stairs and died. There was one called Jessica – she had become a drunk and homeless, then died of liver disease. The horror stories piled one on top of the other. It seemed so unfair, so wrong. These children had had such terrible upbringings, why did they have to die so young? If anyone deserved long, happy lives it was all of us.

My life had moved so quickly since coming to London I never stopped to think about what happened to me as a child. I suppose I'd been running from it ever since they kicked me out. But after my third child, things began to catch up with me. I'd planned to have William, but the moment I fell pregnant I changed my mind. I was worried. I'd been stuck inside with the two younger kids for so long, I wanted my freedom. But I couldn't bring myself to consider an abortion and so we went along with the pregnancy. Something went wrong with the birth – the midwife had to break my waters and in September 1989 William came out bleeding from his head. He looked angry – a look I'd never seen before on a newborn. It scared me – how could a baby be angry? But he was and he stayed that way for a very long time.

For the first two years I struggled every day, getting the two eldest ready and off to school while dealing with an angry, crying baby. I couldn't get out of the house at all, and while all my siblings cavorted outside I was stuck inside, getting more and more stressed. One evening my heart started to race, my breathing became difficult and I felt shooting pains in my chest and all down my arms. Alex was working in the restaurant so I called Tara.

'Tara, you'd better come straight away,' I panted, terrified. 'I think I'm having a heart attack.'

By the time Tara got to me I was a complete wreck – crying and fighting for breath. She called the ambulance, but when the paramedic checked me over he said: 'It's not a heart attack. You're having a panic attack.'

I didn't believe him. This fool didn't know what he was talking about. How could pain be related to stress? I was dying and this man wasn't listening!

Eventually I got so wound up they had to take me into hospital – but there the tests confirmed the diagnosis. It's stress, they told me time and again. With each attack I became increasingly erratic and irrational. Night after night I went through this torture – I couldn't breathe, my heart felt like it was going to explode. Pain shot up my arms and I lost control of myself completely. One after another, the attacks kept coming. By now I was riddled with anxiety and fear. I couldn't leave my front door, afraid of the people outside, I couldn't pick up the phone. I found it difficult even to communicate with the kids. The only place I felt safe was my bed, so I stole away there for days on end, refusing to come out or eat.

Eventually, underweight and severely dehydrated, I was admitted to the psychiatric wing of my local hospital. I was 21 and weighed just six stone. It was there they gave me Temazepam, a really strong tranquilliser, to calm me down. Immediately, my heart rate slowed and my fear dipped – it was pure relief. For the first time in ages my body relaxed and I could think straight. Only now I found myself locked up in a psychiatric ward. I looked at all the other distressed, confused individuals in there and I was scared I was losing my mind.

The psychiatrist came to see me.

'Tell me about your childhood,' he urged.

But I was reluctant to say anything about my childhood – the truth was that I'd spent six years trying to block it all out. Now, however, there was no running. I couldn't even get out of bed. Eventually, and with a lot of coaxing, I opened up a little about my past experiences and after two weeks the doctors diagnosed me with severe anxiety and depression. I was sent home with a large supply of Valium.

At first, nothing changed. I felt scared of everything, even my own children. If William came near me I'd get so frightened I'd move away from him. I couldn't do anything around the house so Tara came and looked after me and my children. This went on for months and months. I was so scared of people I couldn't set foot outside the front door. The tablets worked for a while but then the effects wore off and I'd be battling the panic once again. The fight against my own fear went on and on and the only relief I had, apart from the drugs, was the thought of taking my own life.

Upstairs, in my bed, I'd imagine all the different ways I could kill myself: I could throw myself under a bus, or swallow all my pills at once, or get a knife and slice my wrists. I could jump off a tall building or drown myself. These thoughts ran through my head constantly. It sounds grisly but they actually made me feel so much better because I just couldn't live with the fear any more. The idea of dying felt so peaceful, relaxing – like a long, deep sleep from which I'd never wake up. I longed for that kind of peace. The one thing that stopped me going ahead with my plan was the thought of my kids – I couldn't leave them without a mother. I knew only too well how sad it was to be without a mammy. I knew I had to get better. There simply wasn't any other way.

But it was slow and torturous. It took months before I could communicate with the kids, and a year before I could walk out of my front door without feeling threatened. Gradually, I started to re-emerge into the world, taking it easy at first with little trips to the school or the shops. My appetite increased and energy surged back to my body. But I definitely wasn't the same person I was before. The light, easy-going Kathleen who liked to joke around and play had gone, and now I was altogether darker and more serious. It took many more years to come off the drugs and to get back to someone resembling my old self.

By the time I was ready to live again I was still only 26 and desperate to make the most of my new-found health and freedom. Now nothing could keep me inside. I had been oppressed as a child and those same feelings of oppression had resurfaced as a young mother, sparking an intolerable bout of depression. I was fortunate enough to have the constant love and support of my family and, thanks to my children, the will to live had been stronger than my determination to die. Now it was time to enjoy life.

So I'd go out for days at a time, taking the kids with me in the holidays or just exploring for a day if it was school time. Tara and Libby would come too and we went to the Isle of Wight, Great Yarmouth, Devon, Cornwall, Dorset, Wales and even as far as Scotland. I needed my freedom more than anything in the world. For my health, my happiness and my sanity. I was very lucky to find a husband who appreciated that.

One night, after a long day out in Sussex, I'd just put the kids to bed when the phone rang.

'Kathleen, it's your daddy here,' came the familiar gravelly voice at the end of the line.

'Hello, Daddy.' I thought we were going to have one of our usual maudlin conversations – him drunk and rambling about how much he missed us all, and how much he longed to see us, me telling him to get himself well.

But he surprised me.

'Kathleen, I've stopped the drink,' he said. 'I haven't touched a drop for four months now and I've got the place all nice again. I've painted the rooms, bought new furniture, new linens, new curtains – the lot. Will you come and see me now? I promise you, from the bottom of my heart, I ain't gonna touch another drop. I just want to see my family. Please come. Please come and see your old da.'

I thought for a minute.

'Okay, Daddy, okay. I'll come and see you.'

CHAPTER 22

REUNION

Stepping inside the old house in Lockmeet was like walking back into my past. As soon as I caught sight of the little front door my heart leapt and I was flooded with emotion. All those years I'd tried to put my childhood behind me, to run away from the memories, but somewhere deep inside I knew I could never run away entirely. And a large part of me didn't want to. I needed to confront the ghosts of my past, the memories, happy and unhappy, that made me into the person I'd become.

Daddy had been waiting at the front door as Tara, Libby, Colin and myself drove up the little road in our hire car from the airport. Just from the way he was standing and smiling, I could tell this was the old Daddy back again, the man who'd swung me over his head as a child, who taught me how to ride a horse, who played his harmonica and sung to us at nights. This was the man I'd longed to be with for so long. We all fell into Daddy's arms, laughing and crying at the same time – it had been many years since I'd seen him. He never came to England and I'd always been terrified of returning to Ireland. Now I felt the large arms wrap themselves around me and I was transported back 20 years.

'My children!' Daddy said, wiping his eyes. 'I can't believe you're all here. Look at you all! So grown-up! So beautiful!'

True to his word, Daddy had been off the drink for a good many months and he looked healthy and happy. He was older, of course, a few more grey hairs at the temples, some more lines around the eyes, but otherwise he looked exactly the same as I remembered him. He'd done the house up beautifully, with all new beds and bedspreads, pretty white walls and floral curtains, and the kitchen was swept and clean. We all settled ourselves in quickly and it wasn't long before we were all reminiscing together about old times. Daddy was over the moon to have us all there and he couldn't stop telling us how much he loved us.

We spent two weeks in Lockmeet and it felt like a cleansing time for all of us. We talked about the difficulties Mammy and Daddy had had when we were younger and he couldn't stop apologising for letting us all down the way he did.

'That's all right, Daddy,' we reassured him. 'It wasn't your fault.'

Daddy told us he felt he could have had more support from his own family, and we recalled the time we'd gone to our grandfather for help and he'd turned us away. Grandfather had been so nice to all of us in the beginning but he couldn't see Daddy was sick – he'd ended up punishing all of us for it. It didn't seem fair.

'Was it bad there, at St Beatrice's?' Daddy asked, clearly eaten up with guilt.

'We didn't like it that much,' I told him carefully.

'It wasn't all that great,' Colin agreed. And we left it at that. In a way we'd all come to the conclusion, separately and without any discussion, that we wouldn't tell Daddy the truth. Now that he was on the right path there was no point in upsetting him and potentially sending him back to the drink. He couldn't do anything about it then and he certainly couldn't do anything about it now. So why pain the man?

'Ah, it was terrible the way your mammy left you like that,' Daddy said, shaking his head. 'A mother should stay with her children. It was unforgivable what she done to you.'

It was the only bad word he had to say about her. In truth, I think he was still in love with her.

'You know I would have done more,' he went on. 'But I wasn't well. I was missing your mammy terrible.'

'We know, Daddy,' we chorused back.

'I never stopped loving you all, even though I wasn't the best father in the world. I loved you like mad and it broke my heart when they took you all away.'

When it came time to leave, Daddy begged us to return at Christmas with the children, and so, five months later, I brought my whole family over to see him. The kids adored him – he was still so funny and charming, he could spin a silly story out for hours at night, doing all the funny voices. And he still loved to play his music. We went to the beaches, we showed the kids the fields and woods where we'd played as children and they even got to know the local kids in Daddy's street. My children loved the freedom they had in Ireland – they'd been brought up in London where playing out in the streets was unheard of. But here they were safe to make their own adventures.

It made me laugh when Daddy started to get protective about them.

'Do you really think Maya should be out on the streets with them other kids?' he'd worry, watching my 12-year-old daughter flying up and down the street on a bicycle she'd borrowed from next door.

'I mean,' he went on, 'these kids here, they're wild. Yours are brought up in the city. They wouldn't know how to play without getting hurt.'

It was astonishing! I'd spent most of my own childhood in almost continual danger and he hadn't shown any concern at all.

'Oh, Daddy, just leave them go!' I chided fondly. 'They'll be fine. We all done it when we were children. Let them explore!'

Over the next four years we went back to see Daddy at every available opportunity, sometimes taking the kids, or, if we had some days free, Libby and I would go over on our own. These were precious holidays to us; we were all making up for years of separation. I never blamed Daddy for it – I was just thankful he got himself back on track in time to get to know his own grandchildren. He was the only reason I was back in Ireland – if it wasn't for him, I would never have set foot in the place again. The truth was that I still had a lot of anger for what those nuns and staff did to me and my family. The way they'd treated us was worse than animals. Every month that passed I watched my beautiful children grow and my love for them just seemed to expand endlessly. I couldn't understand how anybody could treat children so cruelly, so unjustly. Even seeing nuns walking down the street made my blood boil. I felt nothing but contempt for those people in St Beatrice's who'd shrouded themselves in holiness to the outside world but then, behind closed doors, acted like brutes and cowards, beating up small children.

It was during one of these visits to my daddy that I found myself at the gates of St Beatrice's. I hadn't meant to go back there at all but Tara and me were taking the children on a road trip and we'd agreed it would be nice to show them the cathedral in the city. When I suggested we walk the road up to Watersbridge, Tara had refused. It was too much for her, but I felt a curious pull towards the place. I couldn't help myself – I wanted to see what the old building looked like. We'd found out that the orphanages had gradually been shut down in the last 10 years so I knew it no longer housed children. So while Tara took charge of the other kids and took them round the cathedral, Maya accompanied me to the old house. That's when I saw the ghosts of the children from my past. So many had turned to drink or drugs to cope with the difficulties of their pasts, and inevitably this led to early deaths. Some had simply chosen suicide as an easier path. I knew now why they'd done it. I too had felt the pleasurable tug of death during the worst days of my depression. There were times I knew it would have been so much easier to die than cope with another day of fear and pain. Thank God I had my kids!

As I turned away, I looked up and down the street. I realised then that I hated this place, I hated everything about it. Such a beautiful city, but I couldn't see that – I could only feel the misery and oppression that had haunted me throughout my childhood. This had been such a place of unhappiness for me I couldn't build any new memories here. Even those moments of elation and love with Shane had been destroyed by the nuns. I wondered where he was now – he frequently entered my head even though I hadn't heard from him at all since I'd moved to London. It didn't occur to me to try and track him down now. What for? I was a happily married woman. To see him again would only invite confusion and heartache. No, I didn't want anything from this place … except … a thought suddenly struck me. There was one person I did want to see. My heart started to pound and I hurried Maya back to meet up with the others at the entrance to the cathedral. There I told them my idea. They immediately agreed and so we all went to visit Grace, the cook.

When we were children Grace used to take us on walks through the town and occasionally we passed by her house. You couldn't miss it – it stood alone in a garden full of flowers and vegetables. I remember thinking back then how pretty it looked. She cared for her home the same careful way she cared for us children. It took me no time at all to find it again – it looked exactly the same.

The cool spring breeze rippled through the pretty roses that lined the path to her front door. I felt elated and scared at the same time. Would she still be here? What if she'd died or had lost her memory? Would she even recognise me? I braced myself for bad news as I rapped the old iron knocker on her white wooden door.

My heart was in my mouth as we waited and waited and waited.

Suddenly I heard the creaking of floorboards and in another second the door swung open and there, in front of me, was the woman who had loved me as a child. My Grace!

For a few seconds nobody said anything. She just looked at us through her clear blue eyes, uncomprehending.

'Grace?' I started.

And then her eyes widened in recognition and her hand flew to her mouth.

'Oh my Lord!' she exclaimed in that soft sweet voice of hers. 'Oh my Lord! It's Kathleen! Good heavens! Kathleen!'

And she wrapped her plump little arms around me in a warm, motherly embrace. When she pulled back her eyes were moist with tears.

'Hello, Grace,' I smiled. 'I've come here with my sister and our children. We wanted to say hello.'

By now Grace was shaking with shock but she hugged us each in turn and then welcomed us into her home as if we were her long lost family.

We took tea in her garden that day, surrounded by beautiful flowers and a garden brimming with herbs. She gave our children chocolate biscuits and let them run around while she told us about her life. She had never had children of her own so she'd become extra close to all of us through the years. After the orphanage closed down she had retired but she still visited some of the children who had stayed in Ireland. There weren't many. A lot had emigrated to England, fleeing their pasts in the same way I had. She was still the same Grace from before – snowy white curly hair and a round, cherubic face. But her clothes hung around her loosely and when I asked how she was getting on she said: 'I'm not very well, Kathleen. I'm having tests right now but the doctors, they say they don't know what's wrong.'

I knew then that I would never see Grace again.

As we left that day I gave her a huge cuddle.

'It was terrible what went on in St Beatrice's,' she whispered to me. 'I saw too many bad things and I wanted to do more. I'm sorry I wasn't able to help you children more than I did.'

'It's fine, Grace,' I told her. 'You did so much for me, more than anyone else. I want to thank you for everything. For being there for me when nobody ever was. You're the kindest person I've ever known.'

Her eyes filled with tears again and she smiled at me. I realised then that Grace wasn't really an old lady, she wasn't even a human being. Grace was an angel. My last memory of her was waving goodbye on her doorstep, her skirts billowing in the breeze, her white hair shimmering around her face.

By now I had gone back to work as a cleaner, the children were in school and my siblings and I were all getting on with our lives. The one person who couldn't move on was Brian. He never did say exactly what had happened to him but I knew it was bad just from the way it ate at him constantly. Then, all of a sudden, one day, when I was 31, I got a phone call out of the blue from the Garda.

They'd had several reports of abuse at the orphanage, including a report from Brian, and wanted to come to London to speak to me. It wasn't just me – there was a large-scale investigation into the practices of the orphanage.

That night I rang Brian and he explained he'd been over to Ireland to report the abuse he suffered. I was so pleased – finally somebody was going to listen to us. Two weeks later the detective came to my house in London. He sat in my front room drinking tea while I told him everything I could remember about what happened to me in St Beatrice's. For the first time in my life I wasn't trying to forget it or put it to the back of my mind, I was recalling it and actually telling another person.

Somebody is finally listening to us! I thought. Finally, someone who matters is listening to us and they are going to do something about it. Until that moment, I never really believed any of this would get out and all those horrible people would get away for those years of mistreating kids. Ireland was such a closed society – the Church ran everything and if anyone ever spoke out against the Church or the clergy they were silenced and the whole scandal covered up. Now I had high hopes there would be justice at last. These people wouldn't get away with it any longer.

* * *

All of us children spoke to the detective, all except Riley – he was off somewhere, we didn't know where. Tormented by his demons, he'd thrown himself headlong into the drugs world, taking everything he could get his hands on – heroin, cocaine, crack, ecstasy. None of it was a true substitute for his mother's love, of course. And none of it could hide the savage truth of his past, but I understood his need for oblivion. We all did. Occasionally he'd pop up, asking for money, and each time he looked sicker and sicker. He barely even smiled any more. We knew he had been abused too, that he had suffered terribly and needed to tell his story, but no one could track him down.

A long time went by and nothing happened. Then Brian's abuser went to court – the details in the case were abominable. Meanwhile our investigation was still ongoing – no details had emerged yet of the nature of the orphanages themselves.

From then on, Brian's life took a strange turn.

He split from his wife, walking out of his house one day – and never went back. He never turned up at our houses either. Instead he started living rough in the parks of London, with just a sleeping bag for warmth at nights.

'Why is he doing it?' I asked Bridget, whom he saw occasionally when he popped in for a cup of tea and a ham sandwich.

'It's the only way he can be happy,' Bridget replied thoughtfully. 'Or at least, it's the only way he can keep going. I don't know if Brian *can* be happy any more. But he's going to live on his own terms for the rest of his life from now. He's decided that. And I suppose that gives him some peace.'

I thought about this for a while. It made sense. All of us travelling children felt more comfortable outdoors in gardens and parks, close to nature. It's how we were brought up. It's what makes us feel safe and comfortable. And I knew that at least, out in the open, nobody could trap Brian ever again. He was free. Truly free.

CHAPTER 23
LOSS

None of us had heard from Riley in months and then suddenly I got a call out of the blue. Just from the strange tone in his voice I could tell something was seriously wrong.

'Kathleen,' he said softly. 'Kathleen, I know you're my sister and I'm going to come.'

It was an odd thing to say.

'Riley? What's wrong? Are you okay?'

A long pause, then: 'Kathleen, I'm going to kill myself.'

My whole body went cold.

'No, Riley, you can't do that. You surely don't want to kill yourself.'

'Kathleen, I want to live but I can't get better. And I can't live like this. It's torture morning, noon and night. I'm destroyed. I want to live more than anything, but Kathleen, if I don't kill myself I'll kill my mother.'

'You surely can't be serious,' I breathed.

'I'm going to kill my mother. The only way for me to stop myself is I have to kill myself.'

As soon as I put the phone down, I was a wreck. I called up all my brothers and sisters, telling them what Riley had said about killing himself. I was fearful for my brother – he sounded so lost, so hopeless. For the next few days I sat by the phone, waiting for news, or at least another call from Riley, but nothing happened.

It was a week later that he turned up at my door, and from the moment I caught sight of him I knew he had given up. His eyes were blacker than I'd ever seen eyes before, blacker than coal. It was like his soul had already left him. He came into my hallway, quiet, just staring at me. I felt his overwhelming sadness then and I wanted to cry. Riley looked at me as if the world had beaten him and at the age of 25 he was ready to die. He leaned back against the hallway wall and slid down till he was crouched on the floor. I looked at his wrist – bizarrely, he had tied loads of elastic bands round it so tightly the skin on his hand was turning purple.

My daughter Maya came out of her room and she saw her uncle then, saw the pure sadness coming off him. He was crying in his heart but his face was blank. We all knew why he was there – he'd come to say goodbye. Maya started taking the bands off his wrist, unwinding them one by one. She did it slowly, gently; I could see she was trying to stop herself from crying. When she'd finished she gave Riley a piece of paper and a pencil – Riley was an artist and Maya always loved his drawings.

'Draw me a picture,' she urged.

Riley obliged.

'I'll draw a picture of you,' he told her.

For five minutes he scribbled intensely on the piece of paper but when he turned it round to give her a look we all got the shock of our lives. It was just a huge collection of eyes.

'What's that?' Maya exclaimed.

'That's an abstract.' Riley smiled. 'It's for you.'

And he gave it to her.

I wanted so much to take away Riley's sadness. But I couldn't – he was already gone. This man in front of me, this beautiful man with the thick brown hair and high cheekbones, had given up on life. It was like looking at an empty shell.

Now Riley was gazing at me, a fond smile on his lips.

I knelt down so we were face to face and I put my hands on his shoulders. In the softest quietest voice, still smiling, he said: 'Kathleen, I love you so much.'

My eyes filled with tears: 'I know you do, Riley, and I love you too.'

'I love all my sisters. Kathleen, will you ring Colin for me and get him to meet me on the bridge?'

'I'll do that.'

Colin agreed to meet Riley on the bridge between our houses, and when Riley went to leave he asked for money. I gave him £20. He looked so desperate, I didn't hesitate. I knew he would buy drugs but I didn't care, I just wanted his pain to go away.

He left then, just turned around and walked away, never even looking back. Once I'd closed the door I broke down completely. I was broken-hearted, seeing my brother like this, destroyed. Riley had been sent to the orphanage as a baby and, by the little I knew from my brothers, he had been abused horribly. He'd been released at 12 years old but by then the damage was done. If only my mammy had gone to save him. If only she'd been able to give him love just once in his life. He couldn't live without love, none of us could.

The seconds ticked by; my mind raced. I wanted to do more for him. I couldn't help it, I grabbed my purse and ran out the door, after my brother. He wasn't far down the road when I called out his name and he turned round. I caught up with him, pulling out all the notes from my purse – it was £60.

'Here, Riley,' I said. 'Here's more money.'

Riley just looked at me, smiling, then he took me in his arms and squeezed me really, really tight. When he let me go, he took the money and stuffed it into his black jacket pocket, then he looked up: 'Goodbye. I love you, Kathleen.'

It was a week later, when I was coming back from a friend's house, that I met Declan, Tara's son, on our balcony.

'Kathleen, have you heard the news? It's Riley. He's died.'

My whole body started to shake. I had to sit down. I knew this was coming but nothing on earth could have prepared me for the reality. My baby brother was dead. He'd taken an overdose and by the time the paramedics got to him he was already unconscious. He didn't even make it to the hospital. He had a heart attack and died in the ambulance.

I was devastated beyond words. We all were – Lucy and Libby were inconsolable, screaming and crying so much they couldn't be calmed. I stayed up, night after night, haunted by that last meeting with my brother. What a waste! He was just a young boy and I knew he didn't want to die. He wanted to live so much but he took his own life because he didn't want to take another. That was brave, so brave.

Tara and I told our mother. We went round there the following day to deliver the horrible news. I don't know what I was expecting from her, but, even now, her reaction shocks me.

'Well, that's the drugs, isn't it?' she shrugged. It was like a knife in the heart. There were no tears, no words of sorrow or regret, nothing. Her own son was dead and she was as cold as if we were talking about a stranger. It was too much for me. I had to get out of there that minute.

As I left I turned to look her straight in the eyes.

'Can you not even give Riley a grieving for two minutes?' I said, more in sorrow than in anger. 'Can't you just give him that last little bit of dignity? Say something nice about him. Why did you have to say something so horrible?'

I wanted to say more but I stopped myself. I wanted to tell her that she was only alive because Riley chose to kill himself instead of her.

I didn't speak to my mother again for years. I could never forgive her callous treatment of her own flesh and blood. And in truth I blamed her for Riley's death. Telling Daddy was even worse. He didn't understand it at all – he had no idea of the years of abuse Riley had suffered in the convent.

'Why would the boy kill himself?' he asked me over and over. It ate him up.

'Riley was sick on drugs, Daddy,' was all I'd say. 'He wasn't well.'

The next time I saw my brother was in the funeral parlour – he was dressed in a suit but his face was all swollen. It was awful. He didn't look like the Riley I knew and loved. But I could see that he was at peace at last. He didn't twitch any more; he was still. All the pain and torment were gone. We kept him there for three days, all of us unwilling to let him go. We spent hours talking to him – me, Libby, Tara and Lucy. We chipped in and bought him the best funeral we could, hiring out a large white carriage pulled by two beautiful black horses. The church was a riot of flowers and we hung up his paintings on the walls for everyone to see. All the brothers carried the coffin during the service – the look of them all was terrible, they were torn apart, carrying their youngest in a box towards the ground. Daddy couldn't come over but our mammy was there – I could barely look at her during the service. He was buried in a cemetery near to us all and for months afterwards I went and sat at his graveside day after day, talking to him, trying to make sense of it all.

Was Riley in a happier place right now? I wanted to believe that so much. I couldn't bear the thought of dying and never seeing my loved ones again. But at the same time I found it harder and harder to believe in a God that let people live in such misery. I didn't believe any more in priests and nuns doing God's work, but then, for Catholics, if you kill yourself you don't go to heaven. No, the Catholic religion didn't make any sense to me. If you're so tormented by life you can't take it any more, why would God punish you by sending you to hell for eternity?

As a child I prayed and prayed for Him to help me, but no help came. So maybe, I reasoned at the time, God wasn't listening. Now I went one step further. Maybe God wasn't listening because there was no God.

It took a whole year for me to grieve for Riley properly. I knew then what loss truly felt like, and it was the worst possible feeling in the world. All us brothers and sisters were in pain, but the one who took it the worst was Daddy. He just couldn't get over Riley taking his own life. In the back of his mind somewhere I think he must have blamed himself, but he never said this. Instead he started drinking again, ringing me at all hours of the day and night.

'Your daddy is really depressed,' he'd slur down the phone. 'You girls, you look after each other and make sure you stick together.'

He'd start crying then: 'I love you. I love you.'

I was fearful for my father: 'Daddy, make sure you don't do anything stupid.'

'I feel like throwing myself off the quay.'

'Don't talk stupid now,' I'd chide, but in my heart I was frightened.

A week before Easter 1998 I had a strange dream. My father

came to me and told me he wanted to show me something. Then he showed me the coffin, *his* coffin, his body laid out inside with his blue suit, smart black shoes and looking more peaceful than I'd ever seen him. Then he beckoned me on; he had more to show me. I saw the gates of the chapel where he'd be buried. I saw lilies on his casket, then out of a clear blue sky a little storm blue up, blowing the lilies off the coffin. It was strange – I was just floating about seeing all of this. I saw people's clothes whipping around them as the unseasonable storm broke, my aunt walking through the chapel gates, her umbrella blowing inside out. When I awoke, I knew what was coming.

And, sure enough, a week later I got a call from my aunt in Lockmeet: 'Kathleen, your father has passed away.'

Though I'd seen the future in my vision it was still a terrible shock to hear it for real.

I was devastated. 'How? What happened?'

'The helicopters are looking for him because he's still lost at sea.'

By the time my siblings and I arrived in Lockmeet, Daddy's body had been found. The whole town had been out looking for him, all his friends, the people he'd known all his life – the boat people, the fishermen, the Garda. They all knew and loved my daddy. For all his problems he was a man so easy to love.

When I saw my father laid out in his casket, I almost fainted with shock. He was wearing the exact suit and shoes he'd shown me in the vision! Daddy looked so peaceful now, it was like he'd only just fallen asleep. I stroked his hair and kissed him on the cheek. At 60, he still looked so young and healthy. The most remarkable thing was the autopsy found his liver was still in perfect condition! After all those years of alcohol abuse, it was a miracle really.

Daddy had known he was going to die, though the inquest recorded a verdict of drowning, not suicide. He had bought and paid for his plot and even had his headstone made, minus the date of his death. It was simple: 'In Loving Memory of Donal O'Shea.'

What really made me laugh was that he'd finally got his own back on his family by arranging to be buried in a Protestant cemetery. Those of his family still in Lockmeet were in uproar, desperate to have his wishes overturned, but my siblings and I stood firm. No, this is what Daddy wanted and we would see his wishes carried out to the last.

The funeral itself was the largest I'd ever seen. Daddy was so well known people came from all over Ireland to pay their respects. The town shut down completely for the day. There wasn't enough room in the church for everyone so people were sat in their cars, listening to the service, which was actually broadcast on the local radio.

The day itself was beautifully sunny, not a cloud in the sky. Unknown to any of us, Daddy had asked for lilies on his casket – just like in my vision! Walking through the gates of the chapel too I felt a sense of serenity as I recognised them from the dream. But I couldn't believe it when, out of nowhere, the skies turned dark and a wind started up. From a gorgeous spring day, the weather turned in an instant into a storm, and, just like my vision again, the lilies were blown off the casket and my aunt's umbrella flipped inside out. It was incredible but it also gave me a warm sense of comfort. Daddy had shown me all of this. He had known he would die, he had known everything that would happen, and he wasn't afraid. He showed it to me because he wanted me to see that he wasn't fearful of death. And in this way I accepted my father's death. As devastated as I was, I felt at peace with his passing.

I returned home after the wake and all the prayers, knowing I would never visit Lockmeet again. The town wasn't the same without him. I was just thankful we had shared the last five years together, that we had reconciled and he'd had the chance to get to know his grandchildren. And he never knew what had happened as a result of his marriage breakdown and his mental difficulties. The fact was, I returned to London feeling lighter than I'd done in years. Now I didn't have to worry about my father ever again. It struck me that I'd fretted for him all my life. Was he drinking? Was he sad? Was he depressed? Now I didn't have to worry. Daddy was dead and he wasn't coming back. As much as I missed and wanted him back, I knew he went to his grave never realising what we all went through. We protected him to the very end.

Still, I'd lost my brother and my father within the space of two years and it was a hard, hard time. Now I clung to my sisters and brothers like never before. We met and talked all the time and recalled funny stories about Daddy and reminded each other of our years of strife on the road, his battle with the drink and his loving, charming ways. This way and between us all, we kept their memories alive, holding them both close to our hearts.

CHAPTER 24

REDRESS

Years went by and still we heard nothing from the police about our complaints against the orphanage. Finally, in 2002 we were told the Irish Government had set up a Redress Board to make amends to all the children housed in Catholic orphanages across Ireland, paid for by the state. We were told to get lawyers in order to put our cases to the Board. A London firm of solicitors took us on and we gave them the details of the crimes that had been committed against us and they began to compile evidence. We were shown medical records as well as psychiatric, school and doctor reports from when we were children. Very little information came from the orphanage itself. In many instances they claimed they'd simply lost our files.

I spent hours poring over the physical details of my childhood. It was noted how much I weighed, how well I performed in school, but nothing was said about beatings or drugs. Could anyone have seen the torment of this little girl from the physical descriptions? Was there a clue there? I wondered how many so-called professionals saw us battered, bruised and miserable children and whether they once questioned the institutions themselves. Or whether they, like the nuns and staff, blamed us? Or our parents? Maybe they just didn't care either way. Grace knew we were being abused. She can't have been the only one. But back then the Catholic Church was so dominant and all-powerful in people's lives. Ordinary folks couldn't imagine the evil that was being done in its name. And so many who may have seen the evidence with their own eyes probably chose not to believe it. That would have been far easier.

In 2004 Tara got a letter from the board, asking her to give evidence in person. She didn't want to go to court alone so I flew to Dublin with her for moral support. For some reason she was the only one out of all of us who was asked to appear before the board. It was terrible. We thought it would be her chance to tell her story but instead she was interrogated like she was the criminal!

The next week we all got letters from the Redress Board awarding us compensation for our suffering. There was no word of an apology, no explanation of what would happen next or whether anybody would be arrested or tried for their crimes. All I got was a formal letter telling me I had been subjected to a level of abuse that fitted their scale of suffering to the tune of 50,000 euros. I didn't want anything more to do with it so I just signed the letter and sent it back.

If only I had examined the letter closer I would never have signed that form. Little did I know I was signing a confidentiality clause that effectively gagged me from ever speaking publicly or naming the people from my childhood. All of us did – we just wanted the whole thing over and done with. The only person who wouldn't sign, who didn't take the money, was Brian.

So I got my compensation, paid off my mortgage and sent my children on a long holiday to Asia. I didn't want the cash for myself but I wanted them to get something out of it at least.

It was only a year later that we started to realise the implications of being bought off. I talked to my solicitor. What was going to happen to the people who had carried out the abuse? To Sister Helen? The answer was nothing. Once we'd signed away our rights we couldn't take them to court because the Redress Board had made an agreement with all the Catholic Orders who ran the orphanages, protecting them from prosecution. Once the claims were all dealt with the Commission published a report – it was a shocking catalogue of sustained abuse going back to 1914. Yet nobody, not one person, was named.

For weeks afterwards, I felt very depressed. But then I sat down at my computer and I started writing, just like I'd done all those years before with my green journal. I thought of all the things we'd been through and I realised that I couldn't let them pass by without in some way recording them. I knew I had to get it all off my chest. And once I started recalling and writing, I couldn't stop. A part of me thought nobody would ever read what I wrote. But then another part didn't care. I had to get it off my chest. Today, *Little Drifters* is the result. Yes, the names and places in this book have been changed because we children have been gagged. But every single thing you have read here is true.

Today I live a happy, joy-filled life, thanks to my siblings, my children and grandchildren. I don't let my past rule my life. I know many are dead but I don't want to be dead with them. I'm not going to be destroyed because of what happened. I'll always have dark days, days I'll think about the kids like little James or Shay. Sometimes, when I'm least expecting it, they'll pop into my head. I'll never forget them, they were part of my life and we loved each other as brothers and sisters. The first daffodils of spring always make me think of the ones we lost. I see their nodding lemon heads and it reminds me of the daffodils that used to pop up along the grass verges to school.

Of all the children that went into that home, I feel fortunate, much more fortunate than most. Some are dead, others are alcoholics or drug addicts and some didn't have families of their own. I know for a fact my life would be empty now if it weren't for my brothers and sisters. We can't do without each other. We love each other's company. Even now we'll take ourselves off into the woods to play chase. They too have families of their own to sustain them, to love them, and though I know every single one of us struggles still with the trauma of our shared past, we embrace life, grateful for every day we are alive.

Look around you today. Have you seen the drunk Irishman passed out on a park bench? Have you noticed the downtrodden lady who shuffles past you with her knotted hair and dishevelled clothes?

Or read about a heroin addict's death in your local paper?

Maybe you've seen me, running around a park, screaming and yelling like a little girl, though I am a grown woman.

Maybe you've met us before – we are the Little Drifters.

You may not have paid us any attention before now or you may have formed a judgement about who we are and the choices we've made. But I write this to tell you that sometimes we had no choice at all.

Not all of us made it. We are the ones still living, some barely, and others in the only way they know how.

This story is for all the Little Drifters, for my brothers and sisters who have been silenced in one way or another over the years – by threats, violence, at their own hands or by legal documents.

No amount of compensation can bring back our stolen childhoods or the innocents who were lost along the way, but by telling this I hope we can add our voices to the history books in an effort to prevent this ever happening again.

To every Little Drifter still with us, I give you my love, my compassion and my fond wishes. Because without each other, and without love, we would all truly be lost.

EPILOGUE

BY KATY WEITZ

A series of media revelations in the 1990s about the abuse of children in Catholic homes led to a number of prosecutions and in May 1999 the Irish Taoiseach Bertie Ahern made a public apology to all the children damaged by these abuses:

'On behalf of the State and of all citizens of the State, the Government wishes to make a sincere and long overdue apology to the victims of childhood abuse for our collective failure to intervene, to detect their pain, to come to their rescue.'

That same year the Irish Government set up a Commission to investigate the abuse in institutions operated by Catholic orders and funded by the state from 1936 onwards. It is estimated 173,000 children entered the industrial schools and reformatories during this time. The subsequent report published nine years later, commonly known as the Ryan Report after its chair Justice Seán Ryan, concluded that the entire system treated children more like prison inmates and slaves than people.

After taking testimony from thousands of children from more than 250 institutions, it confirmed that some religious officials encouraged ritual beatings and consistently shielded their orders amid a 'culture of self-serving secrecy', and that government inspectors failed to stop the abuses. When confronted with evidence of sex abuse, religious authorities simply transferred offenders to another location, where in many instances they were free to abuse again.

It described a Victorian model of childcare that failed to adapt to twentieth-century conditions and did not prioritise the needs of children. Children were committed by the courts using the process of criminal law. The authorities were unwilling to address the failings in the system or consider alternatives. Many of the children who ended up in the orphanages were from poor backgrounds, and a disproportionate number were from travelling families. These, the most vulnerable members in society, were then subjected to a catalogue of torture and abuse, and all because they were deemed to be 'less worthy' because of where they were from. Their low status in society deprived them of their rights.

The worldwide response to the report was one of horror – some described it as Ireland's own Holocaust. It was hard to comprehend the scale of the abuse – for decades, Catholic nuns and priests had terrorised thousands of children with chronic beatings, rape, torture and humiliation. In consequence, the Redress Board was set up under the 2002 Residential Institutions Redress Act to compensate the victims. In total the Board made 15,000 awards to victims in 22 countries. However, the Board has been heavily criticised for a number of reasons. First, many survivors did not apply because they found the process too difficult. Second, the state struck an indemnity deal with the Catholic Orders, protecting individual members from being named or prosecuted. As a result, of the 15,000 awards, only 11 cases were forwarded to the Director of Public Prosecutions. Of these, only three cases were prosecuted. Third, the awards were funded from the public purse. Fourth, the inquiry did not include those women in the Magdalene

Laundries. And finally, the manner of interview for those individuals called to give evidence was in some cases almost as traumatising as the abuse itself. Human rights and survivor groups continue to be heavily critical of the Redress Board, claiming it is no more than a cover-up.

It is estimated that around 30,000 survivors of these institutions fled to Britain, like Kathleen, and, though physically and psychologically damaged, many have pulled their lives together. However, a very significant proportion were so deeply distressed and anguished by their experiences that it has dominated their lives, leading to homelessness and extreme poverty, substance misuse, domestic abuse and mental health problems. This continued suffering has subsequently haunted these victims and their families through the generations.

In 2011 Amnesty International Ireland published its own report on what it described as 'the gravest and most systemic human rights violations in the history of this State'. *In Plain Sight* attempted to uncover not just what happened but why and how such violations could be prevented from happening in the future.

The report concluded:

> The State failed to honour its obligations to children and vulnerable adults it placed in the 'care' of church run, State funded institutions. It failed to investigate and prosecute allegations of child sexual abuse made against priests and religious with the same rigour that it investigated and prosecuted others accused of the same crimes. It failed to protect and support the most vulnerable children in our society, those living on the margins in some way due to poverty, family status, ethnicity or because of some arbitrary judgment that they were morally suspect.

> Instead it pushed them further to the edge of the margins, effectively 'othering' them, deeming them unworthy of social inclusion and rightful legal protection. They were made invisible, turned into outsiders by their own society, and abandoned to multiple abuses and experiences of exploitation.

The Report highlighted the issue of deference to the Catholic Church in Ireland and how this affected people's responses to abuse and suspicions of abuse. It stated:

> Fear, an unwillingness and an inability to question agents of the Church, and disbelief of the testimony of victims until recent times, indicate that wider societal attitudes had a significant role to play in allowing abuse to continue. The end of deference to powerful institutions and the taking of personal responsibility on behalf of all members of society will initiate some of the changes that are necessary to prevent the occurrence of human rights abuses.

The Report noted that many people in institutions in Ireland today are still without safeguards.

Part of the criticism that was levelled against the Ryan Report was that it did not investigate or take testimony from those sent to the Magdalene Laundries, like Tara. These asylums were originally set up to rehabilitate women back into society, but by the early twentieth century the homes had become increasingly prison-like. In most asylums, the inmates were forced to do hard physical labour, including laundry, baking and needlework. They endured a daily routine that included long periods of prayer and enforced silence. It is estimated that up to 30,000 women were incarcerated in these institutions, and the last closed in 1996. But some fear the true extent of the abuses carried out there will never be known until there is a similar inquiry. In June 2013 the Irish Government agreed to compensate the women who, like Tara, were forced to work for the Catholic Church's laundries and bakeries. However, four orders of nuns who ran the workhouses have refused to contribute to the compensation fund.

Today, there are a number of support and welfare groups in Britain, Ireland and around the world working to help victims of Ireland's state-funded institutions. Many, like Kathleen, believe the fight for justice is not over.

FURTHER READING AND SUPPORT GROUPS

The Ryan Report is available to download and read here: www.childabusecommission.ie

The Amnesty International Report *In Plain Sight* can be read here: www.amnesty.ie/content/plain-sight

Support for Irish survivors of institutional abuse living in Britain can be found here: www.irishsurvivorsinbritain.org

The Irish Survivors Advice and Support Network, based in London, was set up to support and empower all survivors: www.irishsurvivorsuk.org.uk

The London Irish Centre Outreach Service has been operating since 2001 to provide support for individuals who suffered abuse as children in Ireland's industrial schools: www.londonirishcentre.org/welfare/london-irish-survivors-outreach-service

Justice for Magdalenes promotes and represents the interests of Magdelene women: www.magdalenelaundries.com

ACKNOWLEDGEMENTS

I would like to thank my agent Andrew Lownie for accepting me, Katy Weitz for believing in me and helping to write my story and Vicky Eribo at HarperCollins for making the book a reality.

I would like to thank my husband Alex, my three precious children – Maya, Alan and William – and their partners Keiran, Hannah and Neema. Also thanks to my two gorgeous grandchildren Sophie and Lara, all their cousins, and Jenny, who is like my own daughter, for their constant encouragements.

Enormous thanks goes to my siblings, especially Tara and Libby who are like my two best friends.

And Shane, my first boyfriend. Fiona and Grace, who both loved me like their own, as well as Gina and Dara, my two constant companions at the orphanage. Thanks too to Teddy and Mona, who really cared, and to Bill for giving his time.

These are the people who showed true love and kindness.

And to my dearest father R.I.P. I will always love you.

Lastly, I'd like to thank my mother. A part of me will always love you for I know you suffered too.

ACKNOWLEDGMENTS

[illegible]

[illegible] and [illegible] to thank my [illegible] children [illegible] and [illegible] [illegible] and [illegible] [illegible] and [illegible] [illegible] and [illegible]

[illegible] especially [illegible] [illegible] who [illegible]

[illegible] and [illegible]

[illegible] and those who [illegible]

[illegible]